NEW SCIENCE LIBRARY presents traditional topics from a modern perspective, particularly those associated with the hard sciences—physics, biology, and medicine—and those of the human sciences—psychology, sociology, and philosophy.

The aim of this series is the enrichment of both the scientific and spiritual view of the world through their mutual dialogue and exchange.

New Science Library is an imprint of Shambhala Publications.

General editor: Ken Wilber
Consulting editors: Jeremy W. Hayward
                      Francisco Varela

BQ
4570
.P76
H39
1987
        Hayward, Jeremy W.
            Shifting worlds, changing minds : where the
        sciences and Buddhism meet / Jer   W.
        Hayward. -- 1st ed. -- Boston   cience
        Library, 1987.
            310 p. : ill. ; 23 cm.
            Bibliography: p. 283-2
            Includes index.
            ISBN 0-9777336-8-6
            ISBN 0-9777336-8-

                                            _IBRARY
                                            UNIVERSITY
                                         ..NDA ROAD
                                         .A, CA 94563

            1. Buddhism--Psychol.   . 2. Buddhism and
        science.   I. Title.

        00040373
        931215   87-9732 //r89

Shifting Worlds, Changing Minds

WHERE THE SCIENCES AND BUDDHISM MEET

Jeremy W. Hayward

NEW SCIENCE LIBRARY
Shambhala
Boston & London
1987

NEW SCIENCE LIBRARY
An imprint of
Shambhala Publications, Inc.
Horticultural Hall
300 Massachusetts Avenue
Boston, Massachusetts 02115

9 8 7 6 5 4 3 2 1

FIRST EDITION

Printed in the United States of America
Distributed in the United States by Random House
and in Canada by Random House of Canada Ltd.

Library of Congress Cataloging-in-Publication Data

Hayward, Jeremy W.
  Shifting worlds, changing minds.

  Bibliography: p.
  Includes index.
  1. Buddhism—Psychology.   2. Buddhism and science.
I. Title.
BQ4570.P76H39   1987   110   87-9732
ISBN 0-87773-368-6 (pbk.)

To
MANJUSHRI VAJRATIKSNA
Joining Intellect and Intuition

CONTENTS

INTRODUCTION

THIS BOOK is an invitation to people who feel some anxiety at the seeming lack of authenticity in their lives and worlds, a sort of blankness of heart in the midst of activity, yet who also feel that genuine discovery of joy is possible. We tend so often to turn away from such possibilities, and from the anxiety they bring with them, by wrapping ourselves in beliefs of all kinds, beliefs in 'spirituality,' 'rationality,' 'materialism,' or 'survival of the fittest.' Some people, perhaps the silliest of all, even believe in "not believing in anything, because it's all bullshit anyway." So-called 'Buddhists' and 'scientists' are no less likely to put themselves to sleep with comfortable beliefs than the rest of us. Indeed, in the modern world the sciences have provided many of the hidden beliefs by which we all do manage to keep ourselves asleep. And in the traditional world of the East, blind belief in Buddhism has perhaps been at various times and places a similar 'opiate for the masses.' But at the same time the sciences as well as Buddhism can provide a pathway to wakening to the freshness of each moment if we take both of them seriously, but not too solemnly. Buddhism and, in recent decades, the sciences provide powerful insight into the nature and creativity of the human mind-body, our self and its world. If we take them personally these insights can bring about profound changes in our lives and our society. The invitation, then, is to journey through this material, not only as interesting information, but also as personally meaningful.

We start our journey with a question concerning the belief systems that each of us, as human beings, hold at the deepest unconscious and biological levels. The book proposes that a radical uprooting of primitive beliefs about reality is necessary in the face of our fast-changing confusion, as well as insight, about our world and ourselves. This rapidly evolving upheaval is reflected in the wide range of discoveries in fields as diverse as physics, evolutionary biology, cognitive psychology, artificial intelligence, linguistics, and anthropology. And the upheaval is felt in the individual lives of many

1

people in the modern world, in the deep anxiety and the desperate questioning of who we are, where we are headed, and what we can believe in.

The search for something to believe in and hold onto, for some certainty amidst rising chaos, is seen in the reversion to fundamentalist beliefs of religious theism or of materialism, in renewed belief in all kinds of fanciful occult phenomena, in fanatical political extremism and nationalism, and in self-righteous individualism. Another manifestation of this desperation is the attempt to demonstrate that the latest scientific work finally proves that the 'mystics' were right all along so that we can put ourselves back to sleep with some vague but comfortable belief that everything really is all right.

The book proposes that only a profound examination of the dynamic, creative perceptual process, by which worlds and selves are made and remade every moment, will provide the clarity and confidence *within* uncertainty that is needed. The body of the book is therefore an in-depth, but nontechnical, analysis of this process, gathering together reports from that group of sciences that are coming to be called cognitive science, or the 'new science of mind.' Added to these data are insights gained from the practice of a method known as 'mindfulness-awareness meditation' on which the Buddhist tradition is based. This is a method of refining attention to become aware of physiological and mental processes taking place at much briefer time intervals than are normally accessible to untrained attention. The results of this analysis and practice may bring about the freedom from dependence on *all* beliefs that mind fundamentally seeks, and provide a genuine revolution in the understanding of consciousness and the possibilities for human awareness and compassion.

Chapters 1 through 3 presents the shifting realities and the world-making role of the observer through the eyes of modern science. These suggest a reexamination of the fundamental belief in an 'external world' and an observing mind altogether separate from it, the belief in the duality of world and mind. Chapters 4 and 5 describe the Buddhist analysis of this duality of subject and object, and of its nondual ground. Experience is analyzed into bundles of elements: forms, or sensory patternings; feelings, or fundamental reactivity to these patternings; perceptions or discriminations of subjects and objects; formations of thoughts and emotions; and, finally, consciousness. Chapters 6 through 11 survey various areas of current sciences of mind, from the point of view of this analysis. Chapter 12 shows how these "bundles" of elements are joined in the temporal process of perception in which the 'external world' and the 'self' that is conscious of it are fabricated anew moment by moment; and Chapter 13 examines the temporal flow of experience and opens up the possibility of gaps in this flow, experienced as glimpses of intuitive insight or nowness. In Chapter 14 we discuss how such glimpses of insight might be integrated with our usual idea of intellectual knowledge. Chapter 15 describes the method of mindfulness-awareness meditation by which the perceptual process has been and can be unravelled, and intellect and intuition joined, and shows that the grounds for the validity of the method of meditation are not very different from the grounds for the validity of the scientific method.

In Chapter 16 we enter a new phase of the journey, asking in what sense even the process of perception is 'real,' and in what sense it is itself a fabrication. The idea of 'emptiness' is introduced: that there is nothing in reality that has inherent existence or independent self-nature separate from the rest. That is, there are no 'things,' either 'mental' or 'physical,' and even the categories of 'mental' and 'physical,' 'existence' and 'non-existence' are seen to be merely conceptual projections within nonconceivable reality. Chapter 17 continues the discussion of 'emptiness' to see how it is different from the nihilist view that there actually *is* nothing at all. 'Emptiness' is an experiential discovery, not merely an intellectual idea, and this discovery is equally one of 'fullness' beyond concept. In this chapter we also see the way in which language and symbol systems take us away from the direct experience of 'emptiness.' In Chapters 18 and 19 we examine the so-called mind/body split in perception from this point of view. We look in Chapter 18 at the tendency of thought to think in terms of closed systems, and in Chapter 19 we see how the 'things' of our ordinary everyday world, even the 'body,' are conceptual constructions, particular forms of perceptual patterning.

Chapters 20 and 21 ask how does perceptual patterning arise as the appearance of self and world, and what is the nature of this patterning's awareness. Chapter 22 discusses the nonconceptual compassion that arises from the openness and interconnectedness of beings. We see that this compassion, together with a sense of irony that there is nothing to rely on, can form the basis for a gradual transformation of society.

The book offers a personal view. As a teenager, I had an intense longing for an understanding of the world that would satisfy my intellectual curiosity as well as a more heartfelt feeling that I recall now only as a longing for genuine value. Reading James Jeans and Arthur Eddington, two of the older generation of physicists who appreciated vastness, I fell in love with physics and studied it as far as I could. This search then took me to a wish to understand life and to four years of research in molecular biology, and then on to a study of modern psychological theories. Still, whatever it was I was searching for seemed to elude my grasp. Coming upon the Buddhist approach to the study of mind was like a breath of freshness, for there I heard and finally began to understand that the search is the answer. What I had been working so hard and earnestly to understand was this world, the world within experience, not some fantastic invention of others. When I began to see that the barrier between experimenter and experiment is arbitrary and deceptive, then the rift between intellect and heart could begin to heal.

In the history of Buddhism there have been many schools and much debate and disagreement. Buddhism is by no means a monolithic doctrine, and there is no central dogma nor one universally accepted authority or text. And the same is true, of course, of the sciences of the twentieth century. At their best and most lively, Buddhism and the sciences suggest continually evolving ways of being, knowing and acting, with no end-point or final answer. Therein lies their delight. So in referring to what Buddhists or scientists maintain, I refer not to any absolute and universally agreed-on doctrine, but rather to what I find pertinent and interesting in this variety of doctrines and research programs. I have tried not to distort the views of each, at the same time suggesting how their insights might be drawn together into a coherent view of human experience expressed in the language of our time. If the reader finds anything of value in this journey it is a tribute to the wealth and generosity of my teachers in the sciences and Buddhism.

My thanks and appreciation go to those who read and criticized the manuscript, particularly Larry Mermelstein, Reggie Ray, Francisco Varela, and Ken Wilber; to the staff of Shambhala Publications, especially Emily Hilburn Sell; and to my family.

1

Changing Worlds

AT A CONFERENCE held in Boulder, Colorado, in the summer of 1979, prominent young research scientists from each of the fields of biology, anthropology, psychology, linguistics, neuroscience, and mathematics met for two weeks to discuss the disturbing and fundamental questions confronting each of these disciplines. The perhaps rather mundane title, Contrasting Perspectives on Cognition, belies the conference's powerful message. Attending, among others, were anthropologist and linguist Alton Becker, neuroscientists Humberto Maturana and Francisco Varela, psychologists Eleanor Rosch and Avram Tversky, linguists George Lakoff and Charlotte Linde, mathematician Newcombe Greenleaf. Although the conference was funded by the Alfred P. Sloan Foundation, there was no pressure to produce. It was understood that this was a time for openness, for trying to reach across the disciplinary boundaries that sometimes seem to be more like an "iron wall" than any barriers between nations. Acknowledging this breaking of academic barriers, one participant said, "I would be branded a heretic for saying these things in my own department back home."

By the end of the conference the realization had dawned that many of the difficulties that these scientists were confronting in their research could be summarized in the words of Maturana: "We, biologists, must put the 'external world' in quotations." By this he meant, quite literally, that the external world is a statement made by an observer, not a reality independent of any observer. And he meant that biologists, not only philosophers, should take this view. The idea that there is an objective world, and separate organisms with separate minds that perceive this world, was no longer an adequate basis for the scientific research these scientists were doing. This was not felt so much as a startling, dramatic revelation, it was more in the nature of an uncanny feeling of slowly recognizing something that one has known in one's heart all along. Many of the participants were deeply moved to realize that there was common ground in so many fields at such a profound level.

"The external world no longer exists objectively"; and "the Universe has turned inside out." These statements characterize a revolution that has been taking place, in the past quarter of a century, in the way men and women might think about the universe and about their lives in that universe. It is a revolution more profound and far-reaching than the two great scientific revolutions of the twentieth century, relativity and quantum theory. I use the term 'revolution' here, not in the modern political sense of something new that is going to violently overthrow the old order, but in the older sense of turning over, looking back to and rejoining the origins. If it enters the minds and hearts of the ordinary people of the modern world, this way of thinking and knowing can bring about a transformation of our society comparable with the transformation that brought us out of the Middle Ages and into the era of mechanical science. But it will be a transformation in which we rejoin our roots in the cosmos rather than separate further from those roots.

This realization has dawned in the minds of scientists in many varied disciplines as well as of historians and sociologists of science. The dawning view is summarized by James Burke, sociologist of science and creator of the prize-winning PBS Television series *Connections*. In *The Day the Universe Changed*, in which he describes the change of mind accompanying the Newtonian revolution, Burke says, "Scientific knowledge, in sum, is not necessarily the clearest representation of what reality is; it is the artifact of each structure and its tool. Discovery is invention. Knowledge is man-made. . . . There is no metaphysical, superordinary, final, absolute reality. There is no special direction to events. The universe is what we say it is. When theories change the universe changes. The truth is relative. This relativist truth . . . makes science accountable to the society from which its structure springs."[1]

To think that there is a real, objective and external Universe, independent of mind and observation is no longer an acceptable attitude with which to approach science, or reality. Rather, as this book will demonstrate, the universe and the self that observes it co-arise in a mutually creative process. That is why it can be said that 'the Universe has collapsed.' I am not here talking about:

> Moon shining above pine covered hill,
> Wood smoke drifting from chimney,
> Birds singing their evening song,
> Tiny fishing boat sails across calm bay.

This we know is fleeting, transient. This will quickly pass never to return, as will the sadness and joy the viewer felt, and felt to be real, at that very moment. No, I am talking about belief in the Universe (with a capital U) as a separate eternal entity behind and more real than that transient present moment. Such an attitude forms an unconscious belief through which, without knowing it, all our other beliefs about our lives, and all our perceptions of the world are filtered, as a pair of tinted spectacles or a fish-eye lens filters ordinary visual perception.

To a very large extent men and women are a product of how they define themselves. As a result of a combination of innate ideas and the intimate influences of the culture and environment we grow up in, we come to have beliefs about the nature of being human. These beliefs penetrate to a very deep level of our psychosomatic systems, our minds and brains, our nervous systems, our endocrine systems, and even our blood and sinews. We act, speak, and think according to these deeply held beliefs and belief systems. So when an upheaval occurs in our group understanding of mind and body (who we are), reality (what there is) and science (one way we explore and come to know what there is) it naturally affects all of us to the very root of our being. This is what is happening now, in the last quarter of the twentieth century. The fundamental assumptions we make about the world—that is, the context of beliefs for our lives—altogether are in question.

BELIEF CONTEXTS

What do I mean by a 'context of beliefs'? 'Belief context' might be compared to the term 'paradigm,' which has become popular among some sociologists and philosophers of science in the past decade.[2] But 'belief context' points beyond the narrower idea of 'paradigm.' First the 'new paradigm' that is popularly sought—the 'holographic paradigm,' the 'evolutionary paradigm,' the 'systems paradigm'— usually refers merely to a *new set of beliefs* that can guide research and explanation in a particular field of inquiry, however broad. It usually takes for granted the old 'objectivist' philosophy of science, and does not by any means refer to the kind of reexamination of fundamental beliefs that is needed. A change in belief context may not necessarily mean adopting new beliefs. Rather it may be a change in the entire relationship we have to beliefs altogether.

The second reason for being cautious of it is that the paradigm idea too has become sullied in recent years by a tendency to an overenthusiasm that tries to rouse a gullible public with a liberal splattering of words such as "fantastic," "startling," "shocking," "dramatic," and so on, into believing that their minds are just about to be blown into a permanent state of drug-like ecstasy. Finally, 'paradigm' is an abstract, highly rational and impersonal term. 'Belief context' points to the personal nature of what we seek: we seek 'belief' by which to live our lives, and 'context,' which gives meaning to our lives.

'Belief context' is closer to the older term 'set,' or the term 'perceptual readiness' used by psychologist Jerome Bruner in his studies of the way we place objects in categories in order to perceive them. Perceptual readiness is the tendency of the organism, human or animal, to be set to perceive in a certain way, that is to have expectancies about its environment that predetermine to some extent what it perceives. Bruner showed many years ago that not only do we tend to perceive something in our environment more readily if we already expect to perceive it, but also that we have much more difficulty than usual perceiving something that we are preset not to perceive.[3] Bruner recently summarized his work in this way: "If what impinges on us conforms to expectancy . . . we may let our attention flag a little, look elsewhere, even go to sleep. Let input violate expectancy and the system is on the alert. . . ." In one famous example of his work, Bruner showed subjects two series of playing cards, one normal and one with the colors reversed, at speeds of a fraction of a second. Subjects not only had a much harder time identifying the color-reversed cards, but they went to great lengths to reinterpret and 'regularize' what they saw to fit with their expectations of the nature of playing cards. Bruner remarks, "I recall one subject reporting that our red six of clubs was a six of clubs, but that the illumination inside the tachistoscope was rather pinkish." After describing his researches on this he says, "All this is banal enough but the implications are anything but that. For it means that perception is to some unspecifiable degree an instrument of the world as we have structured it by our expectancies. Moreover, it is characteristic of complex perceptual processes that they tend where possible to assimilate whatever is seen or heard to what is expected."[4]

'Belief context' refers to the deepest levels of perceptual readiness, going beyond the kind of superficial cognitive attitudes that Bruner experimented with. It reaches to the most primitive beliefs we hold that we are very largely unconscious of but which predetermine our way of living. We might think that 'belief context' is just a sneaky way of bringing back those tainted words, 'metaphysics' or 'religion.' But metaphysics and religion have rightly been questioned by many ordinary people because over the past few centuries they came to refer not to a fundamental reexamination of the beliefs at the root of our minds, but to elaborate, abstract, conceptual layers of further beliefs laid over our minds that take us even further from the reality of our lived world.

Let us look further into the way belief contexts organize our perceptions and our lives. Consider the difference between seeing the headline "AIDS Virus Isolated" in the *National Enquirer* and in the *New York Times*. In the first case most of us would probably not notice it as we walked past the newsstand; we would literally not perceive the headline although our eyes may pass over it. If we did notice it our response would probably be disbelief. On the other hand such a headline in the *New York Times* might well induce a pleased "Aha." The headline itself is the same, with perhaps a difference in the size of type, but our response is entirely different. This difference in response is due to the different context in which the message "AIDS Virus Isolated" is received, the different belief system we have, normally unconscious, concerning the two newspapers and the likelihood of finding a true statement in one of them.

Another example of the effect of mental context is a riddle told by Douglas Hofstadter.[5] A father and his son are driving to a football game. They begin to cross a railroad crossing and, when they are halfway across, the car stalls. Hearing a train coming in the distance the father desperately tries to get the engine started again. He is unsuccessful and the train hits the car. The father is killed instantly, but the son survives and is rushed to the hospital for brain surgery. The surgeon, on entering the operating theater turns white and says, "I cannot operate on this boy. He is my son." The question is, what is the relation between the boy and the surgeon? Take a few minutes to ponder this one before looking at the answer, which I will write in reverse: eht noegrus saw eht s'yob rehtom. I have known even staunch feminists to be stuck by this one and to admit later that they had a firm image of a male surgeon in mind as they were trying to solve the puzzle. This image, with all its associated ideas of male intellectual superiority and so on, formed the unacknowledged belief system that was inhibiting the discovery of a very obvious solution. Even my eight-year-old daughter got stuck on this riddle. When I asked her to describe the surgeon coming into the room she described a male figure.

The human organism is born into the world already embodying all kinds of beliefs, at a primitive feeling level. For example, it believes that when it sees a face with a smile, it can relax, but when it sees a face with a frown there is danger. As it grows older it learns to speak and it is surrounded by messages, both verbal and nonverbal, about how the world is. Thus, without knowing this, without reflecting on it in conscious thought, the organism acquires more and more beliefs about more and more aspects of the world around it. One can hear children constantly making up stories to explain to themselves what is happening around them. The two-year-old will make a mudpie and push it into the face of his cat saying, "He wants to eat it," and break into unrelenting tears when the cat will not eat the mudpie; the four-year-old will *explain* to you that the cat has a bad tummy and that is why he is not eating it; the six-year-old will dress the cat for a tea party with mudpies, but will also tell you that we feed him cat food "because cats eat meat"; for the eight-year-old, the cat is her brother, but at the same time she will give you an almost nonstop running commentary on what is going on in the world around her, and why; by the time the child is twelve, the cat is just a cat, and the running commentary is fully internal.

Thus even young children do not simply and directly live in the world around them. Rather they are, at the same time as living in it, struggling to create explanations of it, to create a belief system. At each stage of their growth they have a belief system that alters as they learn more about the world.

The human being acts at almost all times not according to direct perception of the world around him or her, but according to his or her beliefs, at that moment, about the world. These beliefs provide the context for each person's action, for our perception, and for our ideas about how the world is. The beliefs that we have about the world form layer after layer of preconception, prejudice, or bias. This bias is not a bad thing or a good thing, it just is so. It is the nature of the human and perhaps of all perceiving organisms.

The universe, as we, the ordinary men or women of the street, know it to be, is a contextual belief system. It is taught to us gradually by explicit instruction of our parents and teachers, by what we read and by everything we see, hear, smell, taste and touch around us. And what we believe the world around us to be profoundly affects the way we perceive and experience that world. Thus the two, our beliefs and our perceptions form a tightly interlocking system of mutual feedback and support so that we could just as easily say "I will see it when I believe it" as "I will believe it when I see it." We perceive only what we already believe to exist and we perceive it in the way that we believe it to exist.

This effect, "I'll see it when I believe it," is used in the picture puzzles familiar to us from childhood. We were asked to find the rabbit hidden in a picture of a landscape, or in a pattern of dots, as in Fig. 1-1. We searched and searched until suddenly there was the face of a rabbit, whiskers, long ears, snout, and curved back, formed by the foliage of a bush, or the dots. Sometimes we were unable to find it after a long search and it had to be pointed out to us. It was a shock, there was no question that it was a rabbit, and from then on we could not *fail* to see it, even when we tried not to. If we had not believed that it was there we would probably never have discovered it. Charles Darwin noted, in *Voyage of the Beagle*,[6] that native islanders seemed altogether unable to see the Beagle anchored on the horizon, even when it was pointed out to them, although they were able to see the smaller boats ferrying crew between the Beagle and the island. Presumably such a large ship was not part of the islander's belief context, and therefore they were unable to see it. As we will see later, simple but strangely disturbing facts like these afford profound insight into the nature of perception.

"I'll see it when I believe it" is true of simple perceptions such as form and color as well as perceptions of emotions in ourselves and others, perceptions of personal characteristics and of national characteristics, and perceptions of universals such as the qualities of space and the flow of time. As I was writing this a friend arrived for tea. She asked me to explain what I was writing and I replied, "Even as we sit here and talk, we take it for granted that you are over there, and I am over here, that there is empty space between us, that you and I are essentially lumps of meat with a mind in our head, and that

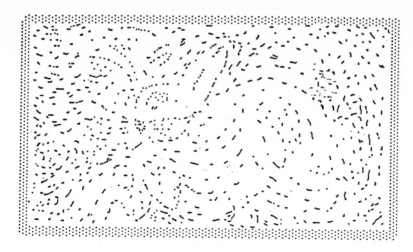

Figure 1-1

the major source of our communication between us is in the words we say. But our belief that we are like that, and the 'fact' that we are like that create each other." She immediately got the point and said, "Yes, and we think it is because we are filled with information that this communication happens." All these are assumptions we make all the time in our daily life, which are now being profoundly questioned by the sciences of mind.

All these beliefs form the context for our society and for science. And they form the unconscious backdrop to what we learn about the world through intellectual effort as well as how we act in the world. And belief in science as the only valid way of gaining knowledge of the world forms a deep context for our society and for each of us individually. When we read in a reputable newspaper or a popular science journal that "the *Voyager 2* spacecraft has discovered stunning revelations about the moons of Uranus" we unquestioningly take these revelations as statements of the truth. Believing well-documented statements made by scientists to be true is not in itself a scientific attitude. However, it does form the context for science. A context of beliefs, a contextual belief system, of this nature is absolutely necessary in order for the endeavor of science to have any meaning for us.

Michael Polanyi has convinced us that the learning of contextual beliefs is a necessary part of the training of a young scientist. His example is that of a medical student:

> Think of a medical student attending a course in the x-ray diagnosis of pulmonary diseases. He watches in a darkened room shadowy traces on a fluorescent screen placed against a patient's chest, and hears the radiologist commenting to his assistants, in technical language, on the significant features of these shadows. At first the student is completely puzzled. For he can see in the x-ray picture of a chest only the shadows of the heart and ribs, with a few spidery blotches between them. The experts seem to be romancing about figments of their imagination; he can see nothing that they are talking about. Then as he goes on listening for a few weeks, looking carefully at ever new pictures of different cases, a tentative understanding will dawn on him; he will gradually forget about the ribs and begin to see the lungs. And eventually, if he perseveres intelligently, a rich panorama of significant details will be revealed to him: of physiological variations and pathological changes, of scars, of chronic infections and signs of acute disease. He has entered a new world. He still sees only a

fraction of what the experts can see, but the pictures are definitely making sense now and so do most of the comments made on them. He is about to grasp what he is being taught; it has clicked.[7]

We all experience this kind of "click" whenever we are thrown into an unfamiliar situation in which we have to learn an entirely new set of habits and perceptions in order to survive. When we start a new and unfamiliar job or if we go to live in a foreign country, we are confronted with a multitude of impressions that simply do not fit into any way of thinking or acting that is available to us habitually. We feel confused and sometimes so disoriented that we feel unfamiliar even to ourselves. We begin to lose our sense of identity and perhaps become quite paranoid. Slowly we learn the language and the meaning of various gestures and terms until finally, just like the medical student, one day we realize with a shock that our sense of unfamiliarity is gone. We have formed a new context in which the previously strange perceptions and words have now become comfortably familiar.

THE ULTIMATE BELIEF: WHAT IS REAL

The deepest belief context underlying the lives of every one of us has to do with the question of what is real. Ordinary common sense leads us to assume without much question that the things around us in the world are real, as they appear to us. If you kick a rock, you hurt your toe. The rock is real, your toe is real, your hurt is real and you are real. I am real and that famous American President, Ronald Reagan, is real. Blue is real and the Mediterranean sea is really blue. Green is real and the grass is really green. The sound of the loon calling across the bay on a midsummer evening is real. My sadness is real and my happiness is real. All of this we assume in our daily affairs.

But for at least a thousand years in the West there has been a contrary view. It stemmed first from Christianity and then from science, but it had its origins in ancient Greek writings. Popular Christianity taught that there is another world, altogether separate from this one, altogether separate from Earth and from Nature. This was the transcendent world of God, the 'Heavenly City,' compared to which this world is like unto a garbage dump. The world of the earthly experience of the senses was to be given up. This world, while apparently real, was assumed to be smeared with some inher-

ent obscuration that brought the inevitable result that the only
worthwhile response to it is to try to get out, to escape into a world
of belief, or to wait for a world after death.

In the past four centuries those who practice science have taught
something apparently as different from common sense as the popular
Christian heaven was. Yet ironically scientists have kept the key point
of Christianity, the unreal quality of the world of the senses. And
gradually their teaching has sunk into the roots of our society to form
the very foundation of the modern world. Like Christianity, modern
science teaches that these things of the world of senses are not really
real, but that there is a more real reality, in Nature, behind these
appearances, a permanent, unchanging reality in comparison to
which the world of appearance is ever changing and is an accidental
product of our sense organs. Unlike the "other world" of Christianity,
which is a world of spirit or mind, altogether without body, this
"other world" of science is a world of matter, altogether without
spirit, life, or mind. This ultimately real world is the world of particles
(little bits of dead stuff), of space and time and of forces (gravitational,
electromagnetic, and more recently the strong and weak nuclear
forces). This ultimately real world, so the nineteenth-century scientists said, exists independently of people's minds, of our existence,
of our observations. And most of us still believe in this world. We
have called it Reality, or the Universe. We believe that this real
Universe exists independently of people in general, but also independently of each man and woman in particular. This is one of the
deepest levels of belief context in our society, and few scientists
realize the extent to which the belief context of their discipline is
inherited from medieval Christianity.

In developing the classical version of science, three hundred years
ago, it was necessary to assume that the mind was like a clear mirror
that did not interact with the Universe at all and therefore that did
not need to be included in the description of Nature. The soul, which
was more or less the individual mind, was understood to have
inherent and ineradicable impurity and fallibility. The method of
experiment and the language of mathematics were to place a barrier
between the individual experimenter and his or her observations so
that the impurity of the soul did not taint the purity of observation.
This approach was most necessary in Galileo's day, when it was so
important for the new method to free itself from the bounds of the
Church and to investigate nature without apparent prejudice. To
exclude mind and human motivation and aspiration from science
was, at that time, a necessary part of the methodology to uncover
Reality, and to cut through the obscuring beliefs of that age.

But now we have no idea how to close the gap between this supposed Reality and the world of ordinary experience. We have come to believe, so deeply that it has soaked into our nervous systems, that science is gradually getting closer and closer to knowing and being able to describe the exact nature of this Universe, this Ultimate Reality. But ordinary people with their natural sense perceptions cannot ever really know the Real World, the Universe. Thus we ordinary people are condemned to a second-hand version of truth, told to us in a simplified and popularized version. Our own world and our own truth seem subjective and petty beside this. We only partially understand the explanations scientists give us unless we have taken a university course, preferably to the Ph.D. level. But we believe them, just as our grandparents believed the teachings of the Church.

We are taught in school to believe that there is an important difference between fact and opinion: an opinion is said to be just some idea someone might have; a fact can be true or false, and we can check out whether it is true or false by reference to the Real World. This is what scientists say they do and that there is a proved scientific method by which they find the facts. So we believe them, and we believe the facts. Our society believes the facts and inculcates them into us before we are old enough to question. The context for science has become the context for modern society—science has for generations provided the belief system on which society rests. I should emphasize here at the start of our journey, that the issue is not science and the scientific method, nor the value of insights that have been provided by this method. The issue is the inherent human tendency to believe at all, and to believe what we are told without question, no matter who tells it, scientist or priest.

Now, more and more people have in fact been led to question the validity of science because the belief context simply cannot deal with the pressing problems of human experience, of mental and physical health, of sanity and the urgent need for spiritual nourishment. But this context is cracking *and the cracks are coming from within science itself*. Science itself is showing the way its own context, and therefore the context of society, might change. And in fact the change in contextual beliefs that our science-created society so desperately needs can probably come about only in this way, not by denouncing science but by understanding the fundamental change that is happening within science.

The revolution taking place now in science is the gradual realization that there is no Reality, no Universe existing eternally, absolutely, and independently of our own observations and thoughts. As Bruner again succinctly puts it, "For my central ontological conviction is that there is no 'aboriginal' reality against which one can compare a possible world in order to establish some form of correspondence between it and the real world."[8] The nature of human mind is somehow implicated in the need for a new context. The scientific method has now been pushed to its limit, and at that limit we find that the human observer reappears in spite of all efforts to keep him or her out. In order to provide adequate explanations for physical and biological phenomena, for scientific explanation itself, and even for human perception, the active role of the observer *has to be included* in the explanations. Mind and its universe are found to be tangled inextricably after all. When we examine the various foundational problems our science, and our society based on it, is now facing we find that many of these problems arise from ignoring this inherent tangling of universe and mind.

2

Quantum Questions

LET US NOW look more closely at the belief context of today's reality. The description of the Universe that most of us today believe we live in begins with 'matter,' a mindless stuff which, building on itself in forms of ever increasing complexity, is the single reality behind all that appears. For our description to be complete we would like to describe the most fundamental nature of this matter and how it came to be. The physics of elementary particles known as quantum theory is the aspect of the modern universe that deals with these topics. And we will now find that according to quantum theory the description of the fundamental nature of that mindless stuff we call 'matter' includes within it inherent doubt as to whether there is in Reality anything corresponding to 'matter' at all.

THE QUANTUM PARADOX

Quantum theory was formulated in the first few decades of this century, when physicists were trying to understand the composition and behavior of atoms and of the elementary particles believed to compose atoms. At that time it was thought that three particles made up all atoms: electrons, protons, and neutrons. Now it is known that there are hundreds of particles of similar type to the protons and neutrons, although much less stable, and physicists are looking to a yet deeper level to find what they hope to be the Ultimate Constituents of Everything. Nevertheless, all these particles follow the rules of quantum mechanics that describe the dynamic motions of the particles and the way they interact with each other.

Quantum theory is the most successful physical theory of all time from the practical point of view. Since its formulation fifty years ago, innumerable phenomena have been explained in tremendous detail, with very great accuracy; and new entirely unexpected phenomena have been discovered, as a direct result of it. Yet quantum theory is

17

founded on unresolved paradox—a paradox that for most of these
fifty years has been simply ignored by most practicing physicists.

This openness at its foundation (one might say hollowness at the
core) has been ignored by most other scientists taking physics to be
the model of rational science, a model that many have tried to imitate
in method and rigor. An important aspect of scientific realism has
been that all other descriptions of nature—chemistry, biology, psychology and sociology—will be ultimately reducible to physics. Yet
when we ask, What then is ultimate reality? according to the science
that supposedly is the only one that can ultimately tell us, we find
the answer: it is questionable in what sense ultimately objective
reality can be said to exist at all.

The problem arises because elementary particles exhibit some
properties that are fundamentally incompatible. A single electron (or
other 'elementary particle') may appear at times to be behaving like a
small lump of matter, the 'electron-particle,' and at other times to
have the characteristics of waves, the 'electron-wave.' The flip from
one state, the electron-wave, to the other, the electron-particle, occurs
when the electron interacts with anything. It might be an interaction
with another elementary particle or with the particles of our measuring instrument.

Now it is extremely difficult to conceive how anything in our
ordinary large-scale world could be both a wave and a particle, or flip
from one to the other instantaneously. A particle occupies a particular
position in space, no matter how large a container it is placed in: for
example if you place a fly (a particle) in a box, it may fly around the
box but it will always be in *some* particular place in the box. But a
wave spreads out to fill the whole space available to it: if you start a
wave motion on the surface of a pond, the wave will soon spread out
to cover the whole surface.

The quantum reality question then is two-fold: first, what kind of
reality can an entity have that flips in an instant from being wave-like
to being particle-like; and second, does the measuring setup have
anything to do with the flip? This is obviously a very simplified
account of the quantum reality problem; nevertheless this account
summarizes the essence of the problem.

According to one count, there are at least seven different interpretations of quantum reality, each one being upheld by major physicists.[1] Of these only one tries to hold onto the idea that the reality of
an electron is indeed like the reality of an ordinary classical particle,
that quantum reality is like commonsense reality. This interpretation

is in many ways more problematical than all the others and is regarded as the least likely by most commentators.

The first possible approach to the problem is that taken by most practicing physicists today and for the past sixty years. This is to say that quantum theory is a powerful technique that has demonstrably worked in every possible area that we have applied it. Therefore it must be true and it is simply a waste of time to worry about apparent problems at the foundations. It was because this attitude was taken so widely that the problems, although hotly debated between Einstein and Bohr in the 1930s, were virtually unknown to a whole generation of physicists. Little mention was made of these problems when I studied physics in the physics department at Cambridge University in the early 1960s, although the difficulty was discussed in the philosophy department. And these questions are certainly not raised to high school students, even though such students would be perfectly capable of understanding and appreciating the serious issues involved. As physicist Paul Davies says, "These statements [about quantum reality] are so stunning that most scientists lead a sort of dual life, accepting them in the laboratory, but rejecting them without thought in daily life."[2]

NIELS BOHR'S FRAMEWORK OF COMPLEMENTARITY

The principal founder of quantum mechanics, Niels Bohr,[3] concerned himself all his life with the problem of its interpretation. Bohr maintained that, whatever it is, the reality of the electron is neither known nor knowable to us as a classical 'object.' He did not say that there *is* no definite quantum reality; he said rather that whatever that reality may be, we can know it only by adopting an attitude, or 'framework,' altogether different from the classical idea of objectivity. For Bohr, the essential point of 'objectivity' has to be understood not as whether there exists a 'reality' altogether *independent* of the human realm of discourse, but whether we can *communicate unambiguously* about our experience. All our concepts come from what happens at our scale, and our descriptions can only be framed in these terms. To give an account of the apparently incompatible properties of the electron, he formulated the complementarity principle: that it is in the very nature of reality that there exist qualities or aspects that human knowledge cannot grasp simultaneously, and that an unambiguous account, i.e., an objective account, of atomic phenomena must be able to accommodate these complementary descriptions.

Bohr's view is not that, *for the time being*, because science has not yet progressed far enough, we do not know what is behind appearances. It is that because of the inherent relationship between man and his universe, he can never know what is behind appearances, if indeed there *is* anything, beyond the framework of complementarity. In particular it is not possible to picture a world behind appearances made up of substantial entities, or 'things.'

Furthermore, an unambiguous description of experience must, according to Bohr, include a description of the entire experimental setup as a whole, as well as the way we decide to divide that setup into an observing system and an observed system. This division is to some extent arbitrary, and how the division is made determines what kinds of characteristics the observed system will display—wave or particle characteristics, for example. But these characteristics cannot then be regarded as properties of the 'reality' behind the appearances. The 'reality' of the isolated observed system only has meaning relative to the whole interaction. As Henry Folse says in *The Philosophy of Niels Bohr*, "what complementarity allows us to say about the reality which lies behind the phenomena is that it has the characteristics of being able to produce different sorts of phenomena in different sorts of interactions, and the way these phenomena are described cannot be used to characterize the reality which causes them. In one sense it would seem that such a characterization would be more adequately expressed by speaking of the powers of an activity instead of the properties of a substance."[4]

Bohr spoke a great deal about the language community in which physics exists and in which physicists communicate, and was very much aware of the degree to which our langauge creates our reality. According to Aage Peterson, Bohr's student and long-time collaborator, Bohr would say, "What is it that we human beings ultimately depend on? We depend on our words. We are suspended in language." Peterson continues, "When one said to him that it cannot be language which is fundamental, but that it must be reality which, so to speak, lies beneath language, and of which language is a picture he would reply, 'We are suspended in language in such a way that we cannot say what is up and what is down. The word 'reality' is also a word, a word which we must learn to use correctly.' "[5] Kierkegaard used to express his existential anxiety by saying that he found himself with seventy thousand leagues of water under him, and to this Bohr would rejoinder, "with a twinkle in his eyes: 'It is much worse—we are suspended over a bottomless pit, caught in our own words.' "[6]

Bohr carried the complementarity principle beyond physics into all of human affairs. He said, "Thus, the integrity of living organisms, and the characteristics of conscious individuals and human cultures present features of wholeness, the account of which implies a typical complementarity mode of description. We are not dealing with more or less vague analogies, but with clear examples of logical relations which, in different contexts, are met with in wider fields."[7] He felt, for example, that the long-standing debate between mechanism and vitalism in biology would be resolved not by taking one side or the other but by going beyond both taking the viewpoint of complementarity. A biological system presents mechanistic characteristics when we analyze it biochemically, but this necessitates destroying the biological unity of the system. When this unity is preserved, typically living characteristics manifest, but the mechanisms are then obscured. These two aspects thus both have to be taken into account for a complete description of the organism, although they can never be observed together, owing to the way in which the observer has to interact with the system in order to observe it.

He then applies this view to the problem of human personality: "I hope that the idea of complementarity is suited to characterize the situation, which bears a deep-going analogy to the general difficulty in the formation of human ideas, inherent in the distinction between subject and object." In another conversation on this Bohr says, "it is quite impossible to analyze things in terms of—I don't know what to call it, not atoms. I mean simply, if you have some things . . . they are so connected that if you try to separate them from each other, it just has nothing to do with the actual situation."[8] Complementarity, then, was Bohr's way of pointing to the inherent wholeness of nature and to the fact that the activity of analyzing and discriminating, so necessary to science, sometimes simply cannot grasp the whole reality of a situation. According to Folse, Bohr's favorite quotation from poetry was from Schiller's *Sayings of Confucius;* "Only wholeness leads to clarity and Truth lies in the abyss."[9]

HEISENBERG'S POTENTIALITIES

Werner Heisenberg, who worked closely with Bohr in formulating the Copenhagen interpretation, was willing to go a little further than Bohr. He did try to conceive what might be the best way to describe its state when the electron is not behaving as a particle. He suggested that in this state we should not think of the electron as having a definite actuality in the physical world. Rather we should think of it as being in a kind of suspended state of many possibilities, or "potentialities" as he called them. As the electron passes through our experimental setup, before it is recorded as a particle at one particular point of the many it could possibly have arrived at, Heisenberg would like to say that it is potentially heading toward all these points. It is only when the electron actually is recorded at a particular point, thus manifesting as a particle, that it has physical actuality at all. This view led Heisenberg to say, "In the experiments *about* atomic events we have to do with things and facts, with phenomena that are just as real as any phenomena in daily life. But atoms or the elementary particles *themselves* are not as real; they form a world of potentialities or possibilities rather than one of things or facts."[10]

'CONSCIOUSNESS' ENTERS THE PICTURE

John von Neumann, a brilliant mathematician who was at the leading edge of many of the most dramatic developments in the 1930s and 1940s, from developing the logical basis of modern computers to strategic game theory, was the first to clearly lay out the logical basis of the quantum reality problem.[11] Von Neumann was not satisfied with Bohr's or Heisenberg's interpretation. He continued to press the point: at which precise moment in the process of quantum measurement does the electron-wave change into an electron-particle? Von Neumann was forced by his own logic reluctantly to come to a surprising—and to some rather distasteful—answer: that it is the consciousness of the observer that causes the change.

Von Neumann reasoned that as the measurement proceeds, the electron passes through the experimental apparatus and hits the recorder, causing a stimulus on the retina of the observer looking at it. The observer's eye and brain is physical and must be regarded as part of the measuring setup. Each point of the process is itself a physical event that must be governed by quantum theory and that cannot therefore itself be responsible for the change from wave to particle. The only special moment in the whole process is the moment at which the *experimenter becomes conscious* of the result of the measurement. This then must be the point at which the electron-wave actually becomes an electron-particle. Therefore it is the consciousness of the observer that is causing the state of the electron to change from being one in which its position is indefinite to one in which it is definite. It is the consciousness of the observer that reduces the electron-wave to an electron-particle. Although von Neumann remained reluctant to accept the consequences of his logic, the view that consciousness creates quantum reality was championed by other eminent physicists, in particular Nobel laureate Eugene Wigner.[12]

To many physicists, especially those who have decided in advance, for deeper reasons, that their universe shall be mindless, this is a very unsavory solution. However, even if we do not try to force such a mindless view on our universe, the big problem is that this interpretation does not say what is meant by the 'consciousness' of the observer. The interpretation is fraught with problems simply because consciousness is far too vague a notion to be useful in this situation. Wigner himself maintains that this whole argument shows that the laws governing consciousness must be entirely outside of the laws governing matter. And so the duality of mind and matter is reborn. Nevertheless, unless you stop with Bohr, the argument does seem to have an almost inevitable logic to it and, as we shall now see, alternatives are equally bizarre.

MANY WORLDS

Hugh Everett and Bryce deWitt were two physicists who objected strongly to the idea of introducing anything like consciousness into physics.[13] In their Many Worlds interpretation, they suggest that instead of regarding the various possibilities as existing in some vague, nonphysical realm, as Heisenberg had done, we should regard them all as *equally actual*. Each time two or more particles interact, or a particle interacts with a measuring instrument, there are many possible outcomes of this interaction. We could multiply such interactions indefinitely up to the level of two people interacting, or an observer reading a measuring instrument. These interactions are happening trillions of times every fraction of a second, and Everett suggests that all possible outcomes of all such interactions are actual in some world. Every moment, the world itself is branching into trillions of further actual worlds. These worlds continue parallel to each other. Some differ by very little from each other. Some—those that branched off a long time ago—are altogether different. The observer, for example you, also branches at each moment. But you do not know you have branched and you continue to experience yourself as one observer in one world. I should make it clear that this is no fantasy of a science fiction writer, this is a serious physical model of ultimate reality, taken seriously and discussed in many prestigious journals.

One problem that the Many Worlds model does solve is the question of whether it is possible that a universe containing intelligent life could have evolved by chance, given the incredibly long odds against it, in the kind of timespan available to our universe, which is approximately fifteen billion years. The Many Worlds answer would be, it doesn't matter how long the odds are because all possible worlds exist anyway. Of course the only ones that are known to exist will be the ones with knowing observers in it, like this one. This is a clever answer, especially since it is altogether unverifiable, there being absolutely no way anyone can verify whether an unobserved universe exists or not.

The Many Worlds model certainly *seems* to solve the problem of needing an observer to bring potential into actual, for all worlds are always actual. Yet it is not so clear that this problem is solved. For we are, obviously, left with the question, Why is it that all of us experience ourselves as residing in only one unbranching world? The answer presumably cannot come from within the model, but would seem to require some understanding of the nature and limitations of human experience. But then we have simply replaced the notion of 'consciousness' by the equally vague and almost equivalent notion of 'experience.' Everett may argue that whether or not a world is experienced is not relevant to physics. But it would then seem to be a very incomplete physics that comes up with many actual worlds and is not able to say why there appears to be only this one.

Only one 'thought-experiment' has so far been suggested by which it might be possible to distinguish the Many Worlds model of reality from the others.[14] In this experiment a computer is built that is capable of remembering and reflecting on its own inner state, like a human brain, and reporting that state to others. The computer is also the measuring instrument in a quantum level experiment. After the experiment is over, the computer is asked what it experienced at the moment the measurement was made. Its answer will be one way if the Many Worlds interpretation is correct and another way if that interpretation is not correct. Whether such a computer could, even in theory, actually be built is a matter of philosophy. But this 'thought experiment' clearly seems to be bringing back in the notion that inner, self-conscious experience is relevant to quantum mechanics, precisely the notion that Everett and deWitt wanted to eliminate once and for all.

The Wigner and Everett models both in the end need to bring in the fact of a self-conscious experiencing organism (of human origin or otherwise) in order to end up with one actual experienced world. Both Wigner and Everett are plagued by the shadow of mind/matter dualism. Although mind was thought to be eliminated at the very beginning, by trying to build the universe from elementary particles of mindless stuff, it seems to be very hard to keep mind out.

WHOLENESS AND THE IMPLICATE ORDER

David Bohm, a long-time student and colleague of both Einstein and Bohr, avoids this shadow by proposing a model in which consciousness and matter take part on an equal footing, a model in which the ultimate level of reality is one of undivided wholeness. For Bohm the insights of relativity and quantum mechanics agree in pointing to a universe which is undivided and of which all parts "merge and unite in one totality." Bohm holds that flow or process is prior to forms or 'things,' which arise out of and dissolve back into this flow. This flow is prior even to the distinction between mind and matter. Bohm says, "In this flow, mind and matter are not separate substances. Rather they are different aspects of one whole and unbroken movement."

Bohm suggests that this unbroken movement contains layer upon layer of more and more general levels of ordering. Newtonian mechanics is embedded within relativity and quantum mechanics, which in turn is embedded in further layers of ordering yet to be discovered. The boundary of each layer of ordering is reached when the phenomena begin to manifest chaotically in relation to the present order. Specific manifestation, appearance of some 'thing' or 'thought,' is the revealing or unfolding of some layer of order out of the whole. Because appearance is hidden within the unbroken whole, Bohm calls this the 'implicate order,' in contrast to 'explicate order.' 'Explicate order' is actual appearance, e.g., the measurement of the behavior of an electron, the sight of a tree, or a thought of hunger.

According to Bohm, all of reality can be enfolded into the implicate order. "In terms of the implicate order one may say that everything is enfolded into everything. This contrasts with the explicate order now dominant in physics in which things are unfolded in the sense that each thing lies only in its own particular region of space and time and outside the region belonging to other things." Another way of saying this is that all parts of the explicate order, no matter how separated by space and time, are interconnected. Particles that are widely separated are in some way connected.

Bohm also suggests that 'matter' and 'mind' are both enfolded into the implicate order, which is thus prior to both. "We are led to propose that the more comprehensive, deeper, and more inward actuality is neither mind nor body but rather a yet higher dimensional actuality, which is their common ground and which is of a nature beyond both." Thought and appearance emerge together as related projections from this higher-dimensional ground.[15]

Bohm's ideas on the 'implicate order,' that there may well be levels of ordering more general and therefore 'deeper' than the level of quantum mechanics to some extent springs from his earlier work as a staunch follower of Einstein in his criticism of Bohr's interpretation. Einstein maintained all his life that there must be a level of reality that we have not yet penetrated, deeper than quantum mechanics, at which 'elementary particles' do after all behave just as the ordinary particles in our world, that is, they behave like 'classical' particles. This was called the 'hidden variables' view. However, more recently there has been a rather dramatic turn of events. In 1964, John Bell[16] analyzed the logic of certain measurements on systems in which two particles interact and then become separated. He showed that if there are indeed such deeper 'hidden variables,' in other words, if there is a level of ordering at which elementary particles do behave classically, then measurements on such a two-particle system would give results incompatible with quantum mechanics. These experiments were carried out finally by Alain Aspect in 1981. The results quite conclusively were compatible with quantum mechanics and therefore showed that there cannot be such a deeper level of classical 'hidden variables.'

Bell's theorem and its subsequent confirmation prove conclusively that we have at this point only one of two possibilities open to us. First, if we want to speak about an objective 'reality' behind the appearances, then that reality must be interconnected over all of space and time. Any two particles that have once interacted must continue to be connected in some way for the rest of time. This means that all particles of the universe are interconnected. Just like other aspects of quantum reality, these interconnections are very difficult to conceive of in terms of the ordinary world of things and their interactions. They would have to act instantaneously, not be mediated by fields of any kind and not diminish with distance.

If we do not wish to accept the idea that at the quantum level all of reality may be interconnected in this strange way, then we must return to something like Bohr's original viewpoint. We will have to forgo the idea that there is an objective reality behind the appearances that are given to us by our experimental setup. But it seems to be commonly agreed now that we have only these two alternatives: either we give up the assumption that there is a world of real particles independent of the observer; or, if we do assume such a world, then these particles must be interconnected. It has become very clear that whatever we think the nature of reality is, one important tendency of thought that must be given up is the tendency to think in terms of separate 'things.' The tendency to regard the world as made up of separate entities, things, having their own separate existence and identity and only accidentally related to other 'things' is perhaps one of the most deep-rooted characteristics of human thought. And Bell's theorem and its confirmation catches this 'thing-thinking' in a contradiction. If we think of the elementary level as consisting of 'particles' having real existence independent of the observer, then these particles are no longer separate particles.

In this chapter I have tried to come to some further understanding of reality and its relation to mind by asking the question of the most exact of sciences, that science that has laid claim to penetrate to the heart of the material world. I have presented the four major interpretations of reality available to us. Of these, two—those of Wigner and Everett—seem to be saying that there is a factor separate from the physical world that needs to be called on to explain the basic fact that each of us lives in a single, actual world. Wigner invokes this factor explicitly and calls it the 'consciousness' of the observer. Everett tries to ignore this factor, but his fragmenting, multiplying Many Worlds are altogether without basis in human experience if we do not bring consciousness in. For both Wigner and Everett, there remains an arbitrary split in the universe between matter and that other, mysterious factor.

The other two interpretations take a different view. Niels Bohr is conventionally reported as saying that our human knowledge of reality is forever limited by the complementarity principle. However, his other writings and conversations hint that he believed that the reason this is so is because of the undivided wholeness of reality, which does not permit the arbitrary making of distinctions. David Bohm takes this point of view much more specifically and elaborates it into a theory of the implicate order. For both Bohr and Bohm, mind and matter, subject and object are in some way aspects of one underlying totality.

TO BE REAL IS TO BE COMMUNICATED

In one way or another, in every one of the most widely accepted interpretations of quantum reality, some account must be taken of the role of the observer, the experiencer of that reality. Physicist John Wheeler, also a colleague of Einstein and Bohr and one of the most articulate and careful of those physicists willing to enter the interpretation dialogue, has succinctly summarized the situation in this way: 'No elementary phenomenon is a real phenomenon until it is an observed phenomenon.'[17] Another way of putting this is to say that what we have called 'matter' is, at the quantum level, not separable from some aspect of the observer's 'mind.' Wheeler singles out that aspect of mind which communicates meaning to another. It is this aspect of mind that is involved when an observer makes a quantum phenomenon a real phenomenon, by recording it in such a way that it can be communicated to others.

Wheeler has given a delightful analogy that very clearly shows how communication can create a reality.[18] Wheeler bases this analogy on a well-known party game called Twenty Questions. In the usual version of this game one participant leaves the room while the others choose a word. The returning participant then has to guess the chosen word by asking a series of questions requiring the response "yes" or "no." In Wheeler's version of the game there is no chosen word. Each answerer can answer as he pleases, the one requirement being that he should have in mind, at the moment of answering, a word compatible with his own response and all that had gone before. Wheeler describes his experience thus: "At first the answers came quickly. Then the questions began to take longer in the answering. It was strange. All I wanted from my friends was a simple yes or no. Yet the one queried would think and think, yes or no, no or yes, before responding. Finally I felt I was hot on the trail, that the word might be 'cloud.' I ventured it: 'Is it cloud?' 'Yes' came the reply and everyone burst out laughing. They explained that there had been no word in the room."

Wheeler interprets his story in this way: "What is the symbolism of the story? The world, we once believed, exists 'out there' independent of any act of observation. The electron we once considered to have at each moment a definite position and momentum. I, entering, thought the room contained a definite word. In actuality the word was developed step by step through the questions I raised, as the information about the electron is brought into being by the experiment that the observer chooses to make; that is, by the kind of registering equipment that he puts into place. Had I asked different questions or the same questions in a different order I would have ended up with a different word, as the experimenter would have ended up with a different story for the doings of the electron." Wheeler points out that just as the power he had in bringing a particular word into being was limited by the "yes" and "no" answers he received, so although the experimenter has considerable power to influence what will happen to the electron by what experiments he chooses to do, this power is limited by the unpredictable answers nature will give. But he concludes, "In the game, no word is a word until that word is promoted to reality by the choice of questions asked and answers given. In the real world of quantum physics, no elementary phenomenon is a phenomenon until it is a recorded phenomenon."

The picture that emerges is of a universe altogether different from the one each of us learned in school; on which all of us, professional scientist or not, base our lives; and which, very sadly, is still being taught today to our own sons and daughters. The idea that behind appearances, behind the beauty of a pair of seagulls flying over a still bay in the evening mist, is a more real world that is empty and dead in which pieces of matter move mindlessly about forming chance combinations; the idea that the mind is somehow separate from all this, observing it passively as in a mirror—these ideas *can no longer be taken as the basis for any ultimate belief about reality.* In fact they are no more real than the ideas of the seagull and the misty bay are real. They are the description of another level of manifestation, one that we connect with when we use instruments that extend our perceptions so far.

But when we use more powerful instruments that extend our perceptions even further, that universe dissolves and another, the one I have been describing, manifests. At this level we find we have lost the whole idea of a solid reality behind appearances independent of the human mind that is observing and theorizing about it. There is no further level for objective science to go, based on a dualistic separation between mind and nature, on the search for an ultimate physical reality altogether separate from a mirroring mind.

But let the reader beware. Please do not jump to the conclusion that we are now going to join our usual idea of consciousness with our usual idea of matter, or nature, and come up with a hybrid oneness. Rather this discussion suggests the need for a deeper analysis of the concepts of an objective reality and separate minds that perceives this reality. And it suggests that this analysis should not assume in advance the duality of the perceiving mind and the reality it perceives. Now the important point for us is that this is not merely some abstract philosophy divorced and separated from the everyday reality of our lives. To base our lives on a belief system that does not take dualism for granted profoundly alters them, and alters the society we create. In Chapter 4 we will begin to look at some traditional ways of life and thought that have not been based on the ultimate separation of mind and nature, the perceiver and what is perceived.

The quantum mechanical revolution that began in the 1920s profoundly shook the nineteenth-century confidence that science is gradually building a more and more complete picture of the objective Universe. It was not just the problems of interpretation at the foundations of quantum mechanics that shook this confidence. It was that reflective scientists began to ask themselves how they could have been so wrong, and yet have been so convinced that they were right. And beyond this, how could they be sure that they were not making the same mistake again. This led to a questioning of the meaning of the whole endeavor of science and to serious doubt as to what extent scientific theories about the Universe do in fact reflect any ultimate truth. This questioning, as we will see in the next chapter, led to an understanding of the extent to which the observer's descriptions must be included as part of the Universe he or she is observing and describing.

3

Masking the Universe

WE SAW IN the previous chapters that it is an open question whether an external world, the Universe, exists objectively. We must ask then, if this is so, what is science talking about? Before the 1920s there was, to practicing scientists, really very little need for this question. The realist view was taken for granted: that there is a Universe external to people, sometimes known as Nature or Reality or some similar noun. It was also taken for granted that science was "uncovering Nature's laws," laws that were absolute, eternally unchanging, and altogether independent of people's minds. The mechanical Universe of Newton together with the laws of electromagnetism developed by Maxwell was on the right road to a complete explanation of everything. To be opposed to this absolute realist view was to be opposed to science, as well as to common sense.

But at the beginning of the twentieth century scientists were profoundly shaken by the publication of the theory of relativity by Albert Einstein.[1] It was not so much the content of the theory that was shocking, but the implications this had for the idea that science had been steadily uncovering the truth about the Universe. Newton's assumptions of absolute empty space, and linear independently flowing time, and of a gravitational force between planets were seen to be not absolutely true, not even only approximately true. Yes, they underpinned calculational methods that gave approximately accurate descriptions of the motions of the planets. But, as fundamental assumptions about the *nature of Reality,* they needed radical revision in the light of relativity. Then, when the paradoxes of quantum mechanics came along in the 1920s the possibility of describing Reality became altogether questionable.[2] The response to this fundamental questioning was to try to formulate a rational understanding of scientific theories and their relationship to Reality. A main objective of this philosophical endeavor was the preservation of the idea of Reality, the preservation of nineteenth-century common sense.

THE FAILURE OF THE STANDARD VIEW OF SCIENCE

The commonsense idea of what science is doing, which was developed by a group of logicians and philosophers of science in the 1930s and which became the standard view of practicing scientists until now, is presumed in almost all popular expositions of science. It is known as 'logical empiricism' because it takes the view that the endeavor of science consists of deduction of laws of physics (or chemistry or biology) by application of the rules of *logic* (rules like, if A = B, then B = A) to *empirical* statements about observations of Nature.

The truth or falsity of an observational statement is to be determined according to whether or not that statement corresponds to a fact. This simple idea is known for obvious reasons as the 'correspondence theory' of truth, and goes back as far as the Greek philosopher Aristotle. A classic example of the correspondence theory is: the statement "Ravens are black" is true if and only if ravens (the real things, not the word "ravens") are in fact black (the actual color, not the word "black").

The correspondence theory assumes that there are, in fact, real things. There are not just black ravens, white snow, and green trees. There are also, actually, in fact, electrons, protons, gluons, quarks, fields, forces, space, and time, biological species, minds, and the Universe. And all of these real things have an inherent existence completely independent of our theories about them and our observations of them.

The attempt to make the standard view irrefutable was an attempt to establish that true statements can be made about these real things, in other words to establish that we can in fact come to know something true about the Reality behind appearances. And the way we were to come to know true facts about this Reality would be very analogous to the way we come to know true facts about appearances: if someone says "snow is white," I look out of the window to see whether the snow (assuming there is snow) is, in fact, white. I look without any bias or prejudice beforehand as to whether snow is or is not white. I look with pure motivation and unclouded perception. Likewise, if someone says "electrons are spherical" I should be able to make an observation of an electron analogous to looking out the window. The possibility of making pure observations, unadulterated by the beliefs of the observer, is the basis of empiricism.

The theory was made highly sophisticated. Sir Karl Popper[3] pointed out that observations never prove a theory to be true beyond doubt: even a million observations of black ravens does not prove that all ravens are black; there might be a white one somewhere. So a theory of falsification was developed: theories can be proved false beyond doubt, for example, one observation of a white raven falsifies the theory that all ravens are black. The logic of probability was invoked to develop a theory of how to judge the most probable scientific theory, based on the idea of falsification. It was proposed that our theories are gradually more and more probable approximations to the final whole truth. But in all this it was the assumption of an objectively real Universe of ravens, electrons, and everything in between that was being protected.

The significance of all this is that this thirty-year attempt to put Reality on a sound and incontrovertible philosophical basis has failed. By the early 1970s Frederick Suppe, summarizing a major conference on the structure of scientific theories, was able to say: "The situation today, then, in the philosophy of science is this: the Received [standard] view has been rejected . . ." And no universally agreed-upon view has taken its place that in any way reinstates the classical view of an absolute Reality waiting to be revealed, or even approximated to, by science. As Suppe went on to say, ". . . but no proposed alternative analysis of theories enjoys widespread acceptance."[4]

OBSERVATIONS DEPEND ON THEORIES

This final recognition of failure came when, in the 1950s, a number of scientists and historians of science acknowledged that observations are themselves inextricably dependent on the belief system of the scientists who make them—they are 'theory-laden.' To give a simple example, when we set up an experiment to test the IQs of various racial groups, the questions we ask and therefore the observations we make may depend to a great extent on what we already believe about the IQs of these groups. And indeed many silly theories have been proposed over the past fifty years of intelligence testing for just this reason. Today the whole idea of intelligence testing is falling into disrepute precisely because it is becoming clear just how much such observations (the test results) are theory-laden.

We might dismiss this example on the grounds that so little is known about intelligence anyway that "tests" of intelligence are bound to be heavily dependent on our theory. But the observations are no less theory-laden in physics, the strictest of sciences, and on sciences modeling themselves closely on physics. Michael Polanyi's description of the education of a medical student in Chapter 1 is an example of this.

In discussing the nature of the electron, physicist Richard Morris writes, "Today [J. J.] Thomson is remembered as one of the great scientists. Yet in Thomson's own time no physicist in his right mind would take Thomson's conception of the electron seriously. Since then, ideas about this tiny particle have changed so dramatically that it is possible to say that there is little similarity between Thomson's electron and the electron as it is viewed by modern physicists."[5] In other words the very nature of an electron as the human family knows it has changed radically at least twice since its initial discovery. And the observations physicists make on the 'electron' depend, of course, on what they believe its nature to be.

For another example, consider the tracing, shown in Figure 3-1, of lines in a photograph. You might be just educated enough to know that it has something to do with physics, or perhaps you know that it traces a photograph of 'elementary particles' in a 'bubble chamber.' But it took hundreds of physicists many years working in several teams around the world, building machines several miles long, all

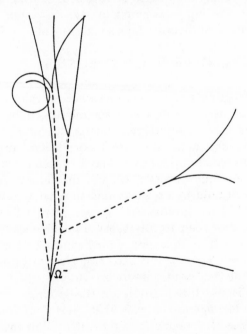

Figure 3-1

this activity intricately wrapped up with theory, to find this photograph. And you would only really understand that it represents the momentous discovery of the Omega-minus particle, if you know what that means, after at least a decade of training in advanced mathematical physics that very few are capable of understanding at all. One simply would not see this Omega-minus particle if one does not hold these theories in one's mind.

The view that observations are laden with our theories, concepts, and beliefs is strongly supported by work on the psychology and neurophysiology of perception over the past decade. The primary assumption that so much of the logical empiricist view is based on is that perception is like a clear mirror, or a camera, with which the mind somehow takes snapshot-like images of the world that are then processed into scientific theories. Recent discoveries on the nature of perception have more or less completely overturned this naive view. We now know, as we will see in detail in later chapters, that perception is a process in which meaning, motivation, and emotional response all enter in at deeply subconscious levels. The final perception of a world includes all these factors in a tremendously complex construction involving billions of bits of information. The idea of a pure, unbiased observation becomes highly suspect at the very beginning.

The view that the perceived world is a construction of the perceptual system, a view widely held by the new cognitive scientists, is a helpful first step toward releasing us from the grip of belief in a given 'outer world' of objects. But, as we will see, it is only a first step. A deeper critique of the processes of perception also questions the opposite extreme of saying that the perceived world is a projection of the structure of the mind, the 'inner world,' that perceives it. This deeper critique will show that the 'outer world' and the 'inner world' are mutually fabricated in an active reciprocating process.

It is ironic that until very recently philosophers concerned with the basis for scientific knowledge rarely took into account the data available from scientific work on perception. Bertrand Russell, a foremost exponent of the logical empiricist view, and one of the leading philosophers of science and human knowledge of all time, says in *Our Knowledge of the External World*: ". . . the first step in the analysis of data, namely, the discovery of what is really given in sense, is full of difficulty. We will, however, not linger on this point: so long as its existence is realised, the exact outcome does not make any very great difference in our main problem."[6] Psychologist Richard Gregory comments, "His [Russell's] denial of the importance of psychological details of perception is very generally shared by philosophers today."[7]

But in a 1983 conference on Science vs. Reality, even Paul Churchland, a well-known exponent of scientific realism, remarks, ". . . our perceptual judgments themselves emerge as theoretical responses to . . . the environment. . . . [We are free] to transform the conceptual content of sensory perception itself, in a potentially endless variety of useful and revealing ways, limited only by the bounds of human theoretical imagination and by the actual intricacies of our causal interactions with the world." Churchland, the supposed realist, is saying that we can actually change our perceptions. He goes on to say that we can transform the content of perception "by learning to respond habitually, to one's pre-conceptual sensory processing, with judgments framed in the idiom of successful scientific theories. This holds promise for expanding our sensory perspective not only of the external world, but of the internal world as well. Introspection can be informed by neuroscience, just as vision can be informed by physics."[8] In talking of "the preconceptual level of processing," Churchland is making reference to the realization that perception is a process, taking time and having several levels, deeply unavailable to normal consciousness yet influenced by our conceptual beliefs about reality.

Churchland appears, however, not to notice the circularity of his argument. If we are free to alter the conceptual content of our perceptions at the preconscious level, cannot our perceptions be already highly influenced by our conceptions at the preconscious level? And what does this say about the purity of empirical observations, and therefore of the possibility of knowing Reality at all? This question must face not only the scientist in the laboratory, but each one of us as we realize the significance of the breakdown of the naive 'camera theory' of perception. We will return to this key point in subsequent chapters.

MASKS ON THE UNIVERSE

We can see how, given this realization, we must then understand that the beliefs of the scientist are going to be built into the picture of the Universe that that scientist constructs, that is, his or her universe. The scientist's beliefs are built in not just through the theory he or she invents but through the *observations* he or she makes, which are supposed to *check* that theory against 'objective' nature, because these observations are already preconsciously influenced by his or her beliefs. The situation is suspiciously circular.

Here I am using a distinction between the Universe and universes, suggested by Edward Harrison, Professor of Physics and Astronomy at the University of Massachusetts. Harrison says, "The Universe is everything. What it is in its own right, independent of our changing opinions, we never know. The Universe is all-inclusive and includes us; we are a part or an aspect of the Universe experiencing and thinking about itself. . . . The universes are our models of the Universe. They are great schemes of intricate thought—grand cosmic pictures—that rationalize human experience. . . . Each universe is a self-consistent system of ideas, marvelously organized, interlacing most of what is perceived and known. *A universe is a mask fitted on the face of the unknown Universe.*"⁹

Harrison reviews the stories of universes of the past and present: the magic, mythic, Greek, medieval, mechanistic, and modern universe of space-time, black holes, quarks, the Big Bang and Grand Unified Theories of Everything. Reflecting on these stories Harrison remarks, "Wherever we find a human society, however primitive, there is a universe; and wherever we find a universe, of whatever kind, there is a society; both go together, and the one does not exist without the other. Each universe coordinates and unifies a society, enabling its members to communicate their thoughts and share their experiences. Each universe determines what is perceived and what constitutes valid knowledge, and the members of each society believe what is perceived and perceive what is believed."¹⁰

This comment applies not only to the changing universes of the Western world through the ages, but it applies also to the universes of societies with altogether different belief systems. The great Chinese civilizations of the Tang or Ming periods were in every way as full in human dignity, creativity, and moral and intellectual development as the great civilizations in Western history. Yet the most fundamental beliefs on which these civilizations were based were entirely different from those of the West. The Chinese belief systems—Confucianism, Buddhism, and Taoism—were not theistic or dualistic at their basis, they did not separate mind from nature in the radical way that Western belief has done in recent centuries. Likewise, the belief systems of Native Americans are profoundly different from those of science. Native Americans, too, did not separate mind from nature. They have not sought to dominate nature, but rather they have sought the harmony of the great ecosystem of which they are a part (and for that matter, so are we.) Yet in their original lifestyles, they too do not appear to have been lacking in human dignity, generosity, or rich creativity. Their belief system provided them with a coherent, valid, and humanly uplifting way of living in their universe.

If there is no conceivable 'Ultimate Reality,' then how can we say that our universe is more true, and therefore better, than another? The realist Paul Churchland suggests the 'global excellence,' the overall simplicity, capacity to make predictions, and usefulness of a theory, as the criterion of that theory's truth. Now it is true that the scientific universe contains cars, medical drugs, packaged food, and many other benefits to people. It contains the knowledge to manipulate our environment and also our minds. So, we might say, the theory works and that proves it is true. But it has also produced a society that so narrowly defines the correct view that that society locks up a fifth of its population in mental institutions for not having that view and therefore not being able to live in that society. And perhaps another fifth are able to live outside these institutions only because of the pacifying drugs we have produced. Beyond this, the litany of destruction we are causing to our environment is famous. Even if we do not go along with the extremes of dire warnings issued regularly by environmentalists, *something* is out of harmony. The ideal of the philosophy of science is to control the environment for the greater benefit of mankind, yet more than any other major culture we seem to have lost control of our own minds. Should we then say a belief system such as this "works"? If we are considering the global excellence of a universe, all its practical results must be taken into consideration, not just the ones that do work—including the psychological and spiritual well-being of its occupants. We might then turn to other universes to see the extent of their 'global excellence.'

Recent generations of anthropologists and historians, influenced by the humbling effect of the relativistic and quantum revolutions, have approached other societies by trying to see the world from the point of view of members of those societies. They have come to realize that the belief systems of those societies form a complete and coherent system, adequate in every way, or at least as adequate as ours, for dealing with their practical, social, personal, and spiritual needs. Yet these people may live in a world actually perceived as quite different from our own. It is not just that they have different beliefs about the world, they actually perceive differently.

The director of the Pain and Stress Relief Clinic of Lemuel Shattuck Hospital in Boston, who earned his doctorate degree at the Macau Institute of Chinese Medicine, T. J. Kaptchuk, says, "The difference between the two medicines (modern Western and traditional Chinese) is greater than that between their descriptive language. . . . [What has been said] about medical perception in different historical periods could apply as well to these different cultural traditions . . . 'not only the names of diseases, not only the grouping of systems were not the same; but the fundamental perceptual codes that were applied to patients' bodies, the field of objects to which observation addressed itself, the surfaces and depths traversed by the doctor's gaze, the whole system of orientation of his gaze also varied.' "[11]

Yet the traditional Chinese system of medicine *works*. And the traditional Chinese society in which this medicine flourished was in every way as fine, dignified, cultivated, sophisticated, artistic, philosophically, and in certain ways even according to Joseph Needham,[12] scientifically as inventive as modern technological society. It had vast global excellence. But the traditional Chinese assumptions about and explanations of the Universe were profoundly different from those of modern science.

I would not suggest that we promote these societies in a romantic way. They of course have had their problems and brutalities just as ours does. I am suggesting that, of these other societies, whether primitive, premodern, or from a different cultural sphere of the world, we can only say, "Their universe *was* like this." We can no longer say, "They *believed* the Universe to be like this but we now know they were wrong." As science historian Morris Berman says of the universe of medieval alchemy, "The above analysis forces me to conclude that it is not merely the case that men conceived of matter as possessing mind in those days, but rather that, in those days matter *did* possess mind, 'actually' did so. When the obvious objection is raised that the mechanical world view must be true, because we are in fact able to send a man to the moon or invent technologies that demonstrably work, I can only reply that the animistic world view, which lasted for millennia, was also fully efficacious to its believers. In other words our ancestors constructed reality in a way that typically produced verifiable results."[13] The contents of each universe depends on what is selected by the occupants of that universe as appropriate to attend to, and to give names to.

NO ULTIMATE REALITY

In summary we have to abandon the belief that there is an objective Universe behind observed phenomena, independent of human mentality, and that science is step by step getting closer to knowing the truth about this Universe. This belief is now seen as a quaint self-deception. This is such an important and radical change in belief context that it bears repeating over and over again. In fact, if we could follow Churchland's suggestion, we would benefit by entering this context change more than any other into our preconceptual perceptual system. For the belief that science is discovering Reality and that twentieth-century science tells the only true story is deeply embedded in every ordinary man and woman in the modern world. Every politician, businessman, farmer, doctor, psychiatrist, and psycho-therapist is taught this in elementary school and holds it as the contextual belief for everything he or she does. Thus every ordinary educated man and woman in our society lives and perpetuates the self-deception.

In a comment on human fallibility and arrogance Harrison says, "In every age people believe that their universe contains whatever is real and significant. In their temples, academies, monasteries, and universities they reject the rest as opinion and illusion. Forget the superstitions of the uneducated and the myths your parents taught you. For behold! Here is the true universe, awesome, vast and wondrous. . . . The scene is timeless. Yesterday a false universe, today the true universe."[14]

Any new context for science must first and foremost take into account the relative nature of universes, and the active role of any conceptual system, including science itself in constructing universes. What, then, remains of the 'reality' which we are supposedly perceiving? Certainly science is telling us something valid at the practical level, it is telling us something about the causal nature of the world we live in. We cannot change our perceptions at will and whim; these perceptions are constrained by some basic structure. But at this point we must recognize that this basic structure must include our own perceiving bodies and theory-building minds. Science is giving us some messages as to what the basic structure may be, and one of the questions that a new context for science must speak to is what is the status of this structure if it is not ultimately real, or 'aboriginal' as Brunner puts it.

In this chapter we have seen, from the point of view of an analysis of the endeavor of science itself, the extent to which the observer must be included as a part of the system he or she is observing and describing, and indeed the extent to which the world we believe we live in is dependent on our theories and deep-rooted beliefs about it. In the last chapter we saw this observer-participation entering at a fundamental level in physics, and later we will see it too in biology, linguistics, perceptual psychology and cognitive science. Later, when we come to look at the nature of perception we will find that this interdependency of world and perceiver is reciprocal and reaches a very profound level. What all this is pointing to is that a belief context based on the separation, the duality, between mind and nature is no longer workable. We need to find a belief context comprehensive enough to encompass all these disciplines that is based on the nonduality of nature and its observer and of body and mind.

4

Buddhism

WE HAVE SEEN that a new belief context for our society and its science will have to recognize the relativity of all belief systems, and the interdependence of 'universe' and 'mind.' In addition, we would want to be able to elucidate in as much detail as possible just how 'mind' and 'reality' manifest, without any unexplainable remainder, from within this interdependence. That is, we would like a causal theory of the appearance of duality or separateness from within interdependence, or nonseparateness. This would be a theory of the causal nature of mental and perceptual processes. Third, we would need a technique, a method, by which nonduality could be directly experienced, as well as the arising of dualistic thought, perception, and reality within that nonduality. Fourth, our new belief context should not give itself a special status but should include itself among those thought forms arising in duality.

Any system of belief falling short on one of these four criteria would not be adequate as a basis for a new belief context that would be acceptable for science. Any system of belief that speaks of non-separateness or nonduality, without providing an understanding of how duality arises, and without methods to realize this directly, would be nonrational belief, not science. If it recognizes nonduality and provides a method to experience that, but had no theory or method relating to the arising of dualistic thought, perception, and so on, it would again reduce to a belief system with faith in 'nonduality,' which soon becomes objectified as a thing—'The One.' Even if we had a causal *theory* of the arising of duality, or separate 'minds' and 'universes' within nonduality, if we did not have a *method* to realize this directly, it would be a possibly interesting theory but speculative and therefore irrelevant.

There are many scientists and social commentators who now recognize the tremendous upheaval that science is going through, and who seek a new way of understanding the foundations of our society.

These writers are aware of the need to include the observer in any understanding of our universe, and there is indeed an awareness that there are traditional ways of thought and life that are based on nonseparateness. But it has not been easy to see how such ways of thought can be helpful, and these ways have tended to be dismissed. This is understandable in view of the distortion that has arisen by the good-hearted attempt to lump them all together, under the rubric of 'perennial philosophy' or 'Eastern Mysticism' (usually capitalized for no apparent reason), thereby robbing them of the precision and clarity that is essential if we are to be able to put any one of them to the test of experience. Those who have considered traditional belief systems for their possible contributions to science have either rejected them out of hand, or have made the 'Eastern Mysticism' error, thus making them seem vague and irrelevant and provoking further irritation in scientists who rightly demand methods of falsification as well as precision.

At the same time this wish for a new approach is understandable when we consider the appearance of deathly solemnity and ossification that many traditional philosophies and religions present to the public—and science is not excluded from this criticism. It is as if solemnity itself were a criterion of divinity or of truth. It is also understandable when we consider the distortion of these traditions that has resulted from the scholarly demand for abstract knowledge about them without direct experience—as if you could convey to someone the quality of the Mona Lisa's smile by sending that person a letter, even one written in poetry. Such an attitude is as presumptuous as to think one can understand the theory of general relativity, well enough to judge its validity, without knowing even the rudiments of tensor analysis, or to judge the validity of evolutionary theory without knowing the details of fossil remains and molecular biology. It is likewise presumptuous to suppose that one can judge the validity of a system of psychology and philosophy without using the necessary methods for its verification, in this case meditation. Scientists and religious people have each tended to fall into this trap with regard to religion and science respectively.

There are indeed several belief systems that have proclaimed the nonduality of mind and reality, and this is the legitimate basis of the 'perennial philosophy.' In particular we find such claims in Buddhism, Taoism, certain heretical strains of contemplative Christianity (such as Meister Eckhart or the author of "The Cloud of Unknowing"), the Advaita Vedanta system of Indian philosophy, and the late Chinese system known as neo-Confucianism.

However, most of these systems fall rather short when it comes to the criterion of supplying a causal account of duality, thought, and perception in ordinary human experience. Many such systems have a tendency to give the impression of dismissing duality as illusion, and leaving it at that. According to Joseph Needham, the great historian of science and civilization in China, Taoism does have a very strong sense of cause and effect.[1] However, like the scientists of the West, Taoists apply their rational search for knowledge more to the outer natural world than to exploring the cause and effect of mental processes, including perception. The Taoist description of mind and its relationship to body is more alchemical and intuitive than psychological and analytical. This is not to say that it was not valid, as is testified by the success of the classical acupuncture and herbal medicine of China, which is largely based on Taoism. But it is not helpful to us as we try to analyze the causal dynamics of mental processes.

BUDDHISM AND SCIENCE

Is Buddhism a possible belief system that can provide a context for science as it recognizes the relativity of universes and for extending the range and depth of scientific understanding? In the following chapters I shall try to show that Buddhism satisfies all four of the criteria that I suggested at the beginning of this chapter. I do not suggest that Buddhism is the only such system.

Buddhism is also satisfactory as a possible new context for modern thought in that its profound psychological and philosophical discoveries have been expressed in a way that is not essentially tied to or organized around any particular cultural form. Buddhism has taken a variety of manifestations since its origins in the small kingdom of Magadha, in the region that is now India, in the sixth century B.C. It traveled from there down to Sri Lanka, and to Burma, Thailand, Vietnam, Cambodia, Tibet, China, Korea, Japan, Indonesia. In each culture that they entered, Buddhist practice and insight took on the cultural and artistic forms and adapted many of the philosophical and religious ideas of that culture. Of course, like any belief system, Buddhism has taken on accretions that are in some sense contradictory to its essential teaching. Its adherents, too, have at times reverted to dualistic worship—worship of an external deity—and to the belief in an external savior. At the same time, with few exceptions the essence of the teaching was not changed even though the external cultural manifestations have varied.

Whereas Taoism, Hinduism, and neo-Confucianism have remained very much tied to particular cultural forms, Buddhism is similar to science in its universal nature. It is an analysis of universal characteristics: of the nature of mind common to all humanity; of the nature of prejudice and narrowmindedness and of the suffering that these cause; and of the possibility of overcoming such narrowmindedness and opening into a joyful existence not based on self-interest alone. As such it cannot in its very nature be predetermined by any particular cultural forms or beliefs. As the Buddhist scholar Herbert Guenther says, "Since the way I travel is said to remove all bias and blindness, its nature must not be predetermined in any way; it must find its determination in the progress along it to a point which is free from all bias."[2] Or as Nolan Pliny Jacobson, Emeritus Professor of Philosophy at Winthrop College, puts it, "Buddhism has always been persuaded that life is one, self-corrective, and self-surpassing, and Buddhism's methods of meditation and analysis are designed to free men and women from the self-serving, time-bound, authoritarian social institutions that now threaten the adventure nature has been making in man."

Jacobson argues that another important characteristic that science shares with the Buddhist viewpoint is that both bring to the forefront the self-correcting nature of men and women, by which is meant "the capacity . . . for changing the way they have been reared, for rethinking from time to time everything they have concluded regarding the dynamic and beautiful universe of which their living is a part." He goes on to assert that "The issue of survival serves to single out for the attention of all humanity the two clearly defined communities where the greatest joys of life have been associated with the process of self-correction. One of these is the community of modern science. The other is the venerable Buddhist legacy, where self-correction has operated on the most personal level for twenty-five hundred years."[3] This notion of self-correction is reflected in the fourth criterion above, that a system describing the causal nature of thought should not give itself any special status. It is the case that both science and Buddhism have built into their very structures the inevitability of self-reflective criticism. They submit their own views to the degree of scrutiny, analysis, and challenge inherent in their methodology, like a sword that cuts even itself.

BUDDHISM IS NOT PHILOSOPHIZING

Buddhist analysis of mind and its relation to reality stems fundamentally from the recognition of human suffering. Buddhism is not interested in mere philosophizing for its own sake, in speculation or mere abstraction. This is illustrated in an encounter between the Buddha and a philosophically inclined student, Malunkyaputta who, one day after a meditation session, came to ask the Buddha ten questions. These questions pertain to whether the world is finite or infinite, eternal or not eternal; whether the mind is or is not identical with the body; and whether an awakened person exists or does not exist after death. In response to each of these questions the Buddha remained silent. He then asked the student whether, when he had joined the Buddha, he had ever been promised an answer to such questions. To this the student answers no. The Buddha then explains that whatever opinion he or anyone else may have about these questions, there is *still* fundamental anxiety and distress, "the cessation of which I teach in this very life." And he likened the metaphysical student to a man wounded by an arrow who, before being attended to, insists on knowing what kind of an arrow it was, where it came from, who shot it and with what style of bow, and so forth. Answers to these questions will not help him, whereas if he were to ask how to remove the arrow without tearing his flesh and what kind of medication to put on the wound, he would be much better off.[4] Mere philosophical speculation, then, is not the point. Nor is mere "Inquiry for its own sake" really worthwhile if it does not have a direct bearing on the terror of the human condition and of the self-deception at its base, a terror the Buddha vividly saw.

The Buddha was born, in about 560 B.C., as Prince Gautama, the heir to the throne of a kingdom in northern India. His father, the King, afraid that his son would renounce the world to take up a religious life, surrounded him with all the luxuries of the world, and tried to prevent him from seeing the suffering inherent in human existence. However, according to the traditional biography, the prince, while being driven in his royal carriage, saw in succession a sick person, an old person, and a corpse. Thus he realized the suffering attendant to birth, sickness, old age, and death—conditions to which all, without exception, are subject. Realizing this, he also realized the fundamental pain experienced by all humans stemming from their realization of their existence and of the inevitability of their death. In modern times this fundamental pain is sometimes referred to as 'existential anxiety.' Anxiety and alienation are said to be the scourge of the modern age. Yet such pain has afflicted men and women since they became self-conscious, since in other words they became human. The search for wealth and territory, for intellectual prowess, for certainty of belief, all stem from this fundamental cause, according to Buddhism.

The Prince left his father's palace and went to search through the various religious and spiritual disciplines available at his time for a possibility of relieving mankind from this suffering. After many years of intense study of various philosophies, and of practice of spiritual disciplines, he attained realization of the ending of suffering, through awakening to the nonexistence of the individual human soul as an eternal 'thing' and, thence, to the basic nondual ground of all existence. After this awakening, the Prince Gautama was henceforth called the Buddha, which literally means, 'one who is awakened.' His instructions on how to follow this path to awakening, which we now call Buddhism, are more properly called buddhadharma. Dharma, in this case means 'way,' 'law of,' 'principle of.' Thus buddhadharma means the way to awakening.

According to some traditions, the teachings of the Buddha were presented in three phases, known as the Three Turnings of the Wheel of Dharma. Whether these three phases actually took place during the Buddha's life, or whether they represent only the later historical developments of the teaching remains an open question. We will not enter into this debate, but will make use of them since this threefold division provides a clear view of the theory and practice of the Buddhist insights and of the unfolding discoveries and realizations of meditative methods. The three turnings correspond to the progressive unfolding and deepening of the student's understanding and realization on the continuing journey of meditative discovery.

The first turning provides an analysis of the nature and characteristics of the ordinary world as we encounter it in our lives and as it appears to the first stages of meditative insight. This turning has itself three aspects: a description of the major characteristics of the world of appearance, known as the three marks of existence, and of the nature of human dwelling within this world, the four noble truths; an analysis of the world of appearance into its elementary constituents, the 'atoms' of experience or 'dharmas,' and of the causal relationships between these dharmas as they enter into and make up ordinary appearance; and a description of the process of perception and world-construction in terms of the dharmas. In this chapter I will describe the three marks of existence and the four noble truths, and in the following chapter we will look at the analysis of all experience into 'dharmas.' Later we will see how these dharmas are combined, in the process of perception to construct the worlds of appearance.

We will then see how the Buddhist analysis can be supported by the analysis of modern cognitive science.

The second turning of the wheel of dharma asked the question, What is the nature of dharmas and of causality itself? This led to the discovery of the fundamental role of conceptualization in dharmas and the process of perception, and thus to the discovery of 'emptiness of conceptions' as a more ultimate truth. Finally, the third turning of the wheel reflected on role and nature of language and on the possibility of speaking of the nature of mind and perception within nonduality. The third turning points to the fullness within emptiness, altogether beyond conceptualization. Later we will discuss the second and third turnings of the wheel of dharma. But let us now turn to the first turning, the description of the nature of human dwelling in the world and the marks of existence.

THE FOUR NOBLE TRUTHS

The Buddha saw the suffering, the fundamental anxiety, of all humans as a kind of plague, a disease that afflicts everyone, no matter what the circumstances of birth or upbringing. He offered his discoveries as a medicine that can cure this disease and release anyone who takes it from the grip of self-delusion into a great joy and openness of mind. Accordingly his teaching was first presented, as the Four Noble Truths, in the fourfold form common to physicians of his time. First there is a description of the nature of the disease, second an account of its etiology, third a prognosis for cure, and fourth a prescription of the treatment. The term 'noble' here refers not to a particular social class but rather to the type of personality that is necessary to face the hard truth about our human condition.

First, the universal disease, suffering or existential anxiety, was described in very great detail. This was not because the Buddha liked to dwell on suffering or was of a pessimistic turn of mind. On the contrary he appears to have been of a rather joyful and positive disposition. It was more likely out of his compassion, and sense of irony, that the Buddha saw that people are constantly preoccupied with trying to avoid facing this anxiety and thereby constantly feeding it. He saw people trying to lose their awareness of their state of existence, and of their inevitable death, in every form of entertainment from the luxuries of the rich to the asceticism of the forest dwellers; from the passions and aggressions of personal life to the not so different passions and aggressions of the battlefield and the political conference table; from the search for certainty in a philosophy of materialism, which was as prevalent and sophisticated in his time as it is now, to the not so very different search for security in religious beliefs of all kinds. Thus he realized, as so many modern therapists have done since, that the cure for our deep anxiety can begin only when we begin to recognize our urge to ignore it.

The disease, anxiety, was elaborated in the three marks of existence, which refer to the fundamental characteristics of all experience and all phenomena. These three marks are impermanence, egolessness, and suffering. Impermanence refers to the fact that there are no permanent things to be found anywhere in the universe—no permanent material objects, no permanent thoughts, ideas or perceptions, no permanent laws of nature, and no permanent beliefs or systems of belief. All, without exception, is changing. We see this wherever we look around us or inside our own minds. The weather changes, the trees and flowers change and decay, our loved ones are constantly changing, our own bodies are changing, growing and decaying. One day we may be happy, with a good family, a group of friends, sensible political and religious views, and a job. The next day one of our children becomes seriously ill, our political views are shaken by revelations of corruption, one of our friends turns out to be suing us, we discover that we have suddenly lost heart in an artistic activity that has brought us joy for twenty years, or we develop a fear of flying that means we cannot keep our jobs. These are the vagaries of life, we say. Yes, but the mark of impermanence points out that there is nothing *other* than the vagaries of life. The idea of 'changing' is not even the best way of talking of impermanence because this implies that there are 'things,' and that those 'things' change. The mark of impermanence says that the universe should not be thought of as composed of 'things' that change. Rather, the universe and all its parts should be thought of as processes of continual becoming and decaying.

At a very deep level we do not accept the mark of impermanence. We surround ourselves with objects that we feel are permanent, and we become attached to them. We hold to certain beliefs that we regard with certainty as true and unchanging. We seek permanent laws of nature and for a final theory of matter or of human personality. All this is an attempt to fix an ever-changing universe, as if we could take a snapshot of it at this moment and it would always be like that. And more important than all this we hold onto the idea of 'I' as a permanent existing thing. This 'I' is not just the body, which we see changing and which—although we try to keep it together with facelifts and cosmetics—we know will ultimately decay. Even the latest efforts to delay the biological process of aging, and to preserve the body in deep freeze until it can be brought to life again, as some people would like to do, cannot produce an eternal body. But we think of this 'I,' mind or soul, call it what we will, as in some way transcending the body. We may believe this mind or soul is eternal, but even if we do not, we believe that through this life there is something that does not change even as we see the body change. We think that the 'I' is the same 'I' when we are forty, and about to be elected to the Board of Directors, as it was when we were twenty, in love and about to get married, and as it was when we were two and learning to speak. We do not accept the truth of egolessness, the second mark of existence.

Because, at a deeply unconscious level, there is clinging to the belief in a world of unchanging beliefs, objects, and minds, there is a continual gap between our beliefs and our belief-conditioned perceptions and the everchanging nature of *what is,* beyond these. This gap brings dissatisfaction, alienation, anxiety, and suffering, the third mark of existence. This, then, is the first of the four truths.

The second noble truth is the cause of the disease. According to the principle of causation, which is fundamental to Buddhism, all phenomena, whether purely 'mental' or manifesting in appearance, arise one from another in an interdependent web of natural causation. No phenomenon is the result of the arbitrary action of a god or many gods, nor the result of mere chance. According to Buddhism, the cause of the profound anxiety felt universally is the equally universal belief in an individual 'ego' or 'self' and in the grasping at any forms of object or belief that can confirm the reality and permanence of this 'ego.'

The idea of an 'ego' or a relatively permanent 'thing' to which the name 'I' refers does not apply only to the 'soul' of the religions. It applies just as much nowadays to the 'ego' of psychotherapy and psychoanalysis, to the 'self' or 'Self' of various new and old esoteric systems, and to the 'individual minds' of psychologists and cognitive psychologists. It is this 'ego' that the therapists try to patch up when someone comes to them exhibiting a more severe form of neurotic behavior than most of us. The goal of therapy is often a 'healthy ego.' This may be helpful in the short run, but in the long run it only further solidifies the false belief in a 'something' which 'I' am. In fact the original neurosis may have begun precisely because the patient was unconsciously beginning to realize the inadequacy of his version of 'I.' The new self-image is 'healthy' only as long as further inadequacies do not show up, which they inevitably do, that is, so long as the fundamental deception is not seen through.

This fundamental deception is further strengthened when psychologists and cognitive scientists talk in terms of 'a mind,' which nowadays is usually localized in the brain. And the ordinary man or woman who may have given up the belief in a 'soul' has now transferred that belief to the idea of a mind, believing that there is a self, localized in his or her body, which is the thing that is conscious, and which all of us take very personally. The ego is very clever and in each generation it latches onto a new idea to convince itself of its permanent existence. For this generation, the belief in ego is belief in the individual mind.

That then is a description of ego, the cause of suffering, the second noble truth. The third noble truth, the outlook, tells us that the disease can be cured. For all its initial talk of suffering, the teaching of Buddhism is fundamentally positive. The Buddha's personal discovery was that beyond the process of ego there is a state of peace and unconditioned openness. This state of being is 'nirvana,' a term that is now well known in the West and equally thoroughly misunderstood.[5] It has popularly been interpreted as some 'other world' or different plane of existence, perhaps an analogy with the Christian heaven. This is quite incorrect, as will become clear in the course of this book. Nirvana is contrasted with the ego-centered world of anxiety and confusion, known as samsara, in which we feel fragmented and alienated from our universe and in a constant struggle against it.

Traditionally, in the earliest schools of Buddhism this state of being was termed 'cessation.' This term was misunderstood by the earliest Western translators to mean cessation of being in the world altogether, and this misunderstanding led in turn to centuries of misinterpretation of Buddhism altogether as a "world-denying religion."[6] Unfortunately this misinterpretation still abounds in the popular press and even sometimes in the scholarly press. 'Cessation' did not, of course, mean suicidal cessation of the world, it meant cessation of the belief in ego, which in fact forms a barrier to fully and joyfully living in the world. Cessation of the self-deceptions of ego means the cessation of the fundamental anxiety caused by ego, and therefore gives rise to the possibility of realizing our nature to its fullest. By 'realize' here is meant not merely intellectual understanding but actual embodiment and actualizing of that understanding.

The fourth noble truth indicates the method by which this realization can come about. The method is a combination of precise analysis with the direct experience of the entire process of perception and its making of universes. This direct experience comes from the practice of mindfulness and awareness meditation. The method of mindfulness and awareness, which I will describe in detail later, enables us to see directly the nature of the belief in ego, the structure and perceptual projections of ego, and the gap between ego's fabricated and projected world and *what is*. With the first stages of the practice of meditation, experience is analyzed and seen to consist not of permanent objects or minds but of elements of perception, called dharmas. And in this dharma analysis neither 'I' nor 'things' are found among the elementary constituents of experience. Thus this analysis leads to the realization of egolessness and impermanence and thence to the underlying openness of mind that is nirvana.

These ideas form the basic tenets of Buddhism, accepted by all schools without exception. They form the major doctrines of present-day Theravada Buddhism, which derives from the many earlier schools of Buddhism that flourished in the first few hundred years after the Buddha's death. The early schools refused to speak of nonduality directly, recognizing the danger of conceptualizing. But the emphasis on 'cessation' did lend a nihilistic flavor to their doctrines, much like the nihilism that can result nowadays from contemplation of the doctrines of science. These doctrines, too, have intellectually demonstrated egolessness, as we shall see, while being unable to know the fullness and living quality of nonduality.

The later schools of Buddhism, the mahayana schools, plunged into nonduality more directly. They provided a more penetrating analysis of the 'emptiness,' or lack of inherent existence or 'selfhood' of all phenomena, including the dharmas of the earlier analysis. As well, in poetry and art they conveyed the flavor, if not the literal content, of the experience of nonduality. The mahayana schools also provided an account of the path of discovery of emptiness and the compassionate action arising from this discovery.

Nevertheless, ego is the fundamental obstacle to the experience of nonduality. Therefore the discovery of egolessness, or lack of inherent existence, of oneself as well as 'external' phenomena, *is* the discovery of nonduality in experience. And it is with the realization of the egolessness of oneself that the discovery of nonduality and its corresponding radical change of perception begins. In subsequent chapters we will look at the insights of modern psychology and cognitive science, which have clearly discovered the structure of mental process and the absence of ego. But before we begin this we will, in the next chapter, look into the way the early schools of Buddhism analyzed each moment of experience into what they saw as the fundamental atoms of experience, the dharmas.

5

Fabricating Experience

IN THIS BOOK we are interested in Buddhism as a psychology and philosophy of life, not with the repetition of ancient doctrines merely because they are ancient. We are concerned with the analysis of what is experienced and what may or may not be beyond dualistic experience. Sometimes the analogy of baking bread is used to illustrate the relation between experience and the traditional doctrines: your grandmother may have had a recipe for making wonderful and uniquely flavored bread. She passed on this recipe to your mother, who still has the recipe and is still able to bake wonderful bread. Now it is your turn. Your mother can show you the recipe, and she can let you watch her while she makes bread. But now you must bake your first loaf. Only you can do it, and you will use fresh flour, fresh water, and a new flame. Then you will make fresh bread.

The traditional doctrines are, from this point of view, not a "Buddhist catechism," although they may certainly be taken this way by people in search of something to believe in or be opinionated about. Rather they may be seen as prescriptions, available to anyone who wants to try them out, as to how to look in order to see and experience directly the view of reality described by Buddhism. Taken merely as items of belief based on authority they do not accomplish the original purpose of the Buddha, whose parting words, on his deathbed to his weeping servant, were, "Ananda, you must be your own lamps, be your own refuges. Take refuge in nothing outside yourselves. All composite things are subject to decay. Journey on the path diligently."[1] When this prescription is not followed, it being easier merely to believe, then Buddhism too becomes entombed as "One of the World's Great Religions."

Merely to repeat doctrines written generations ago in an archaic language and translated into English, via perhaps one or more langauges, is not necessarily helpful except to some scholars, although it may be very religious. It can also lead to misunderstanding, as was the case with the early European scholars, who, having little conception of or acquaintance with nonduality, looked at egolessness through the eyes of duality and saw it as nihilistic, pessimistic, self-denying, and even suicidal. It is certainly true that as soon as we lose the perspective of nonduality, then the doctrine of egolessness can easily become the doctrine of nihilism. This is what has begun to happen in the modern world.

Later we will analyze the psychophysical constituents of experience in terms of psychology and cognitive science, terms familiar to the modern mind. We will see that these studies do suggest that a self is nowhere to be found and that grasping to the idea of a self and its projected world leads to anxiety, mental turmoil, and suffering. But the realization of egolessness has entered our society without being fully accepted at the personal level, and the result has been the propagation of various forms of nihilism.

It could not have been otherwise because while the analytic tools for the discovery of egolessness—namely science—have existed, the method for the direct experience—namely, meditation—has not been known. Until at least glimpses of it are experienced, egolessness can only be thought about. And this thinking will be done from the point of view of ego, and will therefore be bound to regard egolessness as a nihilistic idea. Therefore the practical method is essential. Without method it is like a medical student who learns all about bacterial diseases without ever looking through a microscope. The problem of nihilism has also arisen at various times in the history of Buddhism as schools have become merely philosophical without following the practical prescription for realizing that philosophy. Theory and practice have always gone hand in hand in the living expression of Buddhism.

Because theory is always accompanied by practice, the analysis of experience in the Buddhist tradition has a different flavor from the objective analysis of science. Since Buddhism does not start from the point of view of an observing self, experience is not analyzed from the 'objective' point of view, as if one's own experience were an object outside of oneself, or were the experience of a stranger. Nor is experience analyzed purely subjectively, as if it were the make-belief of each individual and had no common elements from person to person. It is the claim of Buddhism that the felt, direct qualities of one's experience are common to all and can be seen and analyzed impartially, without prejudice or prejudgment, if there is the intention and the method to do this. At the same time 'impartiality' and 'nonjudgment' should not be confused with 'objectivity.' It is rather more reminiscent of Niels Bohr's "unambiguous communication."

DHARMAS

The analysis of experience into elements known as 'dharmas' was one of the main topics of the doctrines of the early schools of Buddhism. Each of these schools developed its own list of dharmas, and to some extent the lists vary from school to school. But they agree in basic principles and to a large extent in the details.[2]

Now, what precisely was meant by a dharma? The term 'dharma' has had many different usages in the Buddhist tradition, and indeed in early Indian philosophical traditions generally, and I do not want to occupy or confuse the reader with an analysis of all of these. We must, however, distinguish between 'the Dharma' and 'dharmas.' The Dharma is the term by which Buddhists refer to the entire body of the Buddhist teaching. The Dharma can also mean the "order of the universe," or "the natural law of how things are." Third, the Dharma can refer to the moral law, how virtuous and nonvirtuous behavior is to be understood and distinguished. All three meanings of Dharma are to an extent connected. To put it simply, the teachings of Buddhism (the Dharma) show the way to discover the 'natural law' or 'order of the universe' (the Dharma) as that law operates in and pervades our lives. Seeing the natural law, one sees automatically what behavior is appropriate to be cultivated and what is appropriate to be rejected. When behavior is cultivated that is in accord with the way things are, and is rejected when it is not in accord with the way things are, then this leads to joy and to an end to anxiety for oneself and for others. For Buddhists, then, morality, or virtuous behavior, is not a question of following a law given by an external law-giver, be it the Buddha, the State, or a God, and receiving external rewards and punishments according to the judgment of a Supreme Judge. It is a question of following the natural order of things.

The difficult part in all this, of course, is to determine just what is "the way things are." And the major, if not the only, obstacle to such discovery is, according to the Buddhists, the self-deception wrought by belief in individual ego. Therefore morality consists first and foremost in seeing through the deception of ego, and second in bringing that vision of egolessness into practical effect in one's relations with others and with society.

According to the analysis of the first turning of the wheel of

Dharma, what is real, all that actually exists, are dharmas, which are momentary elements of experience, flashing in and out of existence and directly knowable to the cognizing mind, which is itself one of these momentary dharmas. Each dharma is not further subdividable; it is an elementary atom of experience. Each dharma 'carries its own mark,' i.e., has a defining characteristic that distinguishes it from other dharmas. In fact a dharma should be regarded as *none other* than its defining characteristic. A dharma is not some kind of substance that supports qualities, it simply *is* that quality. Through a variety of interconnected causes and conditions, particular dharmas arise at any moment and are the experienced characteristics at that moment. And a particular moment of experience is, in turn, *nothing other* than this particular conglomeration of dharmas. All persons, objects, and facts can be understood as combinations of elemental dharmas. The analysis of experience into dharmas is known as 'abhidharma.'

Buddhist scholar Edward Conze summarizes the nature of dharmas thus:

> For an understanding of Buddhist philosophy it is vitally important that one should appreciate the difference between 'dharmas' on the one hand, and 'common-sense things' on the other. In agreement with the majority of philosophers, Buddhists regard common-sense things around them as a false appearance. The 'dharmas,' i.e., the facts which are ultimately real, are normally covered from sight by ignorance, and nothing but the special virtue of wisdom [insight] will enable us to penetrate to them. No rational approach can be content to accept the crude data of common sense as ultimate facts. The scientific propositions of modern science refer to abstract entities of 'constructs,' such as atoms, molecules, electromagnetic fields, etc., and to their properties, tendencies and habitual behaviour. Common-sense data are thus retraced to, transformed into, or replaced by concepts which are both more intelligible and 'fundamental.' Similarly [Buddhists regard] the world as composed of an unceasing flow of simple ultimates, called 'dharmas,' which can be defined as (1) multiple, (2) momentary, (3) impersonal, (4) mutually conditioned events.[3]

The dharma analysis of the early schools gave rise to a profound understanding of the nature of human perception, which, as we will see, is close in significant detail to that of cognitive science. And this understanding of perception was the underpinning of all later Buddhist discovery. The transition from earlier to later schools of Buddhism should be regarded like the transition from arithmetic to calculus, the later schools building on the insights of the earlier, rather than rejecting them. The analysis of experience into dharmas is a necessary first step in discovering the nature of experience and perception. Although, in the end, even the belief that the dharmas exist leads to serious problems that can be resolved only by the realization that the dharmas, too, are subtly conceptual and ultimately empty of self-existence or substantiality. We will get to this at a later time, but for now we will take the point of view that all experience—all that is—is composed of elementary dharmas.

However, even at this stage, we need not commit ourselves to the assumption that dharmas are ultimately real things. Whatever our view in this regard, dharmas are most importantly heuristic devices, taught as guides in meditation practice for the purpose of gaining insight into the marks of existence. Dharma analysis is used in this way in the living traditions of early Buddhism. Students are asked to note each passing moment, first in meditation and then in daily life, and to note which dharmas they detect as entering into that moment.[4] Naturally this requires considerable training. But as his or her attention becomes more finely tuned, the student begins to see the world not in familiar terms of 'things' and 'selves' but in terms of impermanence, of absence of 'selfhood' or 'thinghood.' The understanding of the marks of existence becomes personal and direct rather than merely theoretical.

THE FIVE SKANDHAS

There are a number of ways by which the dharmas may be categorized in order to aid this realization, but one of the most common and fundamental is the division into five groups known as 'skandhas,' or 'heaps': *form, feeling, perception, formation,* and *consciousness.*[5] Each skandha is simply a bundle or a heap of dharmas; and the human personality, as well as the world of 'objects' constructed by perception, is found to consist simply of a conglomeration of these five heaps, ceaselessly changing from moment to moment.

Form (rupaskandha) consists of eleven dharmas. The first ten are the five senses, sight, hearing, smell, taste, touch and the five sense objects, colors and shapes, sounds, smells, tastes, and objects of touch. The eleventh is form without sensory manifestation, which includes imaginary forms, hallucinations, and visions.

Form is the only skandha that corresponds to the external physical-material world. The other four skandhas correspond to the mental side of the mind/body system. Just as in the early view of science, the physical-material world is known as data presented to the senses. However, in this case not only the sense objects themselves such as color and sound are included, but also the senses of seeing, hearing, and so on. This reflects the fact that, if we do not forget the role of our own psychophysical organism in the act of perception, then we find that what appears to mind at a moment of perception of an object of sight is that object *together with* the sense of seeing, and so on for the other senses. We never merely see a flower, we always *experience seeing* the flower at the same time.

Feeling (vedanaskandha) is the automatic affective response to form, before any higher conceptual processes enter in, a bare reaction of 'pleasant' (what one would like to grasp onto and seems to confirm oneself), 'unpleasant' (what one would like to reject and threatens to harm one) or 'neutral' (what has no bearing on one's personal continuation). This does not refer to a distinct emotional response, but to a simple positive negative or neutral evaluation that accompanies cognition of any primary form. While *form* corresponds to the 'physical-material' pole of dualistic experience, and skandhas three through five correspond to the 'mental pole,' the second skandha, *feeling*, connects 'mind' and 'body.' In 'body' it manifests as the inner feeling of the body as pleasurable, painful, or neutral, the 'proprioceptive sense.' Feeling manifests in 'mind' as affective arousal, the instinctual response to the basic thingness of the 'outside' and the basic responses of 'like' or 'dislike' toward our bodily sensations.

Perception (saminaskandha) is also often translated as *discernment*. It should not be confused with the use of perception to refer to the overall process. It is the first discernment or perception that there is a specific object, the beginning of concept formation. It forms the concept of one's 'self' as that 'self' relates to the particular form occupying one's attention. It abstracts the characteristics of any object that has been determined by *feeling* to be of interest to oneself, thus enabling one to name it. Because one can name it one can also grasp onto it and hold it in one's field of attention, i.e., in one's world.

Formations or *mental elements (samskaraskandha)* comprises all mental contents other than *feeling* and *perception*. This skandha comprises the conceptual contents of experience. A variety of positive, negative, and indifferent emotions; simple and complex thought patterns as well as systems of thought such as various philosophical, religious, psychological belief systems; and various mental functions and attitudes are all included in this category.

The positive and negative emotions are also called 'wholesome' or 'healthy,' and 'unwholesome' or 'unhealthy,' factors. Again I should emphasize that the distinction between 'healthy' and 'unhealthy' is not made from the point of view of an externally imposed moralism, but refers to the immediately felt quality of mind, and the direction toward which that felt quality tends. The dharma of 'cheerfulness' bring with it a positive attitude and a tendency to openness. The dharma of 'meanness' brings with it an attitude of depression and a tendency to restriction. The wholesome factors are simply those that tend toward the realization of egolessness, and the unwholesome factors are those that tend to strengthen the tendency toward ego fixation. The point is not to make judgments about this, but to see it impartially.

For example, some wholesome factors are: trust (in cause and effect, the three marks of existence, etc.), nonhatred, equanimity, consideration, mental pliancy. Some unwholesome factors are, first, the 'five root poisons': lust, anger, pride, jealousy, and ignorance. These are classed as the 'root poisons' because they are thought to be the primary negative emotions arising when the initial positive, negative, or neutral feelings of the second skandha combine with the grasping of ego. Positive feelings combined with the grasping of ego give rise to lust and pride, likewise negative feelings give rise to hatred and jealousy, while neutral feelings lead to emotions of indifference. In addition to the five root poisons are various minor afflictions such as opinionatedness, belligerence, miserliness, haughtiness, and so on. Appendix 1 provides a complete list of the samskara dharmas.

The fifth skandha is known as *consciousness (vijnanaskandha)*. In the early schools this skandha was equated with mind (citta) and referred to that which knows or cognizes the other dharmas. Vijnana was sometimes divided into six consciousnesses depending on which other dharmas arose with it. In that scheme there were five vijnanas corresponding to each of the five senses and a sixth vijnana that cognized the mental dharmas. This, as it stands, is a rather condensed category, containing the qualities of illumination and clarity of self-cognition as well as the discrimination and "taking account of" involved in cognition of other. It is also sometimes termed 'heart' to indicate the sense of immediate presence felt as each conglomeration of dharmas arises, abides momentarily, and decays. As we will see, later schools separated out these functions to give a much clearer sense of that notoriously tricky notion, 'consciousness.'

This, then, is a brief introduction to the characteristics of dharmas and their classification in five groups or 'skandhas.' For Buddhists, the five skandhas together comprise all the psychophysical constituents of the human personality. Buddhists find that there is nothing left out that can actually be noted in our experience; the five skandhas constitute all that we call 'I' and 'the world.'

CAUSATION

Dharmas combine to form each moment of experience in an individual stream of being. Of course not all dharmas enter into each moment; some dharmas are even incompatible, such as particular wholesome and unwholesome dharmas. To understand just how the dharmas enter into experience we must examine briefly the Buddhist notion of causality. Although all phenomena are caused, none being miraculous or occurring merely by chance, the Buddhist idea of cause is not the linear one cause—one effect idea of science. As Guenther says, "The Buddhists never admitted the rule 'A causes B,' except as a crude suggestion in nonphilosophical parlance. As a matter of fact, the Buddhist conception of causation is, if we want to compare it with other theories about causation, more in line with [David] Hume's view that in causation there is no indefinable relation, except conjunction and succession and that our tendency to accept such propositions as 'this causes that' is to be explained by the laws of habit and association."[6]

The idea of causation here is one of interdependence. The idea is contained in the Sanskrit term *pratitya samutpada*, which can be translated as 'dependent co-origination.' Literally it means dependence [pratitya] on conditions that are variously originated [samutpada]. It has also been translated loosely as 'situational patterning.'[7] Both 'dependent co-origination' and 'situational patterning' give a sense of the idea that each phenomenon arises dependent on a web of causes stretching backward into the past and outward into the immediate present. There are factors that simply make the phenomenon possible, factors that constitute the absence of hindrance for that phenomenon, factors that appear as objects of perception, and factors that come from the immediately preceding moment of experience. To take a very simple example: in order to see a rock we must have functioning sight, absence of darkness or fog, a rock, and a previous interest in seeing the rock.

Of course most phenomenal situations are more complex than this and the corresponding causal nexus will be more complex. What were the causal factors leading one to drink a cup of tea at this particular moment: the presence of tea, water, and gas in the kitchen; the absence of anything more pressing to do; the presence of a friend; it being time for tea; that one enjoyed drinking tea with one's great aunt when one was a child; the association with the pleasing smell of crumpets toasting on a coal fire; that one dreamed last night of taking tea with a lover; and so on. More significant situations can also be analyzed in this way: what causes one to become violently angry with one's mate? What causes one to sit doing nothing in the meditation hall? And what causes all the thoughts, passions, and irritations that occur as one so sits. As one takes a walk in the country on a stormy afternoon, what causes the quick gust of anxiety, or the sudden glimpse of extraordinary freshness?

Herbert Guenther sums up the Buddhist view of causation in this way:

> In talking about causality in Buddhism, it is of the utmost importance to be aware of the points of divergence from our ways of thinking. In the Buddhist universe events did not happen because of fiats issued by a supreme creator and despotic lawgiver. Nothing whatsoever has been created in the universe. Events come about because they fit into the pattern of a universe based on order, and these events cooperate in perfect freedom and not in obedience to some super-will, nor to some mathematically expressible regularity dependent upon some cause that can be isolated. Causality, if such a term is ever applicable, posits an interlocking system of hierarchically fluctuating cause-factors. That is to say the cause situation was already a 'network' of interdependent, co-existing and freely co-operating forces, and in this network at any given time any one factor may take the highest place in a hierarchy of causes and effects.[8]

From the point of view of Buddhism, causes are always analyzed in terms of the arising of a particular moment of experience. Abstract causal relationships between supposed objects in the 'external world,' whether objects of commonsense appearance such as planets and falling balls, or theoretical objects such as electrons and gluons, are regarded as hypothetical relations between hypothetical objects. They are therefore less important from the point of view of elucidating the facts of experience. The Buddha's discovery of this causal process of the arising of experience, which was the final realization immediately before his enlightenment, is regarded as the essence of his teaching. It was this discovery along with the method of awareness meditation, which sees causality in process, that set off the Buddha's teaching as a unique departure from the various forms of spiritual training common in India at that time.

MOMENTARINESS

All dharmas arise in a moment of experience dependent on the conditions set up by the previous moment and dependent on the network of causes operative at that particular moment. This fact is known as 'dependent co-origination.' Dharmas enter into existence in response to these various cause factors, abide momentarily, and then pass out of existence. The most important aspect of this process, which science has barely begun to recognize, is that experience is discontinuous and momentary. Between discrete moments of experience, of the arising and combining of dharmas, there is a gap during which dharmas have subsided and there is no perception of an 'outside world,' no thought, no dualistic existence based on subject and object, no ego. Normally due to the coarse level of perceptual processing of which we are conscious, we experience continuity. But the awareness of finer levels of perceptual processing seen in meditative training shows discontinuity of experience. The apparent continuity of a world of relatively permanent but changing things is put together by consciousness rather as a movie is seen as continuously changing scenes, even though it is in fact a series of still shots.

The discovery of discontinuity resolves many questions in the understanding of the mechanics of perception as well as in the understanding of the spiritual path. As far as spirituality is concerned, discontinuity shows that egolessness is not some state of mind or of being that has to be 'attained' as something foreign to one's present state, nor is it a 'higher' state of being, nor does it belong to another realm outside of this universe. It is a fundamental, ever-present aspect of one's ordinary being, which is normally covered up due to ignorance and bewilderment, believing in ego's continuity, and which can therefore be uncovered by knowledge and insight.

However, discontinuity raises a new question: How is there apparent continuity? This is connected with the question that has no doubt arisen frequently in the reader's mind: If there is no ego, what is it that experiences continuity? How is it that I experience this particular stream of thoughts and emotions as a continuous stream and that I remember previous moments as belonging to me? Beyond this, what is it that aspires to and realizes egolessness? In some sense the tension that arises in one's mind as one contemplates this question is the essence of the spiritual path: If there is no ego, who or what am I, or am I not? For this reason some traditions remain altogether silent on this issue, feeling that to give any answer would simply further the practitioner's clinging to ego. The Buddha remained silent when the philosopher asked such questions, and the Zen Buddhist tradition of Japan remains silent.

However, other schools did try to answer this question, and one can regard the question almost as the key problem that gave rise to so many different schools in the history of Buddhism. Some abhidharma schools, basing their interpretation of experience on dharmas, tried in one way or another to introduce some special dharma that acted as a kind of glue that held together each individual, personal stream of dharmas. But all these attempts were, in the end, unsatisfactory. Either the special dharma was too vague to have any power to really maintain the sense of continuity, or it was too definite and gave rise in the end to 'heresies' that were accused of reintroducing the idea of a self.

Other schools suggested that the apparent continuity of experience can be likened to the apparent continuity of a tornado. The "tornado" appears to move across the countryside as a unity but is nothing other than the unceasing flux of air molecules and of whatever debris is drawn up into that flux. The appearance of a unity comes from the pattern of motion. Likewise, these schools suggest, 'the personality' and the apparent continuity of 'a person' is nothing other than the ceaseless activity of a stream of dharmas held together as a temporary unity by the force of habitual patterns.

DETERMINISM

This brings us, as the final topic in this survey of dharma theory, to the old question of determinism. The reader has perhaps uncomfortably felt in this presentation that the human person is, in the Buddhist view, much more determined—almost to the point of appearing mechanical and automatic—than we would like to believe. It might seem that there is not much room left for changing the course of our lives. It is certainly the case that Buddhism tries to point out that very much of what we preciously think of as our own free behavior and thought is in fact a habitual and mechanical response to habitual tendencies of which we may not be aware. But this does not mean that we are completely determined in a fatalistic way. In fact, according to Buddhists, it is precisely because our experience is discontinuous and precisely because there is no solid person behind our momentary experience that we do have a chance to change the course of these habit patterns. In that gap of nonduality between moments, there is a possibility that fresh dharmas can enter in. That gap is often first experienced in meditation practice as a feeling of delightful freshness that apparently comes from nowhere.

The pattern of our experience up to the present moment has been conditioned and determined by our past action, just as the present state of affairs on a chess board can be traced back to the beginning move for move. Nevertheless, just as there is a variety of possible next chess moves, so at this moment, there is a variety of possible actions. Another analogy might be the party game called Gossip or Chinese Whisper. The players sit in a circle and the beginning player whispers a message in the ear of the person next to him, who in turn whispers the message to his neighbor, and so on round the circle. At the end, the beginning and ending players tell their messages. The discrepancy between the initial and final messages is often hilarious. If the players are inattentive during the game, the message will simply degenerate into a garbled and incoherent string. But if the players are attentive it is possible for fresh elements to enter into the message in a more harmonious manner so that at the end it is an embellished and enriched version of the original.

In a similar fashion, if we are attentive at each moment of our lives as the "message" of habitual patterning is passed on from one momentary heap of dharmas to the next, it is possible to glimpse the gaps between them so that a fresh element may enter. Perhaps, for example, we are in a familiar situation with our teenage son to which each of us habitually reacts in a set pattern of irritation eventually leading to angry words, often almost identical to the words we used on previous occasions. If we are attentive to the flow of dharmas in this situation it is possible for it to open up, to introduce something fresh—a little relaxation, a hint of humor, a gentle touch, whatever it may be—that might significantly change the relationship between us. But the point is that such a gesture can be effective only if it occurs from the heart, rather than from some past memory of what one ought to do or could have done, and if it occurs at the appropriate moment. And for this to happen one needs to be attentive to the continually changing flux of dharmas. The abhidharma schools referred to such a momentary gap in the flow of moments mechanically succeeding each other as an 'unconditioned dharma.' By this they meant a dharma that is not conditioned at all by previous patterns. It enters in freely and brings with it a sense of freedom from habitual thought.

One term for the unconditioned dharma was 'nirvana.' This expresses the fact that nirvana occurs within the stream of experiential dharmas, which are called 'conditioned' since they arise dependent on the causes and conditions of the previous moments. Yet nirvana is not in itself conditioned experience, rather it is the fact of discontinuity of experience. This is the reason why it is so often expressed in negative terms, as in this most famous passage from an early text, in which the Buddha speaks to his students of nirvana:

"There is, monks, an unborn, not become, not made, uncompounded, and were it not, monks, for this unborn, not become, not made, uncompounded no escape could be shown here for what is born, has become, is made, is compounded. But because there is, monks, an unborn, not become, not made, uncompounded, therefore an escape can be shown for what is born, has become, is made, is compounded.[9] By "what is born, has become, is made, is compounded" the Buddha is referring to samsara, the world of fluctuating conglomerations of dharmas, the fabricated world of mental projection in which, the Buddhists say, we spend our lives in an unceasing round of habit and convention. By "escape from what is born" the Buddha is not referring to escape into some other, 'heavenly' realm, but escape into the clarity of seeing the world as it actually is. And this will become much clearer as we progress on our journey through the path of Buddhism and the sciences of mind.

In this and the previous chapters we have surveyed the basic elements of the Buddhist view and the analysis of personality and personal experience into dharmas. Later we will look to see how the skandhas combine in a temporal sequence to build a perceptual moment. But now it is time to turn to the modern sciences of mind to see another version of the analysis of the elementary components of experience and their interaction. I will organize this discussion according to the five skandhas. It might be felt that I am thereby forcing the discoveries of the sciences into a mold that they do not warrant. On the other hand it might be felt that it is very helpful to have some coordinating scheme for the vast, and often very disorganized, array of data that scientists have come up with. And the agreement between these data and the data of meditation as expressed in dharma and skandha theory is so remarkably close that, if we use this scheme of classification, we can then see at precisely which points the skandha theory goes beyond the sciences and suggests directions for future research. We can also see at which points the modern sciences of mind have gone further than the Buddhists in the detailed elaboration of the skandhas and can therefore enrich the Buddhist understanding.

6

Form—the 'External' World

IN THE PREVIOUS CHAPTERS I have shown that nonduality, the non-separateness of mind and reality, is now suggested by the changing context of science. I have also indicated that Buddhism has a view of mind and reality that rests on nonduality and that Buddhism provides a direct method to rediscover nonduality through the practice of meditation. It also provides a causal theory of the arising of dualistic mental process and perception from within nonduality. It is now time to look into the modern sciences of mind and mental processes, particularly from the point of view of trying to determine, first, whether there is any need for the hypothesis of a self, a permanent ego, or an individual mind. Second, what seem to be the most basic constituents of experience? In Chapter 12 we will see how these constituents of experience may be reassembled to provide an account of the process of perception.

SCIENCE AND BUDDHISM: DIFFERENT VIEWPOINTS

We must be quite clear from the start that there are bound to be differences in the manner of approach to these issues arising from precisely the difference of view between the context of classical science, which starts from the duality of subject and object; and that of Buddhism and the new context, which start from acknowledging nonduality as well as duality. The same phenomena, of mental processes and perception, will be described by science as if from afar, and by Buddhism as intimate experience. Nevertheless in their descriptions of these phenomena, from two different vantage points, we will find that some of the data of cognitive science agrees in significant detail with the dharma analysis of the previous chapter.

It is obviously not possible to prove the nonexistence of something directly. One cannot *point to* the absence of inherent existence of ego, of some inherently existing thing to which the word "I" refers, and say, there you are, I told you it did not exist. When a little girl wakes up crying that there is a monster in her room, her Daddy cannot find something that is the nonexistent monster and show it to her saying, "There you are, there is the monster that does not exist." The only thing Daddy can do is ask her to show him the monster and, each time she points to something, show her that it is actually something else. Likewise with ego, we can only look at everything we think might be evidence of something which 'I' refers to, and see whether an ego is really necessary to explain what we are looking at, or whether there is a simpler explanation.

In this way, by looking at everything that might be evidence of an ego and finding another, more simple, natural, and straightforward explanation for it, science and Buddhism have both become convinced that there is no ego. As I have already pointed out, science comes to this by looking at the mind from the 'outside,' as if mind were an object, while Buddhism comes to it by looking directly at one's own mental process. The result of this difference in viewpoint is that it is possible to come to this discovery, by inference, as a scientist and be personally quite unaffected by it. As a scientist one can continue to live one's personal life dominated by the false idea that one's 'I' exists. On the other hand, to come to this realization through the Buddhist analysis of direct experience is bound to have a very profound effect on the way one conducts one's life. After all, it is one thing to understand generally that that concept which dominates the life of all human beings, namely 'myself,' *is* merely a concept. It is another thing entirely to realize that *this particular* concept referring to *this particular* "me" is merely a concept, and has nothing corresponding to it.

Nevertheless, for readers for whom the scientific way of talking is more familiar, to contemplate the journey that western psychology has been through in the past century or so can be a start toward the discovery of the truth of egolessness. It can also produce quite a negative reaction.

At the conference that I mentioned in Chapter 1 on Contrasting Perspectives on Cognition, the Buddhist view of nonego was being presented in one of the sessions. A famous philosopher of phenomenology, who had become quite irritated as the conference had progressed, leaped out of his chair and said, "Well, I *do* have an ego, and I like my ego, and I will put it in wherever I damn well please." The famous philosopher apparently did not understand that the realization that 'I' is a concept that has no fixed referent is not the same as self-*denial*. It is also necessary to distinguish between the utility on a practical level of being able to refer to oneself, to make plans for one's life and so on, and the fundamental distortion of perception and action that this belief nevertheless introduces.

If we experience a passionate wanting to enjoy, or an angry wanting to get rid of, the energy of arousal is not in itself ego. The particular energy might be an authentic response to the situation that presents itself to us. We may wish to enjoy the companionship of fellow travelers, or we may wish to get rid of a barrier separating us from a companion. However, if one grasps onto that energy, as passion or aggression, and defines oneself as an 'I' who is in love, or an 'I' who is angry, and responds to that concept rather than directly to the energy of the situation, then authenticity is lost. If a man falls in love with a particular woman, tremendous energy of communication and appreciation becomes available to him. However as soon as he says to himself, "I am in love with her," and acts according to that idea, and according to his concepts of himself, of love and of her, then the communicative energy is frozen and appreciation becomes possession. Or when an artist feels an urgent passion to paint a picture, if, having painted it, he identifies himself as someone who paints in that style and tries to imitate himself, then the spontaneous creative energy that painted the original picture is lost. This may seem rather obvious and straightforward in these examples, but the point is that this is happening all the time. Our perceptions and actions are guided all the time by a concept of ourselves that does not refer to anything.

'Ego' is a general term referring to the idea of something existing separate from one's body, that has continuity from moment to moment, day to day, year to year. In fact we feel that 'I' has more than mere continuity, it is the *same* 'I' that exists now as existed a moment ago and will exist tomorrow and will exist next year. It is that feeling we have that even though we change and grow old, *something* remains the same. In the past the term 'soul' was used for this something. Now it is 'a mind.' We believe we have a mind, an individual mind, a personal possession, which somehow does not change as our body changes.

In this and the next five chapters we will look at the work that has been done in recent decades that has begun to be called 'science of the mind,' or we could say modern dharma analysis. I will organize the work of cognitive scientists, analyzing the human body/mind system, rather naturally into categories similar to those of dharma analysis. But I should remind the reader that modern science has a tendency to subtly distort the issue by its insistence on 'third-party psychology': in an attempt to be 'objective' it tries to treat the person like an object. While this began as a healthy reaction to the extreme subjectivism of the religious approach to mind, its limitations must always be borne in mind.

The early work of behaviorist doctrine and the study of input phases of sense perception mainly dealt with the first skandha of form. The study of feeling and of emotion has tended to go hand in hand. But the separation of the two, and the important role of cognition and categorization in emotion, has also been recognized by some scientists who recognize that 'emotion' and 'thought' are more like two ends of a spectrum of emphasis rather than two very different kinds of things. This substantially clarifies the common-sense notion of 'emotion.' It puts the scientific analysis in line with the Buddhist analysis in which 'emotions' are included at the intellec-tual or cognitive level of the fourth skandha, thereby separating pure feeling of the second skandha from the emotion component of the fourth. The automatic processing of thoughts, and the role of con-sciousness as a coordinating function (the sixth consciousness of the Buddhist analysis) has been elucidated by artificial intelligence stud-ies. And finally the intimate relation between language and self-consciousness has been recognized by evolutionary scientists. Each of these topics will be dealt with in turn in the following chapters. We will then go on to see how the various components may be assembled in a temporal sequence giving rise to the appearance of a 'self' and a 'world.' Again we can find some agreement between the Buddhist version of this world-constructing perceptual process and the tentative attempts of some scientists to describe this sequence.

EARLY EXPERIMENTAL PSYCHOLOGY

One of the first experimental psychologists was Hermann von Helmholtz.[1] In the nineteenth century Helmholtz measured the speed of the impulse in human sensory nerves, showing that this speed is a finite value and thus showing for the first time that at least some aspects of sensation and perception are measurable and not instantaneous. Helmholtz also developed the idea of 'unconscious inference': that in perceiving we do not simply read the world as a camera does, but we use the incoming information from the world, combined with stored memories and past knowledge, to *infer* a final perception. He believed that the perceptual system is unconsciously manipulating its input by some form of deductive logic. He says, "The psychic activities that lead us to infer that there in front of us at a certain place is a certain object of a certain character, are generally not conscious activities, but unconscious ones. In their result they are equivalent to a *conclusion*, to the extent that the observed action on our senses enables us to form an idea as to the possible cause of this action; although as a matter of fact, it is invariably simply the nervous stimulations that are perceived directly, that is, the actions, but never the external objects themselves. . . . there can be no doubt as to the similarity between the results of such inferences and those of conscious conclusions."[2] Helmholtz, then, was the first to propose that there can be unconscious processing in the perceptual system. Helmholtz's views were pushed aside by the behaviorist view, which began by denying any internal processes at all. But as we will see, cognitive scientists today are returning to Helmholtz's view and providing extensive evidence in support of it.

Another important contribution to experimental psychology at the turn of the century came from Wilhelm Wundt and his followers.[3] Wundt developed the method of introspection whereby he would ask experimental subjects to introspect their thoughts and feeling in response to simple stimuli, such as the sound of a tone. Wundt proposed that conscious thoughts are a combination of simple elements, mainly raw sense data. He sought the laws by which these simple elements combine in experience. Wundt's psychology is a kind of mental chemistry. It sought the pure and most basic elements of thought through whose combination complexes of mental activity come to be formed.

Wundt emphasized the dynamic nature of consciousness, seeing it as an organizing or structuring activity. According to Wundt, relatively permanent mental contents exist only as hypothetical constructs and the essential features of the mind resides in its character of process. Images and ideas, emotions and feelings, are essentially fleeting events. Consciousness is a structuring activity organizing these elementary events. Wundt distinguished between the total contents of consciousness, which he called the 'field of consciousness,' and those contents being attended to at any given time, which he called the 'focus of attention' or the 'focus of consciousness.' Contents can be brought to the focus by interrupting the automatic flow of consciousness. All this is very reminiscent of the dharma theory of early Buddhism.

However, Wundt did not have the method of meditation for examining the flow of mental contents; his program was flawed, as was much subsequent experimental psychology, by the emphasis on trivial exercises and on content that can be verbalized and reported to another. Later experimental psychologists tried to pay more attention to thought processes during more complex mental activities, but eventually the whole introspective enterprise was rejected because of the difficulty of developing any widely agreed on view of the components of thought, and of the reliability of the method.

Behaviorism was America's answer to the European introspectionists and dominated Anglo-American psychology for thirty years, swinging all the way from Wundt's attempt to find the basic components of conscious experience to denying that such components, or indeed such experience, exists at all in any "objectively meaningful" way. Behaviorism began with J. B. Watson and I. Pavlov at the beginning of the century, but its chief protagonist in the West was B. F. Skinner, who is said to be the most influential American psychologist of all time.[4]

The behaviorists wish to explain all human behavior without recourse to any use of terms referring to mind, consciousness, or their contents or functions. Thus they attempt to establish a science of human behavior that discounts the second through fifth skandhas altogether. Whether or not there are subjective experiences that are best described in terms such as love and hate, anxiety and intention, such terms should not be necessary in a description of the causal sequences of a person's behavior. No terms referring to anything unobservable to an external observer are to be used, and therefore even the inner side of the skandha of form, the sensory organ, is discounted. The world, including the experimental subject, is to be treated as a set of sensory objects. Although this approach may seem very naive to us now, it should be understood in the context of the tremendous confusion in psychology at the beginning of the twentieth century. Psychology at this time had barely freed itself from the shackles of religious belief and the hidden prejudices and assumptions arising from this, as physics had done several centuries previously. The way to sidestep all this, according to the behaviorists, is to turn to the public world of objects and overt behavior. This was a very reasonable approach until it too degenerated into its own version of religious fanaticism.

In the early forms of behaviorism, all human behavior, including verbal behavior, is to be explained as being a summation of learned responses to environmental stimuli. The physical human organism comes into the world with a set of very primitive reflex responses, such as salivation on smelling food. These responses can be trained by simple conditioning, just as Pavlov's dog was trained to salivate when he heard a bell, after he had several times heard a bell associated with the smell of food. Gradually the organism builds up a repertoire of responses that, when combined in response to any environmental stimulus, become its overt behavior. All behavior from simple rote learning of the two times table, to complex learning such as learning a language, to falling in love or committing a murder should then be explainable with reference only to the environmental stimuli and the previously learned responses of the organism to such stimuli.

One of the problems of this approach stems from the fact that so much of human behavior appears to be novel and purposive. When I go to someone's house for dinner, the general nature of our conversation may be determinable—if we are both farmers native to Nova Scotia, we are probably not going to talk in Hindi about our visions of the goddess Kali. But the specific conversation, whether for example we talk about the potato crop or our wives that night, is not predictable on the basis of environmental stimuli. Nor if it were recorded would it be fully explainable on the basis of the pathways of conditioning of myself and my friend. Furthermore, people—especially children—regularly produce fresh insights and actions that have no immediately obvious stimuli in their environment.

To try to deal with this problem, Skinner developed the idea that the way a human organism learns replicates the way a species evolves according to classical natural selection. When a mutant form appears, by chance, that is slightly better adapted to the environment, conditions in the environment support the survival and reproduction of this new form. Likewise, when a new form of behavior arises in a human, conditions in the environment may reward and support this behavior, which therefore will have a greater tendency to appear on a future, environmentally similar, occasion. Skinner argued that the logic of this explanation for the appearance of new behavior in a human is as good as the logic for the natural selection explanation of the appearance of new forms of a species, or of new species.

Behaviorism is at the extreme nurture end of the nurture-nature debate concerning whether inherited (nature) or environmental (nurture) influences are most important in determining the development of a child's personality. In fact behaviorism pretty much denied the importance of inherited characteristics altogether. For example, in the case of a child learning his or her first language the behaviorist view was that at first a baby simply produces random noises. The parents begin to reinforce sounds meaningful in their language, such as mama, dada, and so on. Later children hear sounds being used in reference to physical objects, like "dog" and "chair," and thus begin to associate these sounds with the appropriate physical object. Gradually a simple vocabulary is built in this way, and all more complex concepts are combinations of this simple vocabulary aided by explanations and definitions from parents and teachers. Behaviorism thus also stands at the extreme empiricist end of the empiricist-rationalist debate. Thus, with John Locke, an early empiricist, behaviorists argue that all knowledge—and therefore all that we learn—originates from our experience. This contrasts with the rationalist view of René Descartes that knowledge is inherent in the mind, is already fully there at birth, and is simply drawn out, or provoked, by stimuli from the environment.

There are obviously problems and promises in the behaviorist approach. The main promise is that this system would clear the atmosphere of a tremendous amount of woolly-headed talk. Behaviorism grew up in the 1930s, when the troubles at the foundation of physics were vividly felt, and at a time when all kinds of mad-hat theories were being proclaimed in the name of science (such as the superiority of the Aryan race). In an attempt to establish a firm ground for science, logical empiricism and its more extreme form, logical positivism, proclaimed that only publicly verifiable statements should be used in scientific discourse (positivism claimed that only such statements had any meaning at all), or at least scientific discourse should be reducible to discourse about such statements. So behaviorists, in trying to establish the study of mind on a firm foundation, naturally embraced this philosophy as being the safest and surest. And certainly it was a necessary first step in trying to place the study of minds on a firm basis to eliminate all wishful thinking and groundless speculation. In this way, having first removed all reference to unobservable mental states, those that were *necessary* for a study of mind could be reintroduced gradually.

Behaviorism did clear the ground in this way and it also demonstrated that a great deal of human behavior that had up to that time been taken as innate, and as evidence of the existence of a mind, was in fact the result of environmental conditioning. Nowadays, with the wide knowledge of the methods and results of "brainwashing," which is simply conditioning applied in a political context, people are more familiar with the uncertainty at the core of human personality, and with the potentiality for the personality to be fundamentally changed by conditioning. This has positive as well as negative aspects. Behavior modification therapies can be an effective way of training people away from traits that have become obstructive to their health or their ability to function in society.

The degree to which human beings can be conditioned by their environment was, and still is, shocking to most of us, just because it offends our sense of our integrity and of an inviolable core to ourselves that cannot be changed by any outside influences, a core that we can identify as "this is how I am," in other words my 'self.' To take a rather simple example, the behaviorist approach might make one rather guarded about making statements such as "he has an angry personality." The behaviorist might want to know precisely what behavioral, observable manifestations lead us to say this. Is an "angry personality" an observable state in itself? Furthermore, what observable characteristics lead us to say that he has a personality at all, that is, that he has an entity separate from his body and its behavior that can be identified in such and such ways? Certainly he has a human body and speaks the English language and acts in other ways that I recognize as ways that I and other human beings act, but is there anything *behind* this? The behaviorist might also question the validity of such simple statements as "I want an ice cream." Certainly we can see that if you say "chocolate ice cream" to me, I will salivate. And if an ice cream van goes by singing its jolly song I might run out and buy one. But what is the state of wanting something other than that, and is there an 'I' that is doing this wanting? In questioning such concepts so taken for granted by most of us, the behaviorist is demanding an answer that is not based on wishful thinking.

Clearly this is a primitive but important stage in the discovery of egolessness. Some people might be very offended to read that a tradition that is usually called "one of the world's great religions" is now being likened to behaviorism, seemingly the archenemy of religion. Perhaps this will put into question whether Buddhism is best thought of as a religion at all in the sense that scholars like to classify things. Be that as it may, Buddhism does start from very similar grounds as behaviorism: by questioning many of the mentalistic assumptions that we habitually make about ourselves and others.

However, there are obvious problems with behaviorism that fill one with wonder and awe that an entire generation could have come under its spell. For it is one thing to question the habitual and culturally determined *assumptions* we make about our experience and how we habitually *interpret* our experience, and to see how far we can construct a description of human behavior without such assumptions. It is another thing altogether to deny reference to mental events at all, and then to try to run one's own and other people's lives as if their mental events, their pains, pleasures and even their consciousness are irrelevant because "subjective." However much one may be suspicious of the self-deception of one's mental states, to deny that one has mental states at all—to deny the authenticity of one's own experience, one's own joys and sadness—is surely not likely to result in an adequate understanding of the full scope of human life and mind.

It is important to distinguish between the fact that behaviorism did clear the ground for fresh thinking about minds, and the fact that it was extended to areas outside of its domain. Thinking that a small success in a small arena of scientific investigation can be expanded to become a scientific, political, religious, and educational philosophy applicable to all of society is a leap of blind faith, not of science. When scientists cease to acknowledge the gaps in the explanatory capacities of their own theories, then they cease to "do science" and begin to trespass on the domain of religion: knowledge by faith rather than by reason. We find such trespassing occurring over and over again in the history of science: the extension of Newton's laws to a 'mechanistic' universe; the extension of Darwin's natural selection to a universal theory of social relationships; and the extension of behaviorism likewise to all realms of human behavior.

Behaviorism as the dominant mode of discussion of minds and mental processes is effectively dead, although there are Departments of Psychology, especially in universities and medical schools in the United States, in which behaviorism is still dominant. Nevertheless, in spite of the crude and monstrous ways in which it was given practical expression in medicine, education, and child-rearing, behaviorism did succeed in clearing away many cherished assumptions about the apparently inviolable self. It did show that much that we take to be our 'self'—our habits of expression and behavior—are accountable to conditioning and do not require the assumption of an 'I' that is doing them.

One particular gap that behaviorism was unable to deal with that can be pinpointed specifically is the inability to explain intentional, anticipatory behavior such as deciding, hoping, fearing. If a boy stays away from home one night because he believes, mistakenly, that he was responsible for an accident for which he in fact was not responsible, and fears punishment, how can we possibly explain this on behaviorist grounds? Neither the mistaken belief nor the fear has any basis in the environment. I might, in an impromptu speech, now utter a sentence that anticipates an argument that I plan to make approximately five minutes later in the speech. A football player may make a move that anticipates a move that he suspects an opposing player is going to make in a few seconds. What can "anticipates" and "plans" and "suspects" mean to a behaviorist? Thus it became clear on rational arguments that in spite of its successes, behaviorism would have to give way to some kind of talk about states of mind. We will meet this problem again when we discuss artificial intelligence.

THE INITIAL SENSORY INPUT

Continuing our discussion of the first skandha, *form,* let us ask about the initial sensory input. What is the nature of the interaction between sense organ and sensory object? How does the organism select out parts of its environment to attend to? Another major problem with behaviorism lies in taking for granted the nature of the environment. Behaviorists wanted to be able to treat the organism as a stimulus-response machine that could be completely defined by the responses elicited to a set of defined stimuli. The assumption was that the environment provided the stimuli for the organism and that these stimuli were not themselves affected or changed by the organism. This is the naive commonsense view that the world consists of a number of definite predetermined objects which the organism can perceive and respond to but has no role in defining.

This naive view is altogether subject to question as a result of numerous experiments on the part of cognitive psychologists. Let us look at two of the many examples of such experiments. These show that the input to perception may be quite different from what we *think* we experience, that is, the end-point of perception. First consider the black mark O. Is this the letter O or the numeral zero? That depends on the context in which that mark is placed. If a subject is asked to search for a letter, O, the selection time will be faster if he or she is looking in a series of numbers than if he or she is searching among letters, and vice versa if he or she is asked to search for a numeral zero. How a given sensory input is seen depends on the context in which it occurs. In a second experiment, subjects were placed in a room decorated with patches of gray wallpaper of varying shades, illuminated with red light. Rather than see grays or reds of different brightness, the subjects saw the lighter grays as red, the medium grays as gray, and the darker grays as green, the complementary color to red. Perception was relative to the average level of illumination in the environment.

Or consider this situation: I am sitting at my desk looking out the window; I am asked to describe what I see. Well, I see green trees partly in the sun and partly shaded. Through the trees I see a road with a double yellow line, along which a yellow car passes, moving off into the distance. Beyond the road is a barrier and then the blue water of the bay, across the bay a row of tiny houses on the other shore. No, on reflection, I see a window with six small panes, beyond that the frame of a storm window, and a screen that has not been taken down from the summer; beyond that the trees, road, and so on. But no, I see the patterned wallpaper beside the frame of the window and can just catch the edge of a bookcase on one side, a picture on the other, and the corner of my desk underneath. And this whole scene is framed by an almond shape beyond which there is no visual impression at all. I have described this scene in terms of a set of objects, but of course I also "see" (although I did not notice them until this moment) all the spaces between the named objects, filled with little branches, the crosswires of the screen, and so on, a set of minor objects. Until a strange pattern of branches in one of the trees, shaped like an old man's head, is pointed out to me, I do not recall ever having *seen* that pattern of branches before. That pattern has now become an "object" or "figure" separated out from the background of which it was a part but a moment ago.

Many questions arise from a consideration of such simple scenes: for example, how do we separate objects from the background, and what determines when a figure is part of the background or part of an object, and how is it that the moving car appeared to remain the same size and shape as it passed by? (This phenomenon is known as size and shape constancy.) And even though the car is yellow, we do not confuse it with the yellow lines on the road. It retains its integrity as a moving yellow object.

We are led to ask: out of the variegated array of colors and outlines that we define as the visual environment, how are particular patches selected out as belonging to the same object? In a detailed study of these issues entitled *Perception: From Sense to Object*, J. M. Wilding, in discussing the initial separation of objects from the background, concludes, "Segregation of a complex input into separate objects against a background must be carried out by beginning with automatic processes, *followed by a hypothesis or expectation about the nature of the input* and the relevant features which can be used to assign different areas to the same object. Sometimes these features may be very simple ones, such as an enclosed area surrounded by a uniform background, such as letters or shapes on the page . . . but in other situations quite complex relations have to be extracted."[5] And Wilding summarizes the question of how to describe the initial input in this way, "We conclude that the appropriate description for a given input is *highly dependent on the way the perceiver chooses to process it,* which may vary qualitatively in the way information is interpreted and the degree to which information in memory is tapped, and quantitatively in the number of features extracted from the stimulus and from information in memory associated with it."[6] (Italics are mine in both quotes.) In other words, higher-level attributes such as interpretation, meaning, relevance, and intentions come in even at the point at which the organism defines its input stimulus. And of course none or little of this selection normally occurs at the conscious level.

Of course all these types of argument apply to the auditory and other senses. The naive assumption that our sense organs detect, in the environment, already existing objects simply is not workable. We should not naively adopt either of the simple extremes, of the visual field being an amorphous display of light or sound—the "raw sense data" of old empiricist theories—or of its being already fully determined as objects in a background before the light or sound contacts the sense organ. We are therefore left in a situation of considerable uncertainty as to just what "sense object" or "sensory input" might refer to. We will discuss this initial stage of perception again in Chapter 12. It appears that rather than dealing with a fixed "environment" perceived by a static and passive sense organ, we are dealing with a continually changing dynamic interaction between organ and input in which the "object" is being continually redefined as the environment as well as the internal state of the organism changes. As we will see, this is in accordance with the Buddhist view of the dynamic and open-ended nature of the relation between senses and their sense fields. And this is the first step in our journey of discovering the interlocking and mutually defining nature of organism and environment.

7

Feeling and Emotion

IN THE PREVIOUS CHAPTER we examined some of the ways modern psychology has spoken about the skandha of *form*. The next topic would naturally be the second skandha, *feeling*. But it is very difficult to separate out this skandha and deal with it entirely independently of the third, *perception*, and the fourth, *formations*. The second and third and some aspects of the fourth skandhas will therefore form the topic of this chapter.

First, the second skandha includes the proprioceptive sense, the inner sensation of the presence of our bodies. This normally goes completely unnoticed, and even when it is pointed out to us it is hard for many of us to acknowledge that there is in fact such a sensation. Yet neurosurgeon Oliver Sacks documents with great pathos the case of a young woman who lost this most intimate and precious sensation. She had absolutely no sensation of her body, no idea where her arms or legs were if she could not see them, no idea whether her face was smiling or in a deep frown. She herself explained that it was as if her body had become blind and deaf to itself. In the end, gradually after more than a year's intensive therapy, she learned to walk and use her arms again, but only so long as she could see them. And her body remained altogether absent so that sometimes she would break down and cry, "If only I could *feel*. But I've forgotten what it's like." Eight years later she remained "disembodied"; her body remained for her unreal and unpossessed.[1]

Feelings and emotions, collectively known as 'affects,' are not obviously susceptible to rational analysis. Philosophers choose thoughts and rationality rather than feelings to define the idea of self, while artists tend to find the seat of the soul in the emotions. For Descartes, truth was to be found in what was most clear and distinct, and certainly that cannot be said of feelings. Thoughts, when untainted by emotion (which they rarely are) are able to discriminate one thing from another and to combine according to logical rules. Because of this one can more easily test them against one's perceptions to determine their truth or falsity. Furthermore, thoughts can be related immediately and specifically to language, and therefore again seem to be the most human of our characteristics. Emotions have a vague quality and very often cannot be precisely described in words. Likewise the insights people feel from emotions are vague and easily challenged by the demand to put them into words, to be precise, to say exactly what is meant. For these reasons, thoughts seemed to the philosopher to be superior to emotions, and therefore seemed more likely to be the seat of humanness. But to ordinary people emotions are very intimately connected to our sense of 'I.'

Emotions are usually felt to be very real and definite, almost solid things. We think we have a repertoire of emotions: the emotion of anger, the emotion of love, the emotion of jealousy and so on. 'Anger,' 'love,' and 'jealousy' are all nouns; we think of emotions as things we can experience, like a rock or the sky. And when we experience these things we are in the corresponding state: when we experience anger, we are angry. We would not say to a friend, "I am experiencing anger toward you." We would simply say, "I am angry with you." Thus, when the emotion is a part of our present experience, we name it and identify ourselves with it. 'I' becomes that emotion.

Emotions, then, are things we can become, or at least the qualities of which we can identify with. Of course this identification is partial and temporary. It is temporary because the emotion ends or changes, and then we no longer identify with it. We say, "I am sorry I was angry with you, I am not angry any more." We do not say, or think, "The 'I' that was angry is no more," which would be more accurate. The identification is only partial because we usually also have an internal running commentary going, which continually defines and redefines how 'I' feel. It is only in very rare and intense emotional situations that we lose that sense of being self-conscious about being angry, or lusting, or enthused.

How then is it that we take on these partial and temporary identities that we call emotions? There has in the past been a great deal of confusion among psychologists about emotion, how to define it, what are its causal bases, and what are its functions for the organism. However, in the past two decades some clarity seems to have emerged and there is some agreement on the main outlines.[2] We can divide our discussion into two main headings: the experience and the expression of emotion. In terms of experience there is general agreement that there are two major components, a somatic component that provides the basic energy and primitive feeling of the emotion; and a cognitive component, involving concept and judgment, that provides the more specific characterization of the emotion. In terms of expression, discussion tends nowadays to focus on the evolutionary aspects of emotion, seeing a continuity between other animals and humans, of emotional expression and of the basic patterns of action motivated by emotion.

First let us look briefly at the evolutionary view of emotion, regarding emotions as the behavioral expression of complex patterns of behavior that have evolved as adaptive responses to a complex environment and that are directed toward the survival of the organism and its reproductive continuity. Robert Plutchik arrives at eight basic adaptive behavior patterns that, he says, "may be found in some form at all levels of evolution, do not depend on particular neural structures or body parts, do not depend on introspection, and are defined in terms of gross behavioral interactions between organism and environment." These eight are (1) *incorporation*—acceptance of stimuli, such as food, from the outside world into the organism; (2) *rejection*—getting rid of something harmful that has already been incorporated; (3) *destruction*—an attempt to destroy a barrier to the satisfaction of some need; (4) *protection*—occurring under conditions of pain, or threats of pain or destruction, this is the attempt to avoid being destroyed; (5) *reproduction*—the response associated with sexual interactions; (6) *reintegration*—the pattern of reaction to the loss of something possessed or enjoyed, generally described at the human level as grief or sadness; (7) *orientation*—the pattern of behavior that occurs when an organism contacts a new or strange object; (8) *exploration*—the more or less random activities organisms use to explore their environments.[3]

The significance of these functional patterns of behavior is that their corresponding subjective descriptions as felt emotions provide a set of basic emotions, much like the root emotion dharmas of the fourth (formations) skandha, out of which the numerous more complex secondary emotions are built. The basic emotions corresponding to Plutchik's eight behavior patterns are (1) fear, (2) anger, (3) lust or joy, (4) sadness, (5) acceptance-trust, (6) disgust, (7) expectancy-anticipation, (8) astonishment-surprise. Other psychologists of emotion have also tried to define a set of basic emotions and come up with a set similar to Plutchik's. Plutchik goes on to suggest how complex emotions may be built up as combinations of the basics. Of course, not all psychologists agree with Plutchik's approach, and in fact the whole field of emotion theory is quite controversial. Nevertheless it gives us an example of the kind of work that is being done, and an interesting point of comparison with the Buddhist analysis.

The table of emotion terms Plutchik used is in Appendix 2. With this list he did empirical studies to determine how, when they are used to describe people's experience, these terms can be rated according to their similarity to reference terms chosen from the eight basic emotions. In this way he was able to order the terms as in the list. They come in similarity clusters around the eight basic terms. The last group (content, cooperative, trusting, tolerant) falls quite naturally close to the first (accepting, agreeable, serene, cheerful), and so the entire list can be arranged in a circular continuum evenly distributed without any gaps. I have indicated this by repeating the last term (tolerant) at the beginning of the list. It is as if the emotions form a continuous spectrum of energies, like a rainbow, which can be labeled at somewhat arbitrarily chosen points. Merely scanning this list, if we take it personally, gives us insight into our own experience: how emotions are connected and grouped together, and how one might lead to another.

It is interesting to compare this list with the list of dharmas of the fourth skandha (formations). There are obvious similarities, but Plutchik gives no suggestion as to how we might use such a list in a way that promotes the well-being of ourselves and others. This, of course, is the whole point of the abhidharma division into wholesome and unwholesome groups. The cognitive labeling of the spectrum of energies, which gives rise to recognizable emotions, is to some extent arbitrary, varying from culture to culture. In the English language more than 400 words occur that could be regarded as emotion terms. Nevertheless, there are some clear reference points, as exemplified in Plutchik's eight basic emotions. So we can begin to see a great deal of sense and empirical basis to the abhidharma analysis.

In this analysis, the primary reference frame is threefold according to the fundamental quality of the energy in relation to others: neutral/ignoring; attractive/grasping; repulsive/aggression. The second and third are then divided again: attractive is divided into passion/lust and pride/aggrandizement; and repulsive is divided into anger/belligerence and jealousy/resentment. This fivefold set—ignorance, passion, pride, anger, and jealousy—are known as the root afflictions (Sanskrit: *klesa.*) They are afflictions, or obscurations, from the point of view not of some externally determined morality, but of open awareness, expansive and without prejudice. The klesas tend to focus and narrow awareness, drawing it into knots, or complexes, that in the end become obsessions, habitually repeating in circles with which therapists are very familiar, and locking up energy that would otherwise be available for awareness.

Now that we have a characterization of emotion from the behavioral standpoint, let us look at the question of what might be the causal basis of the experience of these emotions. Although many psychologists agree that both the somatic and the cognitive components are involved in emotion, there is a range of view on just how these two components interact and how significant each is in determining the nature of the emotion. There is also divergence of opinion on which bodily structures are responsible for the somatic component. The main candidates here seem to be the autonomic nervous sytem, the limbic system of the brain, and the neuromuscular motor system. Activation of the first raises the general arousal level of the organism; stimulation of the second activates a very basic range of affects, fear–terror and so on; and the third controls the posture, facial expressions, and actions of the organism. All three of these physical structures are clearly associated with emotions in some way.

Arousal of the autonomic nervous system together with the chemical environment generated by the endocrine (hormonal) system which bathes it, in particular, stimulation of the sympathetic nervous system, causes the blood to flow faster, the heart to beat faster, and the stomach and intestinal activity to slow down. It is the releaser of energy into the system, the organism's emergency system. This is counterbalanced by the parasympathetic nervous system, which conserves energy and shuts down the emergency system. It is arousal of the sympathetic nervous system that is experienced as an influx of energy at the visceral level, the "gut reaction."

While arousal of the autonomic nervous system is clearly an important element in some emotions, it has been shown that not all feelings that are subjectively classified as 'emotional' are paralleled by arousal. The autonomic nervous system cannot then be the only somatic component of emotion. Another major candidate is the limbic system of the midbrain.[4] The limbic system has been called the "old mammalian brain" since structures similar to the human limbic system has been found in most mammals, from rats and rabbits to horses and other primates. It receives messages from the sensory systems connecting the organism to the 'outside' as well as from the 'inner' visceral and muscular systems. When this system is activated a wide range of basic affects is experienced such as hunger, thirst, pain, repugnance, and the general arousal patterns of terror, fear, sadness, depression, foreboding, familiarity or strangeness, reality or unreality, wanting to be alone, paranoid feelings, and anger. It mediates messages received from the sensory system and is responsible for the coloration of such sensory inputs with the all-pervading qualities we call 'moods.' Areas of the limbic system have tentatively been identified as mediating a range of basic moods: rage-fear; fight-flight; pleasure-pain; expectation-actuality; tension-relaxation; we might note here the similarity to the set of basic affects described by Plutchik and others. It is also involved in expression of the more complex emotions, and therefore may be an intermediary between these and the basic affects. It also appears to contribute significantly to the primitive sense of personal identity. In this sense there are similarities between this group of characteristics tentatively associated with the limbic system and the third skandha that bridges the second skandha of feeling and the emotional components of the fourth.

The third major somatic system that has been taken as the chief bodily seat of emotion is the motor system. Here the obvious correlation between emotional states and facial expression or overall body posture is pointed to. Facial expression and posture can be a response to a felt emotion, but they can also induce emotions. If we hang our heads down, slump our shoulders, and frown, we are likely to become depressed. If we already feel depressed, the simple expedient of lifting our chins can often cheer us up.

Although the role each of these systems plays in the experience of emotion is clearly of interest, we will not enter here into the debate of how this role is played out in actuality. Perhaps we can reasonably assume that since claimants for each of the systems can show evidence to support their claims, it is most likely that all three systems are involved in some way. The main point for us is that there clearly is some basic element of biological energy contributing to what we experience as emotions.

These then are the biological systems responsible for the basic energy of emotions and their primary qualities, which generally take the form of basic, almost nameless feelings of attraction or wanting (hunger, thirst, familiarity, reality); repulsion (strangeness, repugnance, terror, anger); or fundamental anxiety (depression, foreboding, paranoid feelings). How, from these basic energies, do all the variety of emotions arise, to which we give specific names, and with which we identify? The answer seems to be that the specificity of emotion comes through the cognitive processes. In perception of the 'outside world' cognition forms conceptual hypotheses as to what is 'out there' and finds the best fit to whatever gave rise to the arousal of the perceptual system; in the perception of emotion, cognition forms conceptual hypotheses as to what is 'in there' and finds the best fit to that. In this case it is to a combination of the basic quality of the aroused energy of the somatic system and the conditions that gave rise to that arousal that a conceptual 'best fit,' i.e., an appropriate emotional label, has to be found. The conditions giving rise to the basic arousal might be external, the perception of some object, or they may be internal, the perception of an internal image or cognitive representation, or a previous emotion. The choice of the 'best fit' is determined by an analysis of the meaning of the arousing conditions.

George Mandler, Professor of Psychology at the University of California, San Diego, describes the process in this way:

> Emotional behavior has, as one of its necessary concomitants, the production of autonomic system arousal. This arousal is nonspecific and merely sets the stage for emotional behavior and experience; the particular quality of the emotion is determined entirely by the meaning analysis, which the arousal and, more important, the general situation and cognitive states engender. The joint action of both of these systems, arousal and meaning analysis, has outputs to consciousness as well as to action systems, including language output. Thus arousal provides the emotional tone for a particular cognition, and cognition provides the quality to the emotional state. Specific events relevant to "emotional" experience have two functions: first, they set off arousal; second, they induce a particular meaning analysis of the situation in which the individual finds himself.[5]

The final evaluation as a particular emotion might occur passively or actively. In the passive case, the perception of a basic arousal energy, say positive-pleasurable, would simply interact with a cognitive interpretation of the situation, say as joyful, producing a positive emotion of joy. In the active case, the perceived situation would activate a previously experienced and stored emotional structure (an arousal-meaning combination) which would then be reexperienced as a response to the present situation. For example, seeing someone might, on a previous occasion, have aroused a basically negative energy combined with a cognitive evaluation leading to the emotion 'jealousy.' In this case seeing that person again might simply stimulate the previously existing structure, 'jealousy.'

The entire process I have described will usually not be conscious. The result in consciousness is the experiencing, *and naming*, of a particular emotion. The ability to give an appropriate name to the final emotion will be a large factor in the recognition as that particular emotion and the storage as such. Even the emotional judgment of a situation as "good" or "bad" can often be, and may well always be, simply the conscious labeling of the basic energies of approach or withdrawal. Once they have been set up in our organisms, such basic evaluative structures may be activated independently by situations, giving rise to automatic responses to those situations as 'good' or 'bad.' But these evaluations originate in the prior labeling of withdrawal-approach energies. Mandler suggests that in all probability a very great deal of our habitual evaluative judgments develop in this way. Again it is rather remarkable to observe the similarity of this analysis with that of abhidhama.[6]

Those who live their lives in one language culture may develop the idea that emotions are real things that actually exist and that are identical for all humans. But anyone who has experienced more than one culture knows that this is by no means the case. There are words labeling emotions in English, French, German, Spanish, Japanese, and no doubt every language, which do not have corresponding labels in other languages. As Mandler points out, there is no word in English that quite corresponds to the German *angstlich*, or the French *ambiance*. An analysis of the notion of 'love' in the western tradition from Greek times to the present has shown that the idea of 'romantic love' or "being in love," with its connotations of separation and unrequitedness, was altogether absent until the age of chivalry in the late Middle Ages.

Or consider the Japanese term *wabi*. Although this is a common term, it has particular relevance to the contemplative practices of Japan such as the Ways of Tea, of Archery or Flower Arranging. Soshitsu Sen, a master of the Way of Tea, has this to say about wabi: "The foundation of the Way of Tea is based on the aesthetic of wabi, which is sometimes translated as rusticity. But this aesthetic should not be confused with a love of the rustic. Wabi is a state of mind. It is better expressed by words such as frugality, simplicity, and humility." By way of trying to illustrate this concept, to evoke the feeling of it in English-speaking people, he says, "People seek flowers in full bloom; yet, while loving their beauty, we must appreciate the effort that brings forth these same flowers to full bloom. A tiny sprout pushes forth, knowing that it is spring. It has no choice; it must grow or perish. The truth of nature can be known from the life of a flower. A person who has not experienced the rigors of austerity like the grasses cannot hope to understand the essence of wabi. It is only natural to appreciate the beauty of flowers in their season, but it requires a finer sense to uncover the beauty of the grasses beneath the snow."[7] Some readers of this passage might not even recognize that the author is talking about an emotion at all, and there seems to be no equivalent word in the English langauge, and perhaps no equivalent feeling to an English speaker. Yet the experience of wabi is as real to a Japanese person as "getting high" or "feeling blue" is to an American.

The emotions we experience are dependent on the labels that are available to us. And the labels that are available to us are a mutual, and continually changing, product of the human community in which we learn our language. Furthermore, many languages do not even have an exact equivalent to what an English-speaker means by 'emotion.'

So far we have analyzed emotions into a cognitive component and a component of bare energy, or arousal. Further analysis of arousal must investigate the causes leading to arousal. Mandler's analysis of this follows a path that goes back at least to a proposal of Donald Hebb, the Canadian neuropsychologist, in the early 1950s.[8] This analysis involves the notion of interruption, or discrepancy. When there is discrepancy between one's expectations of how the world is and one's perceptions, then there is arousal. In terms of interruption this is saying that our actions usually anticipate the way the world is from moment to moment. That is we expect continuity of our perceptions, or, if there is going to be a change in our perceptions we, in our representations, anticipate that change. If everything is going according to these expectations, then we experience simply an even emotional tone of which we probably are not conscious.

However, as soon as there is an interruption of our expectation, then the organism's emergency system—the sympathetic side of the autonomic nervous system—is turned on and we experience arousal. It makes a great deal of sense from the evolutionary point of view that an organism would be genetically programmed to respond with arousal—increased energy level, increased attention, and preparedness for fight or flight—when the environment does not appear to be in accord with the expectation. The autonomic nervous system will then have the dual function of not only cranking up the energy level of the organism when interruption occurs, but also of informing the organism that the world is not the way it was expected to be.

Mandler suggests that the notion of interruption is not necessarily negative. Our expectations can be interrupted negatively, as when an amount of money we have been expecting turns out to be less than we expected; or positive, as when the amount is greater. However, at the more unconscious perceptual level, it would seem more likely that the first level of arousal would be negative, fundamental anxiety, since the nature of the discrepancy would at first not be recognized. Only when the discrepancy is recognized would there perhaps be a sense of relief, which might be felt as pleasure. And this could happen quickly enough so that it has not yet been labeled as an emotion of a particular kind before the arousal has turned into a pleasurable one.

This then is Donald Hebb's suggestion, that fear is the natural response to perceptual discrepancy. Hebb performed experiments to demonstrate this. In one, a group of young geese were habituated to the outline of an adult goose. When the outline of an eagle was passed over their nest the young geese showed a typical fear reaction. Quite natural, you say, young geese have an inherited disposition to fear eagles, a very sensible protective measure. This would be a natural result of evolution, since if geese did not fear eagles, their predators, they would be unlikely to survive. However, Hebb then habituated other young geese to the shadow of an eagle. Now, when the shadow of an adult goose was passed over their nest the young geese again showed a typical fear reaction. Hebb's conclusion was that young geese are "wired" not to avoid eagles but to avoid something unexpected: if they expect a goose they will avoid an eagle, if they expect an eagle they will avoid a goose. This makes even more sense from the evolutionary point of view. Instead of each species having to inherit fear and avoidance reactions to every likely danger, there can simply be a general inheritance of avoidance of discrepancy.

It appears then that the first response to perceptual discrepancy is fear, or panic, and this is followed by arousal, which is felt as basically positive or negative depending on the way in which the discrepancy is resolved. This then leads to the cognitive component, which is first an evaluation of 'good' or 'bad' depending on the type of arousal energy. Mandler suggests that good-bad evaluations take basically two forms: innate and culturally learned (he in fact suggests three, but his second and third both come under the category of culturally learned). Examples of innate evaluations are our withdrawal reactions to bitter tastes or loud noises. Examples of culturally learned reactions are legion. Our responses to the world are almost all colored by like or dislike, and most of these likes and dislikes are culturally learned. Beyond this basic coloration of good-bad, like-dislike, our emotions are given more specificity—joy, enthusiasm, excitement, or anger, jealousy, and so on, by further conceptual categorization.

This then is an outline of one kind of theory of emotions as it is being developed by cognitive scientists today. It is a theory of a natural flow of energy based on causal interactions between the internal state of the organism—its cognitive processing system and its autonomic nervous system—and its perception of an 'outside.'

As I have pointed out, Mandler's emphasis on the autonomic nervous system as the energetic source of emotion is a limited view. And his supposition that arousal always precedes cognitive appraisal seems to refer only to the type of situation involving environmental interruption that he specifically describes. There certainly seem to be occasions when an emotion arises only after a conceptual judgment of a situation has already been made, as for example when we tell a child that we are angry and then begin to feel aroused. It has also been pointed out that emotions can be felt almost completely at the cognitive level with very little arousal of the energetic level. That is, the experience of emotion often comes entirely from the fourth-skandha (formations) level, with very little direct awareness of the second skandha, bare feeling. However these criticisms seem to be more a question of degree of emphasis than a fundamental questioning of the principles involved.

We might expect that if indeed emotions are closely influenced at a nonconscious level by cognition, then the reverse should also be the case. That is, we would expect that cognition can also be influenced at a level below consciousness by emotionally biased stimuli. That this is in fact the case has now been shown quite extensively. First, a variety of experiments repeatedly have shown that emotively toned stimuli presented at a level that makes them undetectable consciously—subliminal stimuli—can have a significant effect on the perception of a neutral image. Second, it has been extensively demonstrated that conscious decisions are frequently made on the basis of cues that have preconscious affective components rather than on the strictly logical argument that is consciously taken to be the basis.[9]

On the first point, one kind of experiment that has been performed repeatedly is the following: subjects are shown a card showing an emotionally neutral scene, such as a boy playing a violin, at exposure levels increasing from 20 to 500 milliseconds, too fast to be consciously noticed. For half the subjects the picture also contained in the upper right-hand corner the head and shoulders of a threatening and ugly male person. For the remaining subjects the peripheral figure was a smiling face. After each exposure all subjects were asked to draw and comment upon what they had seen. The reports of a significant number of the first group were distorted in a negative way, by recalling one or both of the figures as animals, by representing the central figure as dead, broken, or overlaid by a dark shadow. As Norman Dixon, Professor of Psychology at London University, comments, "these data support the view that the meaning of pictorial stimuli, presented below the threshold for veridical recognition, determines how they are perceived in a non-veridical way." These results are so predictable, Dixon reports, that they are used in a test known as the defense mechanism test as part of the selection procedure for applicants for pilots in the air forces of Norway and Sweden and considered for those of Denmark and West Germany—those who show significant effects of the threatening figure on the perception of the central figure make poor pilots, "with an above average chance of being involved in flying accidents or of becoming non-operational through absenteeism or psychosomatic illness."

In another study, reported by Dixon, normal (not psychotic) subjects were asked to control the intensity of a spot of light visible to one eye by manually moving a lever. The subjects thought that they were simply adjusting the lever to indicate moment-to-moment changes in their visual sensitivity to the spot. However, unknown to them, emotional and neutral words were being presented to the other eye, at an intensity below threshold, and movement of the lever was altering the intensity of these words, as well as that of the visible spot of light. Without knowing what was happening, the subjects used the lever to reduce the intensity of threatening words. Dixon comments that "a feature of psycho pathological determination of so-called voluntary behavior is that the subject remains unaware of the fact that his performance is being influenced by factors of which he is not conscious," as is demonstrated in these experiments.[10]

Many experiments of this type indicate the presence of a phenomenon called 'perceptual defense mechanism,' in which there is alteration and distortion of the final, conscious perception as a result of preconscious responses to emotive stimuli. That these mechanisms happen somewhere in the process leading from the initial stimulus to the conscious perception, and not in the following pattern of response *to* that perception, has been clearly demonstrated.

Of the many, varied, and vivid demonstrations of an affective element in decision-making discovered by Kahnemann and Tversky, here is but one example. "Imagine that you are about to buy a jacket for $125 and a calculator for $15. The calculator salesman tells you that the calculator you want to buy is on sale at the other branch of the store, twenty minutes away, for $10. Would you make the trip? Most people say that they will. Another group is asked a similar question. This time the cost of the jacket is changed to $15 and the cost of the calculator to $125 in the original store and to $120 in the branch. Of respondents presented with this version, the majority said that they would not make the extra trip."[11] In both cases the savings are identical, $5 for a twenty-minute trip. But it is far more satisfying to save $5 on a $15 purchase than on a $125 purchase. Most people go for the satisfaction rather than the logic. In this and many other similar experiments it becomes clear that rational choice is being influenced by emotional weight without the direct knowledge of the chooser, corroborating the intimate link between affect and cognition, emotion and thought.

An important point from the point of view of skandha analysis is the separation between (1) the bare feeling, the second skandha; (2) the tendency to action based on that feeling, the third skandha; and (3) the subsequent emotion based on appraisal of the meaning of the feeling to me, the fourth skandha. These three stages do seem to have been separated by modern psychology. C. E. Izard, at the University of Pennsylvania, has this to say: "It is critical for differential emotions theory that we recognize that emotion-feeling can exist in consciousness at different levels of awareness. At the lowest level of awareness, we are barely conscious of the feeling and may have considerable difficulty articulating it even upon reflection. . . . At the highest level of awareness, the feeling dominates consciousness and we can readily cognize it—symbolize it, ponder it, or try to nurture, attentuate or suppress it. In these latter processes, the emotion-related cognition can be very important."[12]

Magda Arnold, author of a two-volume work on *Emotion and Personality*, has this to say on the difference between feeling and emotion: "When I say the fragrance or taste of a wine is *pleasant,* I do not necessarily want the wine; in fact, I may never take it. In tasting its fragrance, I possess the pleasant sensation and no possession of the object is asked for. But when I say I *like* wine, it means I *do* want it when the occasion is given. The aim of the *emotion* (liking or simple love in this case) is possession of the object, while the *feeling* of pleasantness simply indicates smooth functioning in the subject. Hence, emotion aims at the object, feeling reflects the state of the subject. For a sensory feeling to become an emotion it is necessary that the preceding judgement—how this sensation affects my functioning—should be followed by a judgement how the object which occasions the sensation affects me *as a person.*"[13] This is a remarkably accurate description of the difference between the bare feeling of the second skandha and the definite emotion of the fourth skandha, and it indicates the role played by wanting or grasping to the object in relation to my *self* (Arnold's "me *as a person*")[15] which enters at the third skandha.

We have seen in this chapter that the way scientists are thinking about and categorizing feeling and emotion does follow the skandha principles. Buddhists have not, of course, spoken in terms of the nervous and limbic systems, the 'third-person' physiological parallels of the affects. But insofar as feeling is the link between form and the higher skandhas, the scientific theories make a significant contribution to the Buddhist understanding on this point, just as the work on sensory input contributes to the understanding of the skandha of form. In the next two chapters we will look at the 'intellectual' skandhas, the fourth and fifth—formations and consciousness—beginning with work that has been done on the processing of thoughts.

8

Formations of Thoughts and Images

IN THE PREVIOUS CHAPTER we looked at the emotions of the fourth skandha—formations—and the role that cognitions play in the experience of emotions. In this chapter we will continue our examination of the fourth skandha, focusing on the cognitive side, on mental images and representations, that is, on thoughts and their manipulation.

In Chapter 6 I pointed out the way the criticisms of behaviorism seemed to point choicelessly in the direction of taking account of 'inner' experience. This inevitable direction is acknowledged today even by psychologists and philosophers who stand completely by the scientific study of minds. Of course artists, humanitarians, religious people, and others have been saying this all the time. And the reader may well have breathed a sigh and said, "Finally, so what else is new?" But we must look at this development from the point of view of science's refusal to take anything for granted. Not wishing to take for granted that 'a self' or 'a mind' exists, the behaviorists and their inheritors threw the baby, immediate personal experience, out with the bathwater, uncritical belief in inherited folk tales about minds and souls. Now scientists are recognizing the need to take another, but more selective, look at that baby. But if scientists do not assume that there is a self, organizing and controlling these processes, then they must try to understand how the chaotic impressions fabricated by our senses, affects, and thought processes are organized into a coherent world.

What, then, is now deemed necessary? First, criticism of the behaviorist theory of language learning led to the description of apparently innate cognitive structures of learning. Second, it is supposed that there has to be some form of 'innate ideas' and mental imagery, some way in which the organism represents its world to itself. The organism cannot any longer be thought of as being born

95

"blank" and passively gathering ideas and language ability from its environment.

ACQUIRING KNOWLEDGE OF THE WORLD

While behaviorism was clearing the ground of traditional assumptions about souls and minds, Jean Piaget, a child psychologist in Switzerland, had kept alive in Europe a nonbehaviorist psychology since the 1930s.[1] Piaget effectively criticized the behaviorist view of learning and demonstrated that innate cognitive structures must exist in the newborn child for us to be able to understand language and concept acquisition.

Piaget produced extensive evidence on the way children acquire abstract concepts such as those of self, external reality, space, time, and causality. He suggested that there are basic structures of thought that seem to be common to most children and that go through developmental stages at different ages: the sensorimotor stage at infancy, the intuitive stage at early childhood, the concrete operational stage at middle childhood, and the formal-logical operational stage at adolescence. The details of these stages as described by Piaget have been challenged in recent years. The details do not appear to be so universal as he claimed, particularly across different cultural and social groups, and the timing and necessity for each stage is not so clear. Nevertheless it is recognized that the general principle of a gradually unfolding of genetically programmed cognitive structures is correct.

The potentiality to go through these stages must be present at birth, each stage then being elicited by some combination of the inherent genetic development of the child, much as an embryo develops, and the child's interaction with the environment. Piaget describes the organism as an autoregulating system—one that strives for equilibrium as the internal and external environment continually changes. This 'equilibration' happens through a process of *'assimilation'* and *'accommodation'*— the child first assimilates new knowledge about the world using his or her old cognitive structures, and accommodates that knowledge by adjusting his or her cognitive structures to make a better fit to his or her knowledge.

In the nature-nurture and the empiricist-rationalist debates, Piaget took a middle path. Unlike Locke and the behaviorists he did not believe that all knowledge could be learned from the environment "from scratch," and he demonstrated this empirically. At the same time, unlike Descartes and the strict rationalists, he did not believe that *all* knowledge is inborn, or innate. Piaget's work suggests that the structures by which knowledge are acquired by the child develop as a combination of genetic unfolding and environmental interaction, as do the logical types of knowledge that a child can appreciate at each stage. The actual knowledge a child acquires is, however, derived from environmental interaction.

The work of Piaget and his followers over six decades has had tremendous impact on psychological understanding and on the education and understanding of children. Children do not come into the world as little blank slates that can be impressed at the will and whim of teachers and parents. In fact they bring with them an inherited cognitive apparatus that develops at its own pace according to its own rules, much as the baby teeth are replaced by adult teeth between the ages of six and eight years, and sexual changes take place between eleven and fourteen years. This evolution of structures takes place naturally in the psychobiological organism. The hypothesis of a self, or a self-image, according to Piaget, is developed along with other concepts, and changes its character parallel to other concepts. But the actual existence of a separate self or mind to guide this development is not required at all.

Furthermore, the notion of an 'external reality' develops along with this developing idea of a self. According to Piaget, the child's mental processes first construct a concept related to a world, and then project that concept out believing that it does indeed exist in the outer world. As David Elkind, editor of a volume of Piaget's essays, says, "*Once a concept is constructed, it is immediately externalized so that it appears to the subject as a perceptually given property of the object and independent of the subject's own mental activity.* The tendency of mental activities to become automatized and for their results to be perceived as external to the subject is what leads to the conviction that there is a reality independent of thought. The absolute separation between mind and matter is an illusion, but one that can be overcome only by examination of the development of thought in the child."[2] From the point of view of this book, this view places somewhat too much emphasis on the subjective side. Because we realize that there is a serious question about the absolute reality of an external world, there is the temptation to think that the individual mind is more real, and that the 'external world' is somehow a creation of this individual mind. However, as we go on we will see that the individual mind cannot be thought of as any more ultimately real than the external reality it supposedly

projects. The two, individual self-consciousness and its corresponding external reality, coemerge and have identical relative statuses. But
we must go step by step in the development of this understanding,
and Piaget's deconstruction of the absolute reality of the self and its
external world is a first step.

REPRESENTATIONS OF THE WORLD

Beyond the developing cognitive structures proposed by Piaget,
there is a tendency to assume that the organism holds internal images
or representations of its world. There are many directions of inquiry
that can be interpreted to show that, so long as we are thinking of
the organism as something separate from its environment, having an
'inside' and an 'outside,' then we have to assume that the organism
in some manner makes 'inner' representations of the 'outside' to
itself. According to these representations it acts more or less appropriately, and therefore we assume that the representations are harmonious and coherent for it, and mean for it 'the outside world.' It
will become clear in later discussions that this is only an assumption.
It is a natural assumption to make, given our habitual belief in an
external world and in thoughts that somehow reflect that outside
world. Since it allows us to think of thoughts as symbols that can be
manipulated by the rules of logic, it is also an assumption that
appeals to the new generation of cognitive scientists who wish to be
able to model mental processes on the analogy of a computer. Since
this point of view has led to some interesting insights we will take it
at face value for the time being, and leave the criticism of it to a later
chapter.

Studies of perception show that the perceptual system presents
data to the organism in a form very different from what the organism
feels that it is experiencing. Data are in the form of light radiation of
various frequencies reaching the retina, air waves hitting the ear-
drum, complex chemicals binding to the taste buds, etc., but what is
experienced is 'things' in space and time. In the representational
view it is presumed that somehow the organism constructs these
'things' by making hypotheses derived from past experience or from
inherited structures about what is out there. It seeks an image that
best fits the data. And there may be any number of possible best fits,
of which the organism chooses one, more or less by guesswork. We
have no idea what the 'outside world' is other than that it is the
presumed object of the organism's representations. So it is really a

very loose way of talking to say that the organism 'makes representations of the outside world.' But we will adopt this way of talking at this stage of our discussion, modifying it later when we consider the limitation of the whole concept of an 'inside' and 'outside' of the organism. This is the first hint of a subtle circularity that goes on when we try to think about thought.

In an argument for innate structures, Noam Chomsky suggests that there are innate, inherited structures that are responsible for the ability of children to acquire a language.[3] Chomsky challenged two aspects of the behaviorist view. First he pointed out that a natural language is grammatically extremely intricate, and it is simply ridiculous to imagine that a child can, in the few years needed to completely master this grammar, master it only by interaction with environment. If one actually looks at the types and frequency of verbal interactions between a child and his or her parents and siblings, these are simply not frequent or intense enough for such tremendously complex learning to take place. Therefore, Chomsky concludes, there must be innate grammatical structures in the child.

Chomsky also argues for such structures in another way. He regards the behaviorist idea that every utterance we make is completely determined by the environment as nonsense. When I meet a friend on the street, I might say any one of hundreds of things to him, which might be determined neither by the immediate environment, nor by what I had been doing or thinking immediately before I met this friend. In fact the human being exhibits great creativity in conversational situations. However, the grammatical structure of what we say *is* determined by rules, and if they cannot be learned from the environment, these rules must be innate. Furthermore, a child may be brought up in any language environment, not necessarily that of his or her parents, and learn the language as well as a native: an American child brought up in Japan by Japanese foster parents would speak Japanese as well as a child born of Japanese parents. Therefore, Chomsky reasoned, the grammatical rules must be universal to all languages. While to find these universal rules empirically from natural languages has proved a formidable task, the basic principles that Chomsky and his colleagues have pointed to are clear.

Finally, arguments for the presence of a representational system come from Jerry Fodor, Noam Chomsky's long-time colleague. Fodor follows Chomsky in saying that there must be innate universal grammatical rules for an organism to be able to learn a language in the short time it does so, and with environmental clues that are so vague, in terms of the complexities of grammar, as they are for a child. But Fodor goes even further to point out that these rules must be encoded in the organism like a language, what Fodor calls the 'language of thought.' The argument is really quite simple, but Fodor argues it so precisely and cogently that the book that contains this argument, *The Language of Thought,* is regarded as a turning point in cognitive science, even by those who disagree with it.[4] The point is this: that learning a language involves learning what the sentences of that language mean; learning what the sentences mean involves learning the range of application of those sentences, which in turn involves learning that these sentences follow certain grammatical rules. But to learn that a language follows certain rules we must already know the rules (of course all this is occurring at a level normally inaccessible to consciousness). Therefore we must already possess a system complex enough to be able to express the rules, i.e., a language. And of course this language cannot be the spoken language the organism is trying to learn, including his or her first language. Therefore the organism comes into the world already equipped biologically with a symbolic, representational system as complicated as a language, and this Fodor calls the 'language of thought.'

Of course this argument by no means implies that each organism should have just one biological language system. Fodor himself suggests that there may be several parallel processing systems, each somewhat independent, each processing a different input corresponding to a different domain of interaction of the organism with its environment, e.g., a visual processing system, a linguistic processing system, etc.

Howard Gardner has examined this issue in considerable depth from the point of view of 'intelligence.'[5] He suggests that the whole long history of the idea of a 'general intelligence' may have thoroughly missed the point. It is this concept of a general intelligence on which the idea of 'intelligence quotient' is based as well as the silly little tests on which often depends the future education of our children—as if all human possibility depends on the ability to do crossword puzzles. Based on extensive researches, Gardner suggests there are probably a number of quite unconnected 'intelligences.' He points to the following types of intelligences: linguistic, musical, logical-mathematical, spatial, bodily-kinesthetic, personal. Each of these intelligences could well have a corresponding 'language of thought.'

ARTIFICIAL THOUGHT-PROCESSING

Now the question naturally arises, How are these internal representations manipulated and processed in the organisms? Another line of inquiry going beyond behaviorism in the 1950s was that of cognitive psychologists, who were studying how people process simple information. It began to become increasingly clear that raw sense data entering the system—sounds, colors, shapes, and so on—were not simply absorbed and perceived as in a mirror, but that some kind of processing was taking place; experiments showed that abstract concepts are formed, channels of perceptual input (e.g., the two ears, the two eyes, etc.) are selectively attended to, a variety of strategies are used to arrive at categorization of information arriving at the senses. Information-processing models provided a way of thinking about what might be happening between the behaviorists' stimulus and response without needing to reintroduce any separate mental substance, or any little man in the head doing the processing. With the rise of computers, the model of the brain as computer was born, and this model is the dominant model of thought processes today.

With the modeling of thought processes on the functioning of computers, the possibility of artificial intelligence (AI) naturally arises. How far can one simulate apparently intelligent behavior with a computer? The modern version of AI began in 1956, when the term 'artificial intelligence' first came into circulation. But the idea can reasonably be traced as far back as the seventeenth-century philosopher Thomas Hobbes, and David Hume of the eighteenth century. For the past thirty years AI has been a topic of growing interest and power to elucidate some of the mechanisms of mental process.[6]

Proponents of AI made some dramatic claims in the early years: that by 1967 computers would be world chess champions, discover important new mathematical theorems, compose music acceptable to music critics, translate foreign languages, and so on. In the early 1970s a reaction set in, progress was bogged down, the exaggerated claims embodied in names for computer programs such as "General Problem Solver" were being debunked. But by the mid-1980s it was clear that considerable progress had been made in the understanding and application of how to model mental process by computer. At the same time, just because the issues have been clarified, the potential limitations of this model of mentality have also become clearer. There are definitely two camps on the AI question, the proponents and the opponents, and dialogue between them can be irrational, emotioncharged, and sometimes vituperative. Wherever we find this kind of division in science, we can be sure that someone's deeply held contextual beliefs are being challenged. And since it begins to touch what our society regards as the essence of being human, namely reasonableness and rational thought, AI is worth examining.

The essential assumptions of AI, according to John Haugeland, author of an excellent and relatively impartial book on AI,[7] are:

1. Our ability to deal with things intelligently is due to our capacity to think about them reasonably (including subconscious thinking); and
2. Our capacity to think about things reasonably amounts to a faculty for internal "automatic symbol manipulation."

The first part of this statement summarizes what many people believe today: that the essence of minds lies in their being able to *think*. Very often we find the terms 'intelligence,' 'mental,' and 'thought' interchanged as if they were synonymous as far as it makes any difference. In other words, the extent to which they are not synonymous is thought to be trivial and the result of irrational belief and the absence of clear thought. This assumption does not come from within science at all. It goes back to the seventeenth century, to the days of Locke and Descartes, and to the elimination of feeling, intuition, and the body as valid means of knowledge. It is because of this assumption that artificial intelligence is not called artificial thought processing, which would be a more appropriate name for it. But many AI scientists nowadays would not see the difference between the two.

The second part of the statement indicates how AI has so far been successful. It was Thomas Hobbes who first said, in the seventeenth century, that thinking is computation.[8] That is, thinking consists essentially of operations on symbols, and that thinking is rational when it follows methodical rules. Hobbes thought of thoughts as 'little parcels,' i.e., things, that are moved around in the brain according to rules similar to the rules of arithmetic and geometry.

There were two problems in Hobbes's approach, the first being that Hobbes was unable to say how these little parcels in the brain derived their meaning, and the second being that Hobbes needed to assume that there was someone, a homunculus, in the brain who was manipulating the little parcels. To some extent Hobbes could bypass the problem of how thoughts get their meaning by assuming that the homunculus was an interpreter and already understood the meanings of thoughts, thus pushing the problem one step away.

Later, David Hume suggested that in fact there is no need at all for a homunculus, that thoughts combined because of laws inherent in themselves, just as planets move because of the law of gravitation, which is inherent in the properties of planets. But then Hume was certainly left with the problem of how thoughts, or words, acquire their meaning. I will not deal here with this problem. Suffice it to say that neither the AI specialists nor the linguists nor the philosophers had been able to provide any satisfactory understanding of it, until very recently, because it always returned to the question of meaning *to whom*, and the "whom" is precisely the problem.

Hume wanted to eliminate the homunculus because he saw that it automatically led to an infinite regress: if there is a part of the mind, the little man or homunculus, that is reading thoughts and manipulating them, then the little man must itself be intelligent, and then we have the same problem of understanding the little man's intelligence as we originally had in understanding our own, so we will end up with a little man in the little man's head, and so on. The only way out of this difficulty seems to be either some kind of dualism, that the understanding mind is on some altogether different plane of existence—Descartes' solution—or we have to say that thoughts are somehow able to read and manipulate themselves, i.e., thoughts do the thinking.

The question for AI then becomes, Can thoughts be mechanically processed in such a way as to provide the appearance of intelligence and rationality? Therefore can we reasonably come to think that intelligence and rationality *are* the mechanical processing of thoughts? Clearly Hobbes and Hume both thought so, and given the basic assumption of science that everything in the universe is lawful, most scientists would like to think that the answer to this question is, "Yes." Its success so far is twofold: AI has provided a way of thinking about thinking that enables us to clearly see how, at least in theory, all rational thought can be mechanical; and it has succeeded in delineating some areas in which apparently intelligent processes can, in actuality, be reproduced by computers.

The first success—providing new theoretical frameworks to think about thinking—is regarded by many psychologists as the most exciting and promising aspect of AI. In particular AI provides a way of understanding how thoughts can themselves think. The analogy of a committee is used: the committee may be composed of many people who do not know the overall goal of the committee, who carry out their allotted tasks blindly and in a sense stupidly, but the end result can be an intelligent committee. Likewise intelligence can be a group effect of many thoughts, or subgroups of thoughts, whose sum total is intelligent. In this way we see that a little man in the mind is not necessary to read the thoughts; the thinking process as a whole can be self-thinking.

Conscious thinking may be, in fact almost certainly is, only the tip of the iceberg of mental processing. Conscious thoughts are only the last in a chain of processes many of which are not normally—and may not possibly be—accessible to consciousness. As Daniel Dennett puts it, "it would seem that there shouldn't be any homunculus, any subsystem, that is itself *in charge*. And in fact I think there's lots of evidence, now, and somewhat disturbing evidence, which shows that if there were any homunculus in our cognitive committee *with which we would be inclined to identify the self intuitively*, it wouldn't be the boss [italics mine]; it would be the director of public relations, the agent in the press office who has only a very limited and often even fallacious idea about what's really going on in the system. He's the one whose job it is to present a good face to the world, to issue press releases and generally try to tell everybody on the outside what's going on. He can be wrong, he can be massively misinformed, he can be massively ignorant of what is really going on in the system. And many results of experiments in cognitive and social psychology now strongly suggest that our own access to what's going on in our minds is very impoverished. We often confabulate, we tell unwitting lies and we are often simply in the dark; we have no idea at all."[9]

As for the areas of successful application, Margaret Boden in *Minds and Mechanisms* summarizes the current situation thus; "Suffice it to say that programs already exist that can do things—or, at the very least, appear to be beginning to do things—which ill-informed critics have asserted *a priori* to be impossible. Examples include: perceiving in a holistic as opposed to an atomistic way; using language creatively; translating sensibly from one language to another . . .; planning acts in a broad and sketchy fashion, the details being decided only in execution [the beginnings of learning from experience]; distinguishing between different species of emotional reaction according to the psychological context of the subject."[10] Any process which can be precisely analyzed verbally or by symbols analagous to words (known as 'quasi-linguistic symbols') can be presumed to be reproducible in a computer program.

Critics of AI point out that often, although computers appear to be doing things that used to be regarded as the epitome of human intelligence—such as play a decent game of chess, or diagnose and plan a course of medical treatment—computers do not do them in the same way humans do.[11] Furthermore, they point out, the human is embodied in an organism that has evolved over tens of thousands of years and this embodiment is crucial to the kinds of knowledge available to it and enfolded within its body. These are important and valid arguments, and it must be clear to the reader that I am not here taking the "strong AI" point of view that all mental processes can even in principle be simulated on a computer. However, what has been established is that a mechanism, namely, logical processing along the lines of a digital computer, is available for understanding these kinds of thought processes without need for the hypothesis of an 'I.' As John Haugeland succinctly puts it, "There's no inner eye (or homunculus) to read quasi-linguistic symbols 'written' in the brain; and we now know that none is needed."[12] Because such mental processing is *possible* without need for an 'I,' therefore we cannot take the fact that humans can, for example, play chess or diagnose medical problems as evidence that they *necessarily* have an 'I.' In our search for an ego we will not find it in the closet of rational thought-processing. This is ironic in that for many people the ability to think *rationally*, i.e. according to the laws of logic, like a digital computer, is the mark *par excellence* of our humanness.

Note especially that this whole argument is independent of the content of thoughts being processed: the thoughts can be mundane thoughts about what to have for dinner, exciting thoughts about the processing of thoughts, or profound thoughts about higher levels of reality or Grand Evolutionary Theory. They are all merely thoughts, 'quasi-linguistic symbols' "written" in the brain, all processed in the same way. As we have seen, Buddhism also has pointed out the automatic nature of thought-processing and the equal status of all thoughts in this process. And the processing model of AI provides further details on how some of this processing can be taking place.

PICTORIAL REPRESENTATIONS

So far we have been dealing with "quasi-linguistic" symbols, that is, with thought processes that can be represented, or reduced to a propositional form analagous to a language or mathematical symbol system. The reader might be tempted to wonder whether thoughts also occur in other forms, one that cannot be reduced to linear symbol systems, such as pictorial or tactile forms. This has been the subject of considerable controversy in recent years. Intuitively we might feel that we do at times think by manipulating pictorial images, without verbal description as intermediary. But AI proponents who wish to believe that all thought processes can be modeled on digital computers are very loath to accept this.

Some indications that internal images are part of the mental apparatus of the organism comes from an ingenious series of experiments by Roger Shepherd and Jacqueline Metzler, in the early 1970s. Subjects were shown two nonsense figures presented in different orientations and asked to decide whether or not the figures could be placed exactly on top of each other. The time the subjects took to accomplish this was recorded and plotted on a graph against the angle one figure would have to be turned through in order to lay it on top of the other. It was found that the time subjects took to answer the question was exactly proportional to the angle through which the figures had to be turned. Thus the subjects seemed to be doing precisely what they said they were doing: imagining the two figures and imagining turning one of the figures around until they could lay one on top of the other. And the time it took them to do this was proportional to the actual angular separation between the images on the paper. Thus it becomes very reasonable to suppose that the organism has some means by which it is able to represent visual forms in consciousness and to manipulate those forms as if it were manipulating similar physical forms.

Later, these experiments were repeated and refined by Stephen Kosslyn, who is the leading advocate for the existence of an imagery function altogether separate from the linguistic-like mode of representation. In other experiments, Kosslyn showed subjects a map on which there were several locations—a rock, a tree, a beach, and so on. Subjects were asked to imagine the map in their minds and then to answer questions about it. For example, one might be asked, after fixing on one location, say the tree, to move as quickly as possible to the rock. It was found that the time the subject took to perform this exercise in mental imagery was directly proportional to the distance on the map between the two locations. This suggested that the subject was actually reading an image of the map rather than remembering a verbal description of it.[13]

What the medium of these representations is we do not know, although it is clear that there cannot actually be physical forms somewhere in the nervous system reproducing the physical forms being perceived. However, experiments show that the internal images stored in memory or called up when a subject is asked to imagine something are very closely related to the internal images formed in response to a perceptual input. For example, in one such experiment a subject was placed in front of a translucent screen marked with a spot. The subject was asked to gaze at the spot, at the same time imagining a tomato. Unknown to the subject, an image of a tomato was projected onto the screen at levels below the threshold for perception. The intensity of the image was gradually increased. When it was well above the perceptual threshold the subject maintained that the tomato was purely imaginary, confusing his own image with that on the screen. In other experiments, when a subject was asked to imagine a tree and at the same time gaze at a spot of light of gradually increasing intensity, the intensity of light needed for the subject to perceive it was far greater than when he was not imagining the tree. On the other hand if the subject was asked to imagine a sound, this did not interfere with his perception of the spot.[14]

Although controversy surrounds Kosslyn's theoretical interpretation of his experiments, particularly his attempts to model them on computer, the experiments themselves are not in doubt. They seem to indicate quite clearly, except to strong AI proponents, that there is some capacity to represent an 'outside world' pictorially as well as verbally. Whether, as Kosslyn claims, this is completely separate from the capacity to represent that world linguistically is not clear. However, there seems to be no reason to suppose that the pictorial capacity is not available to other animals as well as humans. From the point of view of Buddhist analysis, this controversy somewhat misses the point. Representation of an 'external' world in the 'internal' world of the organism by *any* symbol system, in which one thing (a word or image) stands for another thing (an object in 'the world'), is the essence of ego, when that representation is believed in and taken to be *the world*. The Buddhist notion of *concept* applies to all forms of such symbolizing by substitution of a representation. Thus in building up a theory of how the organism creates representations of the world, pictorial or linguistic, cognitive scientists are building a picture of the fourth skandha of ego, formations.

All of the work that I have been describing here has been using the structure of conventional digital computers as the main model of thought processing. All thought processes are analogous to, or in the strong form of AI are, step-by-step, logical processes organized by one 'central processor.' It is this cental processor that supposedly manipulates symbolic 'representations' of the outside world. But there are serious problems with this model. For one thing, memory consists of lists, which have to be searched item by item whenever the central processor wants to use something from memory. So, for example, if a face is recognized, this is done by comparing the visual input with all visual images of faces stored in lists. The descriptions of faces are, in turn, stored by listing details. But this simply does not seem to be how natural memory works. Faces are recalled swiftly by their overall characteristics rather than by going over a list of details. We are able to recognize a person who may be quite heavily disguised, a task which cannot be based on going over lists of details. And then there is the larger problem of how such a 'central processor' could learn by trial and error, seemingly a fundamental component in animal learning.

In recent years a new way of tackling problems such as these, known as 'connectivism,' is developing. Functions such as face recognition and learning by trial and error have been modeled on systems altogether different from the central processing logical machine. These systems consist of many small simple processors, connected in network fashion, much like the networks of neurons in the brain. Although networks of only a few hundred junctions have so far been tested, compared with the billions of neural junctions in the brain, they appear to be successful in modeling these more global operations that organisms do with such ease all the time. Such models are much more like the actual structure of the brain, and in them there is no 'central processor' at all. The learning and recognition are a cooperative process of all components of the network. Furthermore, the connectivist view does not need to assume that the network is manipulating 'representations' of the outside world; the entire state of the network is continually self-modifying in response to the 'outside.'

We have seen, then, in this chapter that already many of the functions of logical thought processing that we take to be typically human are capable of being carried out in a purely automatic fashion, and as the connectivist approach is developed we can expect that many more will follow. In Buddhist terms we could say that many of the thought and image processing functions of the fourth skandha could be entirely automatic. And this is indeed the Buddhist point of view.

In the next chapter, we will examine the consequences of remembering the observer-dependence of our descriptions. This will bring us closer to a way of speaking about cognition that not only takes into account the actual structure of the nervous system but also makes no presuppositions about the independent existence of an 'internal' cognizing mind and an 'external' world.

9

Self-Organization

IN THE PREVIOUS CHAPTER we followed the arguments, based on a naive commonsense idea of what goes on in our heads, that the organism somehow represents an 'outside world' to itself and that this is how it 'knows' that world. We saw that if we follow the logic of that view then certain types of perceptual and thought processing can be understood on a computer analogy for the brain. However, there is a fundamental problem with this view regarded as a theory of the origin of knowledge about the outside world. The problem is that it takes for granted that there is indeed an already determined outside world for the organism to represent to itself. It also takes for granted that the organism is structured in such a way that it is able to take in pure information from that 'outside world' and assemble that information into a picture of the world. This view has recently been powerfully criticized by Humberto Maturana, Francisco Varela, and their colleagues, who point out that both these assumptions *are* merely assumptions, and that they are not borne out by a deeper analysis of the perceptual situation.[1]

THE AUTONOMY OF THE LIVING

To appreciate the potential revolution in understanding cognition implied by the work of a relatively small group of research workers, it is necessary to follow the manner in which Maturana and Varela build a new way of speaking about the nature of a living being and its relationship to its environment.

First one must ask, What is the characteristic of a living being? Now biologists for generations have tried to answer this question. In fact the term 'biology' literally means the study of the living. However in many biology textbooks one finds a quite cursory attempt to define 'living' in the introductory chapter, the remainder of the book being a description of the various aspects of things that are commonly agreed on as living. Such attempts to define 'living things' have usually and traditionally been in terms of lists of characteristics, such as exchange of materials with the environment, reproduction, and so on. Maturana and Varella suggest that the uniqueness of a living being is not in such lists of characteristics but in its organization. By 'organization' they mean the most essential aspects of a thing, "those relations that must be present for a thing to exist." The example is given of a chair. For something to be regarded as a chair it must have a flat portion to sit on, legs, and a back; this is its organization. It does not matter whether the chair is made of wood or plastic, is put together with nails or screws; these elements are its 'structure' but not its 'organization.'

Taking this point of view, Maturana and Varela define a living being as a unity in which its components are organized in such a way that they take part in the continual process of recreating that unity. That is to say, a living being is self-organizing and self-producing. To convey this idea, Maturana and Varela use the term 'autopoesis,' derived from the Greek 'auto,' meaning 'self,' and 'poesis,' meaning 'producing.' The prime example of an autopoetic unity is the single cell. Thus, through the organization of its various structural and metabolic components such as nucleic acids, enzymes, mitochondria, and so on, a living cell is organized as an 'autopoetic' or self-organizing and self-producing unity. The maintenance of autopoesis defines the scope of activity of the cell, and as soon as autopoesis breaks down, the cell is no longer living. Multicellular organisms may not in themselves be autopoetic; they do not produce themselves but have to go through a single-cell phase to reproduce. But they are self-organizing and autonomous, that is, they define their own principles of organization. And they are built from single cells that are autopoetic; therefore autopoesis is the mechanism that makes life possible.

COUPLING

Such an autonomous unity does not, of course, self-organize in isolation. It is continually undergoing interaction with an environment, moving through that environment, exchanging materials with it. In fact the environment for any particular organism is defined by the types of interactions that organism can have that will maintain its self-organization. Over a period of time the organism, and the environment it has thus defined, will go through a series of mutual changes that always maintain the integrity of the organism. Failing that, self-organization breaks down and the organism is no longer living. Maturana and Varela call this type of interaction 'structural coupling.'

The important point is that, in such coupling, the changes that the internal state of the organism goes through are determined only by its need to maintain its self-organization. Changes in the environment do not determine the structural changes of the organism, they simply trigger appropriate structural changes that will preserve the self-organization intact. In this sense, there may be many possible structural changes available as an appropriate response to a change in the environment, and there may be many environmental changes that can produce a particular structural change. There is by no means a one-to-one correspondence between the environmental changes and the changes in internal structure of the organism. The way a particular organism responds to a particular environmental change will depend on what internal structural changes are available to it at that moment, and this in turn will depend on the history of its interactions with a changing environment.

This way of viewing how an organism interacts with its environment in order to maintain the internal coherence of its organization powerfully changes the way evolutionary biologists can think about the process of evolution. The standard view of 'natural selection' is that over the course of many generations, organisms that *best fit* the environmental conditions are selected, and it is assumed that those organisms that do fit *best* in this way are pretty much determined by the environmental conditions. In the view that we are reviewing here, there may be many ways in which an organism may respond to an environmental change so as to maintain its coherence of internal states. Thus those organisms that survive, at an individual or species level, are not necessarily the *best* fit. They are simply those organisms that have continued to find a pathway that has enabled them to maintain their self-organization. There are many such possible pathways, and thus species must be thought of as arriving at their current forms by processes of *'natural drift,'* to use Maturana's term, rather than by being rigidly instructed by the environment what form they must take at each step of the way of natural evolution.

COGNITION WITHOUT REPRESENTATION

What does this have to do with the way an organism comes to know its environment? Varela maintains that a nervous system is an autonomous unity in the sense explained above. That is to say, when we consider what a nervous system is like, we realize that it is an incredibly complex system of tens of billions of neurons forming a web with various patterns of ordering at various levels, a 'tangled hierarchy,' as Varela calls it. This complex web connects the sensory and motor surfaces of the body, and it is through these surfaces that the organism interacts with the environment. The nervous system itself is a closed system changing from one internal state to another in such a way as to maintain its internal coherence and balance. Any change in the environment is felt by the nervous system as a perturbation at the sensory surface, and the nervous system responds to this perturbation by adjusting its internal state to maintain its internal coherence. In order to maintain this coherence, it adjusts its relation to the environment via the motor surface.

As suggestive evidence that the nervous system should be thought of in this way, Varela presents the striking case of color 'illusion,' which was first noted by Otto von Guericke in 1672. If, from two separate projectors, we project red and white light overlapping onto a screen, we see a pinkish-colored screen. If we now hold up our hand between the red light projector and the screen we would expect to see a white shadow of our hand against the pink background. What we in fact see is a blue-green shadow. Where does the blue-green coloration come from? It certainly does not come from the parts of the screen outlined by the shadow of a hand, for this is illuminated by pure white light. We can only conclude that the blue-green color arises from the way our visual system is responding to the overall illumination, and to the boundary between the shadow and its pink background. If now we turn off the red projector but leave on the white one, the part of the screen that was in the shadow of the hand is now seen as white, even though there is no change whatsoever in its illumination. I mentioned an experiment similar to this in Chapter 6, in our discussion of the skandha of form. I pointed out that this was the first step in our discovery of the mutual interaction of sense organ and sense field. We are now taking this point much further.

We see the reverse effect if we take an orange from a room illuminated with fluorescent light into the sunshine. The orange still appears orange even though the fluorescent light and sunlight contain very different wavelengths. In the case of the hand shadow, the color experience at a point in the shadow area changes, while the illumination at that point remains constant; in the case of the orange, the color experience remains constant while the illumination changes significantly.

Varela points out that to call this effect an 'illusion' is nonsense. It is a fact of visual perception that must be taken into account in any viable theory. To regard it as 'illusion' presupposes a theory about perception that excludes this phenomenon and then has to have something to say about it. And the theory that is presupposed is the common idea that the experience of color corresponds to a particular wavelength reflected from the objects 'out there.'

According to Varela, these and similar experiments show that contrary to widespread belief there is almost no direct relation between the wavelength of light illuminating an object and the subjective experience of color. The experience of color is therefore not a 'representation' in the observer of something 'out there.' Rather, in this case, it is a response of the entire retina triggered by something in the environment but not determined by it. Varela summarizes the situation saying, "the slippery quality we call 'color' cannot be explained if we seek to account for it in terms of properties of objects to be grasped by the observer."[2] Rather we can account for the experience of color by showing how it is constituted through the internal coherence of neuronal activity in the nervous system.

REMEMBER THE OBSERVER

Why then do we tend to want to think as if the organism were internally representing a fixed world 'outside'? The solution to the quandary comes from recognizing that we are dealing here with two quite different domains of description, both defined by an observer. The key point, according to Maturana and Varela, is that "Everything that is said is said by someone."[3] That is to say, we should never forget that any description is always from the *particular* point of view of *someone*, and we should always be careful not only to recognize this simple fact, but also not to mix two different descriptions made from the points of view of two different observers. In particular we can describe an organism behaving in an environment in two quite different ways. The first way is as a nervous system adopting an internal state in response to a trigger from the environment so as to maintain its internal integrity. The second, from the point of view of an observer standing outside of it, is as an organism in an environment responding to various characteristics of that environment. These two ways of describing this organism should not be mixed, and it is such mixing that gives rise to confusion as to what may be going on inside the organism when we are taking the point of view of an observer outside of it. The point is that either of these two ways of describing the organism as a unity is valid, but there is nothing in either of the two descriptions that says that there should be some correlation between them. It is only the observer who is aware of both descriptions, who demands this correlation; in that sense, the correlation exists only in the observer.

It is confusion between these two possible stances of an observer that leads to the notion of the organism 'representing' its environment to itself, when all it is doing from its own point of view is to adjust its internal states to maintain their integrity and balance. To take another simple example: if a hand comes into contact with a hot stove it will be quickly withdrawn. An external observer will say, "The organism withdrew its hand because it knew there was something hot there." But the point of view of the nervous system is that stimulation of a sensory surface caused an imbalance in the system that was then compensated for by a response at the motor surface. The nervous system knew nothing of a stove, or of anything other than the triggering perturbation at the sensory surface and its own consequent imbalance. It can clearly be seen that it is unnecessary to assume that there is anything in the nervous system that 'represents' the hot stove in this situation.

Maturana and Varela provide an analogy that helps to clarify their argument. Suppose, they say, that someone has always lived in a submarine. That person has various sonar and radar instruments, and he has learned to navigate the submarine using these instruments. Suppose one day we see the submarine rise to the surface through a difficult terrain of rocks and strong currents, and pull into dock. We may say to the navigator, "Congratulations, you navigated some difficult terrain there." But he would reply, "What is all this about difficult terrain, rocks and currents. I simply followed my dials and pulled the appropriate levers in order to keep my horizon indicator level, my speed indicator positive, and to avoid warning signals on my sonar." As external observers we may talk about the way the submarine 'behaved,' but from the point of view of the navigator, who is analogous to the nervous system, he simply responded to the internal states of his instruments in order to maintain balance.

What all this means is that in our description of how an organism 'knows' its environment, we must always be careful to take these two alternate descriptions into account. It means, as Varela says, "explicitly taking into account the conditions of our descriptions, whereby we switch back and forth between the organism as a system in its own internal logic, and the organism as a unity in its interactions."[4] It is in this process of description that the observer sees the constraints in the environment that the organism must satisfy in its continual search for internal stability. For example, in the case of color the human is able to respond, if at all, only to a certain range of wavelengths. But within these constraints the responses of the organism can be quite varied, and which one it will follow is determined by the present structure of its nervous system. And the present structure is a result of its past history of such interactions. Thus the process of an organism coming to know a world, and thereby bringing forth that world, is analogous to the process of 'natural drift' in evolution. It is not an instructional process in which the already given environment determines precisely what the organism will come to know.

A 'MIDDLE PATH' FOR COGNITIVE SCIENCE

This new view of cognition provides what Varela calls a 'middle path' for neuroscience. The middle path he refers to is a path between the two traditional extremes: 'representationalism,' which assumes that there is a fully determined real world 'out there' that the organism is able to represent in itself if, through its senses, it receives sufficient information about that world; and 'constructivism,' in which the organism constructs its perceptual world completely from within. The middle path sees the organism channeling out a world, much as snow melting in the springtime channels out a pathway down the mountain. The path that the organism forges is broadly determined by constraints that are mutually arrived at by the organism's past interactions with the environment. The origin of knowledge resembles, in Varela's terms, "a tinkering, a dynamic sculpturing." Varela concludes, "The key to this process is that the consequences of any interactions are to be found, not in the nature of the perturbation that triggered them, but in the way the structure compensates for such interactions according to its dynamic landscape; the overall result is change of structure in a continuous maintenance of the integrity of the system in its medium."[5]

An observer says that an organism 'knows' its environment when it exhibits appropriate behavior in that environment. For example, we say that someone picking berries knows which ones are edible if we observe him select berries that do not make him sick; we say someone knows how to drive a car if that person is able to exhibit behavior that will enable the car to proceed from one place to another. And we say a child knows his or her two times table if, when we ask "what is two times three," he or she answers, "six." The representational theory of knowledge would say that the person has gained sufficient information about how the world is to enable him or her to build an adequate representation of that particular aspect of the world—a car, or numbers—which he or she is able to bring to mind when called on to do the task. The constructivist view would say that the organism already has innate structures, for example concerning the number system, that are activated by and projected onto the environment.

These are rather complex examples involving language that we will come to later, so let us take the simple classical case of a dog salivating when it hears a bell. In the case of the dog the representational theory would say that the dog associates an image of a bell with an image of food and therefore salivates. But we can see from the analysis of Maturana and Varela that this is a very muddled way of thinking. The nervous system of the organism at each moment is responding only to the perturbations of the environment at that moment. The dog's nervous system responds directly to the sound of the bell at that moment, and the responses available to it are a result of its past history of interactions with the bell and food. It is the structure of its nervous system at that moment that determines how the dog responds, and there is no need to bring in the hypothesis of an internal image. In fact, according to Maturana and Varela there is not even any mechanism by which the nervous system can store such images, since it *is* just its current state. That current state is dependent on its history of interactions and it is because of different histories that different responses, or different 'knowledges' about the environment, are possible.

A representationist might argue that part of the history of the nervous system involves the building of representations, which are then stored as part of the current state of the nervous system. But such a hypothesis depends on the assumption that there is an already predetermined environment to represent, and this is precisely the assumption that the present view questions. The nervous system simply does not at any time come into contact with "dogs," "bells," or "food," and therefore there is no opportunity for representations of such things to be built and stored in it.

As I have pointed out, one of the most important consequences of this view is that the organism, through its actions on the medium in which it is immersed and with which it is coupled, draws out its own world at each step of the way. Thus at the same time as the organism is defining itself through its continuing path of interactions with its medium, so the world for that organism is being defined. Thus world and organism arise in a mutual process of a continually changing mutual coupling. Neither world or organism can be considered logically prior to this process. In a manner again reminiscent of Niels Bohr, Varela draws out the implications of this view for our own human circumstances. It involves, he says, "giving up the entrenched habit of trusting the world as some fixed reference point to be represented, or else of taking the subject as an initiating agent and thus also as a reference point. If we are right, our human life, our experience right now, is but one of many possible creods [channels, like the channels formed in melting snow] of knowledge, where the immense background of our biological structure and social practices is inseparable from the regularity we discern in both world and self. When we follow this logic all the way through, we can understand the world in which we find ourselves as neither separate nor distant. But also, as one where we have no fixed reference points left."[6]

LANGUAGE

While we cannot speculate about the inner experience of a dog, we may want to ask, in the case of humans, why do we seem to experience a world of "dogs," "cars," and other "things." Maturana and Varela argue that this comes from another order of coupling with the environment, the social coupling giving rise to language. They turn their attention to higher order couplings in which the environment of a particular organism contains other organisms of the same type. In this case, from the point of view of any particular organism the coupling with its environment includes coupling with other organisms. Thus organism and world are mutually defining through their coupling, and that mutual definition includes the other organisms in the world of each one. One finds this mutual definition abounding throughout nature in what is often referred to as cooperative, or even altruistic, behavior. Insect societies warding off intruders, wolf packs hunting together, antelope posting guards to warn the herd of danger, various combinations of adults caring for the young—in all such cases the animal is defined in part by its coupling with others.

Such coupled behavior between animals of the same species may be seen by an observer to be examples of communication. To themselves, the animals are carrying out habitual patterns of coordinated behavior that have developed as a result of particular pathways of mutual coupling, both in the history of the species and in the individuals. But to an observer such behavior is communicative in the sense that such behavior mediates cooperation that would not otherwise be possible, and the communication is the cooperation.

Taking the stance of the observer, we can now say that communicative behavior conveys meaning, and can be called 'linguistic' in the sense that its meaning can be described by an observer. To give an example: I write at home in an office on the second floor. In the morning before breakfast I light a wood stove downstairs. After breakfast I go up to my office and often do not tend the stove until I begin to feel chilly. However, my old cat, who likes to spread out in front of the stove, usually arrives at my office door meowing at just about this time. Now I could say that the cat is trying to tell me that the stove needs tending, his meowing is conveying meaning to me. However we could also simply say that the cat's meowing is the structural coupling of the cat, myself, and the stove that has developed over the winter months. Likewise a human observer can say that the barks of two sheepdogs convey meaning as they skillfully move a herd of sheep. But again we adequately describe this situation as reflecting the historical coupling of dogs and sheep in a social situation. Thus humans are not the only animals to have developed linguistic types of behavior, that is, communicative behavior that can be interpreted by a speaker as conveying meaning.

However, humans seem to be the only ones to have developed language. Language occurs when one act, a speech act, is used to stand for another act or 'linguistic behavior.' So, for example, the word "table" is about all the various acts that we may do in relation to a flat surface that we can put things on. Language then creates another interpretive domain, the domain of 'acts about acts.' Through the discussion of the mutual coupling of organisms in their social environment, that I have only sketched out here, Maturana and Varela show that language can be understood as arising naturally and in continuity with the other forms of communicative behavior that we observe in the animal world.

The essential point about language here is that it involves standing back and taking the point of view of an observer in relation to our own actions. So we do not just put something on a table, but we can also say, "I am putting something on the table." So, in this sense the domain of language acts obscures the domain of acts that the language acts are about. We begin to exist in a world of language.

This standing back from our own actions, creating a division between our direct actions on the world and our speech acts about those actions, constitutes taking the standpoint of an observer toward our own actions. In the case of the human organism, the observer and the observed system may be aspects of one and the same self-organizing structure. We experience ourselves as having 'thoughts,' 'images,' 'representations,' because we separate off some aspect of our being that acts as 'observer.' That is, our consciousness becomes divided and we become 'self-conscious.' It is this observing, describing, aspect of our mental processes that we believe is our 'self.' Without such a split in our consciousness, there would be no experience of separately existing internal images, thoughts, or representations in relation to an outside world. There would only be direct action which brings forth a world. Our experience of having an 'internal' life of thoughts and images is a direct result of the evolution of a dualistic split in consciousness, of our experiencing perceptions and the internal descriptions of our perceptions as separate. And it is precisely this creating of the standpoint of an observer through the use of language that leads to self-consciousness. But in order to see this we will have to examine more closely the nature of consciousness and language and the connection between them, and we will do this in the next chapter.

10

Consciousness

WE HAVE SEEN IN the previous chapter that Varela and Maturana have effectively argued against the idea deeply rooted in current cognitive science, as well as in common sense, that the organism represents the outside world, in its cognitive interactions with its environment, as images to an internal 'mind.' So once again we might ask, who or what is this famous 'I'? If we have been taking this analysis at all personally, we might be feeling a little uneasy at this point. Are we about to lose our closest, most intimate friend, our companion while walking and sitting, eating and drinking, waking and sleeping, light of our life, dream of our dreams? We might begin to feel quite frightened or unaccountably cheered up and relieved, or perhaps a mixture of both.

At this point someone might very well ask, "What about self-consciousness?" Doesn't the fact that we are conscious of a feeling of self imply that there is a self? Consciousness is obviously a topic that we are going to want to deal with sooner or later, for two reasons. The first is that, in our search for a self, there is really nowhere left to look. And the second reason is that, self or no self, consciousness demands our attention, so to speak. We will deal with the possibility of consciousness without self later.

SELF-CONSCIOUSNESS AND SELF

For now let us consider the question of whether self-consciousness implies a self. Put like that the answer, after all we have been through, is obviously, "No, consciousness of anything does not by any means imply existence of that thing." We have already seen, in the statement from philosopher Daniel Dennett, that what we call self-consciousness is the tip of an iceberg which it knows virtually nothing about, and which could very well be another name for self-deception. We saw in the discussion of thought-processing that consciousness is simply the last event in a lengthy sequence, and almost certainly has very little idea at all of what is going in that process. And we will see this again in more clarity when we discuss the details of perceptual processing.

You might insist, What about consciousness of *self*? But, again, does consciousness of a phantom limb by an amputee imply the existence of that limb? Does consciousness of a ringing in the ears imply the existence of a bell? Does consciousness of anger imply the existence of anger? Well, you may answer, consciousness of these things may not imply existence of exactly what we think we are conscious of, but it does imply existence of *something*: consciousness of a phantom limb implies damage to nerve endings in the still present parts of the limb; consciousness of ringing in the ears implies inner ear infection or high blood pressure; consciousness of anger implies, as we now know, a structure of arousal and negative meaning analysis. Could we, then, say that consciousness of 'self' implies a particular conglomeration of thoughts, feelings, and bodily sensations, various unconscious mechanisms for processing these things and, apart from this, what?

CONSCIOUSNESS IN ANIMALS

Let us then try to focus on the 'consciousness' side of these components of our experience. For we certainly cannot now deny, as the behaviorists once tried to, that there is a distinction between being conscious of a thought or internal image and not being conscious of it. We have seen—and we will look at this again when we examine the details of the sequential process of perception—that most processing of thought is not conscious. This on the one hand tends to reduce the importance of consciousness to the organism. On the other hand it raises the serious question, what *is* the function of consciousness? The first thing to consider is whether consciousness is unique to humans. In answer, it has been very strongly suggested by people who have spent a lifetime carefully studying animal behavior, that animals as well as humans must be considered to have to some degree consciousness of mental imagery. Donald Griffin, professor at Rockefeller University and president of the Harry Frank Guggenheim Foundation, has documented numerous studies in which the behavior of animals can be explained simply and straightforwardly with the assumption that animals entertain mental images and have thinking processes which in a human would be regarded as rational. But without such assumptions these animal behaviors can hardly be explained at all. Here are two of Griffin's many examples.

Krebs and his colleagues studied how great tits, a species of bird, coped with the challenging problems of foraging for concealed food. The researchers hid mealworms in containers of several different kinds and covered them with tape. The birds learned quickly that they could find food in some kinds of containers by pecking through the tape. When it discovered that a particular type of container sometimes contained mealworms, one great tit would search for similar containers. More important, other birds then also began to look for similar hiding places. In other words, these birds learned a great deal about where to locate food by observing where their companions were finding it.

Griffin observes that many students of animal learning have noted that animals often act as though they were expecting something; he gives this charming example. "One of the most dramatic examples is still the one described by O. L. Tinklepaugh, who trained monkeys to watch the experimenter place a favorite item of food, such as a piece of banana, under one of two inverted cups that remained out of reach until a barrier was removed. The purpose of the experiment was to measure how long the monkey could remember which cup hid the piece of banana. When a monkey had learned to do this almost perfectly, in some experiments the banana was replaced by lettuce during the waiting period when the monkey could not see the cups or the experimenter. As Tinklepaugh described the results, the moderately hungry monkey now "rushes to the proper container and picks it up. She extends her hand to seize the food. But her hand drops to the floor without touching it. She looks at the lettuce but (unless very hungry) does not touch it. She looks around the cup . . . stands up and looks around her. She picks up the cup and examines it thoroughly inside and out. She has on occasion turned toward the observers present in the room and shrieked at them in apparent anger."[1]

After perusing Griffin's many, many such examples taken from the work of numerous observers over a fifty-year period, it would seem to be mere human arrogance and chauvinism to deny that animals have some kind of conscious mental life. Behaviorist psychologists failed in their attempt to explain human behavior without mental representations and images not only because we all know we have mental images, but also because much of the behavior of humans, observed from outside, simply *cannot* be understood without assuming a mental life. Now we find extensive reports of very similar behavior in animals. All these behaviors clearly have value to the species and could have appeared in the course of evolution. And all these behaviors can only reasonably be explained if as observers we make the natural assumption that, just like us, animals have conscious mental images. And this seems to be understandable in simple adaptive terms: both the great tits and the monkeys clearly benefit by expecting food where they have found it on previous occasions and searching around if they do not find it where they expect it. In other examples animals learn to avoid hunters, to work together intelligently in hunting groups, and to work together to avoid predators.

In an extensive and very detailed study of the biological roots of the evolution of human consciousness, ethologist John Crook demonstrates convincingly that primate societies have evolved complex behavior and communication patterns, as well as societal organizations—hierarchies, dominance relations, and so on—that are close to patterns found in human groups. Furthermore, he suggests, in primitive societies one finds correlations between societal structures and behavior, and the ecological conditions that indicate an adaptive process taking place. That is to say that the appearance of these societal structures can be understood as a natural process of co-evolution between the social group and the environment. Beyond this, according to Crook, when one follows the patterns of historical change taking place in a group, one can see how the social organizations themselves, as well as the way those organizations become legitimized through culture, have responded to ecological opportunities and competitive challenges. Complex social structures do not simply appear full blown but gradually evolve through (to use Varela's term) the structural coupling between the group and its environment. Thus the principle of natural drift can be invoked to account for their appearance in a way similar to the appearance of the variety of species. The point here, however, is that by tracing the historical development in detail as Crook and other sociobiologists have done, the natural development of such structures becomes very plausible.[2]

This is not meant to be an endorsement of the sweeping claims of some sociobiologists. Crook is simply saying here that a continuity can be clearly seen between the organization of human and other primate societies; that the basic structures of human societies throughout the world have certain characteristics that can be understood from these continuities and have a biological basis.

We can clearly see a role for consciousness in the evolution of these primitive societal characteristics. Animal behaviorist Nicholas Humphrey has argued that consciousness of one's own sensations and emotions enables us to understand the sensations and emotions of others and therefore to predict their behavior. He says, "For man and other animals which live in complex social groups, reality is in large measure a 'social reality.' No other class of environmental objects approaches in biological significance those living bodies which constitute for a social animal its companions, playmates, rivals, teachers, foes. In these circumstances the ability to model the behavior of others in a social group has paramount survival value."[3] Evolution is not necessarily confined to survival of the individual but, through a process of cooperation and exchange (known as 'reciprocal altruism'), also favors societal groups of animals. The ability to imaginatively model the behavior of others may also be an important factor in the ability of animals to cooperate with one another, and thus to achieve a unity of organization in the larger group.

All this argues strongly that conscious mental imagery can very well have arisen in the natural course of evolution, and the mere fact of its presence in no way implies the existence of a real separate 'self' that is being conscious. Consciousness, in this sense, which is not yet self- or divided consciousness, is not a thing, nor is it a substance; it is a natural communicative process shared by animals and humans.

THE CONSTRUCTION OF THE SELF-IMAGE

Consciousness of self, that is, that the organism exists as a recognizable entity separate from its surroundings, has not been clearly shown to exist in other animals. It may well be peculiar to the human species and quite possibly connected with the development of language ability. The human organism is clearly born with an inherent tendency to form self-images, which are composites of mental images with affective structures and bodily postures. The self-image is the organism's mental representation of itself as a unity in its interactions with others, in its planning for the future and imaginative attempts to repair the past.

Jack Engler, clinical director of the Schiff Psychiatric Day Treatment Center of Cambridge Hospital and a supervising psychologist on the faculty of Harvard Medical School, has made extensive comparison of the view of 'ego' in psychoanalytical object relations theory and Theravada Buddhism. He describes the similarity thus:

> It may come as a surprise that though they value ego development differently, both Buddhist psychology and psychoanalytic object relations theory *define the essence of the ego in a*

similar way as a process of synthesis and adaptation between the inner life and outer reality which produces a sense of personal continuity and sameness in the felt experience of being a 'self,' a feeling of being and ongoingness in existence. Object relations theory explains this experience of personal continuity and selfhood as the outcome of a gradual differentiation of internal images of the 'self' as distinct from internalized images of objects and the eventual consolidation of these various images into a composite schema or self-representation. For both Buddhist and object relations psychology, the sense of "I," of personal continuity, of being the same "self" in time, in place and across stages of consciousness, is conceived as something which is not innate in personality, not inherent in our psychological or spiritual makeup, but is *evolving developmentally out of our experience of objects and the kinds of interactions we have with them.* This "self" which we take to be "me" and which feels so present and real to us is actually an internalized image, a composite representation, constructed by a selective and imaginative "remembering" of past encounters with significant objects in our world. In fact, the self is viewed in both psychologies as a representation which is *actually being constructed anew from moment to moment.*[4]

Human beings are inherently social and cultural. Without human culture we are not human, and human culture is both the product and the means of human evolution. In order for the human organism to take on the attributes of being human a strong, responsive, and coherent self-image is necessary. This self-image develops, just as other cognitive capacities do, in part through the unfolding of inherent cognitive and affective structures and in part through its constantly changing interactions with others. As the organism and its environment change, so does its self-image. The course of development of these self-images is broadly similar from person to person and has been amply and extensively demonstrated by investigators such as Piaget, Erikson, and many others. As the organism goes through ever-changing experiences its self-image assimilates and accommodates these experiences, in the fashion described by Piaget, into a self-image which, though ever-changing, goes through recognizable stages. According to Thomas McCarthy, "[The stage model specifies] an invariant sequence of discrete and increasingly complex developmental stages, whereby no stage can be passed over and each higher stage implies or presupposes the previous stages. This does not exclude regressions, overlaps, arrested developments, and the like. Stages are constructed wholes that differ qualitatively from one another . . . no later phase can be [stably] attained before earlier ones have been passed through, and elements of earlier phases are preserved, transformed, and reintegrated in the later."[5] Wilber goes on to say that "This type of developmental-stage approach has been fruitfully applied to psychosexual, cognitive, ego, moral, affective, object-relational, and linguistic lines of development. . . . It is generally acknowledged that most of the stage-models presented by conventional psychology and psychiatry claim to be invariant and cross-cultural (in a general fashion); and within broad limits, most of them have adduced enough evidence to make their claims plausible."[6]

However, the inveterate tendency of thought to think in terms of things is no less evident in the case of self-images. The constantly changing flux of mental images, affects, and perceptions that form the self-image is gathered together under the name 'I,' with its pseudonyms "me," "myself," and the names our parents gave us. We make the unconscious assumption that this 'I' refers to one unchanging thing and attach to it whatever is the contents of consciousness at each moment. Thus we say, "I am hungry," "I am doubtful," "I am sad," "I think, therefore I am," and so on.

There is a constant tension between the conservative tendency of the self-image, trying to remain fixed, and the changing flux of inner and outer perceptions that have to be constantly assimilated. This tension too is a natural tendency of open systems, but for the self-image at the moment, for the 'I' of the moment, it is experienced as anxiety. If the changes in self-image demanded by the environment at a particular moment are not severe enough, the tension it experiences will not surface to consciousness. But as soon as significant changes are demanded, anxiety, pain, frustration, anger, or fear erupts. In terms of Mandler's theory of arousal we could say that the interruption, or discrepancy, of most fundamental importance to the human organism is the interruption of the current version of the self-image.

When the self-image becomes fixed on particular patterns of mental image, linguistic representation and affective structures that bind strongly and form strong foci of energy (the kleshas, in Buddhist terms), neurosis results as these patterns provide less and less responsiveness to changes in the perceived environment. The formation of such neurotic fixations has also been documented with tremendous precision over the past fifty years, beginning with the insights of Freud and Jung, both of whom tried to some extent to base their theories of neurosis on human biology as it manifest in the dynamics of mental processes. Particularly strong fixations tend to occur at the turning points or stages of psychological development described by McCarthy and Wilber, and these then give rise to the behavior patterns recognized as 'neurotic.' However, the fixating tendency of the self-image goes on all the time as the tendency of the self-image toward self-preservation, and the tension between this and the ever-changing flux of mental representations and perceptions gives rise to the underlying nameless anxiety sometimes known as 'existential anxiety.' We find, then, to answer our original question, that far from being evidence of the real existence of a 'self,' self-consciousness, or the consciousness of mental self-image, and its fixating tendency is the primary cause of the basic anxiety underlying human life.

LANGUAGE AND THE SELF-IMAGE

It seems highly probable that the evolutionary processes that led to the development of an organism that could become conscious of a self-image, that could become self-conscious, are very closely related to those processes that led to the development of an organism with language. The evidence that we can adduce from science for this is rather spotty, although it seems to be a rather widely held view among scientists. The scientific study of language is extremely primitive. The most interesting and characteristically human aspect of language is meaning, and meaning is meaning to an experiencing subject. Therefore since it has so far explicitly excluded the experiencing subject from its areas of investigation, science is having a very hard time with language. However, there are some ways, again indirect, that we can look into the relation between language and self-consciousness, from within science.

There is now extensive research showing that complex and intricate nonverbal systems of communication exist in a tremendous variety of species. It appears that animal societies of all kinds are bound together by such systems of communication, about predators, food, mating, nest-building, migration, and play. But we are talking here, of course, of verbal language. It seems most probable that verbal language first appeared as onomatopoeic sounds denoting objects or intentions, such as "food!" "danger!" "run!" These sounds drew their meaning from the environment of situation and nonverbal communication in which they were embedded. As I mentioned in the last chapter, Maturana and Varela have argued that at all levels of evolution, language must be considered not a property of the individual organisms, but a characteristic of the history of interactions of a group of organisms that share a sensory domain, coupling with each other and with their environment. When spoken language does not have such an environment it has no meaning. As linguist John Lyons says, "If the appropriate paralinguistic elements are omitted [e.g., variations of pitch, loudness, duration, eye movements, head nods, facial expressions, gestures, body postures, and so on], the partici-pants in a conversation get confused, nervous or angry; they may lose the drift of what they are saying and become more or less incoherent, and they may stop talking altogether."[7] Furthermore, as George Lakoff and Mark Johnson have shown, the meaning and truth of a statement is relative to a particular person in a particular situation and depends on a process of categorization that rests not on the properties of objects themselves, but on interactional properties that make sense only relative to human functioning.[8] To take a very simple example of Lakoff and Johnson, what counts as a chair depends on the situation in which it is to be put to use: a bean-bag would be fine, at least in California, for an after-dinner discussion group, but not, even there, for a formal dinner.

In their book *Metaphors We Live By*, Lakoff and Johnson show that to a very large extent, probably more than 90 percent, our language and our thought process is metaphorical. Some of the many examples they give are: argument is war; emotions are spatial; theories are buildings; ideas are food. These metaphors emerge from our experi-ence of our bodies in interaction with the physical and social environ-ments. Metaphors form complex webs or coherent structures, and these metaphor webs are the cultural presuppositions in which all our experiences are embedded. Understanding takes place in terms of entire domains of experience that are conceptualized into struc-tured wholes. It is by forming these webs of conceptualization to represent our experiences that we pick out what is important in them for us, categorize them, understand them, remember them, and bring them to bear on future experiences as part of the background.

How are these categorizations and webs of categorizations formed? For many decades psychologists, working with the behaviorist model, tried to develop a theory of category formation based on the assump-tion that the child starts "from scratch." The child supposedly recog-nized patterns in the world and formed new concepts corresponding to these patterns, which were then named according to associations he or she heard in the environment of adult speakers. This is based on the 'blank slate' idea of mind propagated by the empiricists beginning with Locke. Concepts are defined merely by lists of attributes, e.g. a dog is a hairy, four-legged animal that barks; a human is a featherless biped, etc. Each concept is clear and distinct, that is, everything is either a member of that class or it is not, it cannot be more or less a member. There are no hierarchical relations between concepts, none is more natural or significant than another. Questions such as, "Is a penguin a bird?" or "Is this love?" have to be answerable "yes" or "no." Although he or she will recognize this mentality, the reader will also recognize its lack of relation to how the mind seems to work naturally.

Thus, as with the behaviorist theory of language learning in general, this attempt pretty much failed. Cognitive scientists tried to build a world of concepts that followed the neat orderly simpleminded logic, and they failed. As Eleanor Rosch comments, "The 'mature western mind' was presumed to be one that, in abstracting knowledge from the idiosyncracies of particular everyday experience, employed Aristotelian laws of logic. When applied to categories, this meant that to know a category was to have an abstracted clearcut, necessary, and sufficient criteria for membership. If other thought processes, such as imagery, ostensive definition, reasoning by analogy to particular instances, or the use of metaphors were considered at all, they were usually relegated to lesser beings such as women, children, primitive people, or even to nonhumans."[9]

It is now recognized that the child must be born into the world with a tendency to form concepts according to some natural categories, hierarchically organized. The most well-known work on this was done by Eleanor Rosch, who showed that in all common categories there is a *basic* level of concept that is, perceptually, the most easily recognized the most readily named, the most easily remembered and recalled, and the first learned by a child. These basic level concepts give rise to *superordinate,* or more general concepts, and to *subordinate,* or more specific concepts.[10] For example, in the realm of animals, dog or bird are basic, animal or vertebrate are superordinate, and Pekinese or Robin are subordinate; in the realm of vegetables, carrot or turnip are basic, vegetable or root-vegetable are superordinate, "Prince Edward Island Blue" potato is subordinate. Young children learn the basic concepts first and tend to prefer to use these so that, for example all four-legged domestic animals may be "dog" for a while. And adults, too, tend to prefer to use basic concepts wherever possible. Rosch suggests that in perception the first recognition of an object is in terms of that object's basic concept, with its subordinate and superordinate categories coming later. As we will see, this is confirmed by work on the stages in perceptual processing. Thus it appears as if the conceptual web has nodes, like a fisherman's net in which there are a few large knots from which strings radiate out to join up with smaller knots; or like a series of spiders' webs joined together, the center of each web being a basic concept, a node.

As is usual in these kinds of discussions based on cognitive science, the role of the perceiver, the categorizer, has been left out. It has been shown that one of the first concepts to develop in a child is the distinction between 'me' and 'other,' along with the concepts of 'threat' or 'succor,' 'want' and 'don't want.' All these concepts seem to develop between the fifteenth and the twenty-fifth months, just the months when the child is first learning language. From these the sense of self develops as the web extends. As John Crook summarizes it, "The child's emerging sense of self is dependent upon the growth of its cognitive abilities in categorization, its experiences of contingency and agency in interaction with care-givers, and its experience of the emotional quality of its own conscious states. The human species has been well endowed with the basic powers that promote the *conceptualization* of the self as agent, a cognitive construct that is fundamental to the operation of the self process and communication between self and other. . . . 'Identity' is not some immutable property of the species but an often painfully constructed *set of conceptualizations* and attendant feelings that relate the individual to his transient experience of the world" (italics added).[11] "It seems very probable, then, that the primary division in the language web is formed by two large nodes, namely, 'me' and 'other.' Indeed, as we will see when we discuss the process of perception, the recognition of a vague general sense of 'other' as 'hostile' or 'friend,' 'affording pleasure' or 'affording pain,' seems to come before object recognition in this process.

Finally in the discussion of the relation between self and language we must look at the work on "split brains."[12] Patients suffering from certain forms of epilepsy can be helped by severing the link between the two halves of the cerebral cortex. After recovery from such an operation, which might take a year, the patients appear to behave normally, both to themselves and others. The patients do not sense that there is anything peculiar about their perception or their experience of consciousness. However, careful examination of their perceptual processes reveals some remarkable and significant facts.

The left and right visual fields from both eyes are processed by the right and left halves of the cortex, respectively; therefore we can separate the functioning of the two halves by presenting images to only the left or right visual field. When a normal person looks at the center of a line of print, that person sees the entire line. The left half is processed by the right hemisphere, and vice versa. Somehow this processing is coordinated so that we see, and know that we see, the entire line. A "split-brain" patient sees only the right half of the line. He does not even see the left half as "blank," he simply experiences nothing there and does not know that he is experiencing nothing. As far as that patient is concerned, his experience is complete, without gaps. One might wonder, What gaps exist in the apparently complete experience of all the rest of us?

If an image is presented to the left visual field, the split-brain subject is unable to say what is there, in fact *says* that nothing is there. That is, the subject is not conscious of there being anything there. Yet if asked to draw what is there with the left hand, the patient can reproduce a copy of the image. Or if asked to select a similar object with the left hand, he can do so. If two different figures are presented simultaneously to the left and to the right, e.g., a dollar sign to the left visual field and a question mark to the right, then the patient will draw a dollar sign while saying that he or she sees a question mark. If a word such as "eraser" is flashed to the left side, the patient is able to select an eraser from a pile of objects. Thus the right brain is able to understand words, but the subject is not conscious of this understanding and is not able to say the words. The subject is able to respond emotionally to images presented to the left visual field without knowing why. While a series of neutral images was being presented to the left field in one experiment, an image of a nude woman was inserted without warning. The subjects blushed or stammered without knowing why they were doing so.

From these results it appears that knowing that you know something is closely connected with being able to say that you know it. That is self-consciousness and language are closely connected. As neurologist Oliver Sachs says, "We have, each of us, a life story, an inner narrative—whose continuity, whose sense, *is* our lives. It might be said that each of us constructs and lives, a 'narrative,' and that this narrative *is* us, our identities. If we wish to know a man, we ask, 'what is his story—his real, inmost story?'—for each of us *is* a biography, a story. Each of us is a singular narrative, which is constructed, continually, unconsciously, by, through and in us— through our perceptions, our feelings, our thoughts, our actions; and not least, our discourse, our spoken narrations."[13]

None of this work is conclusive, but it all tends to point in one direction, that is, that the thing we call 'me,' which we separate and conceptualize as the subject of our experience, is a product of language, a node in the language net, and it lives in that world of metaphor that Lakoff and Johnson have uncovered. Where there is no language describing the world of metaphor to itself, there is no self-consciousness. The role of the language web in determining conscious experience also plays an important role in the Buddhist theory of perception, and I will have more to say about this later.

At this point it might be helpful to try to distinguish various different ways that the term 'consciousness' has been used. We might distinguish three very different usages. First there is the consciousness of animals. Although the precise nature of this must remain speculative, we might suppose that this consciousness would be oriented for the survival of the organism, and therefore would be centered around that, and in that sense is 'self-centered.' But there appears to be no consciousness of self as separate from world, therefore consciousness is not experienced as divided, it is not 'self-consciousness.' Second, self-consciousness—the consciousness of normal waking humans—involves a consciousness of 'self' and 'outside world' without any awareness of the perceptual process, of the coarising of these two or of the split between them. We might note here that the Sanskrit term used by Buddhists to denote the fifth skandha, consciousness, is *vijnana*. *Vi* means divided and *jnana* means knowing, therefore vijnana means "divided knowing."

There is a third aspect included in the common use of 'consciousness' that is awareness beyond language. It is the claim of Buddhists that, through the practice of meditation, the entire perceptual process can be brought into awareness, including the moment of the first split between 'self' and 'world.' The awareness that perceives this process and the ground within which it arises is not dependent on language and is not oriented toward a self; therefore it is known as 'nonreferential awareness.' I will have more to say about this later. But it is important to mention this awareness here to make clear that the above analysis of the role of language should not be taken to imply that all that in Western terms goes under the name of 'awareness' or 'consciousness'—two terms that are often used synonymously—is necessarily dependent on language.

In nonmeditative situations we may come close to this type of awareness in so-called "flashes of insight." We know, at least in the case of humans, that there are circumstances in which ideas appear to arise without direct contact with the environment; dreams and hallucinations are obvious cases. In many such cases these images may be simply stimulated by the internalized language and thus in effect be indirectly generated by the language process, as I have been describing. However, there are cases of creativity, flashes of sudden insight, that would be hard to explain in this way. It is often reported that at such moments the sense of separateness from the world is not experienced, that rather one's interconnectedness with 'other' is predominantly felt. It is also reported that insights arising under these circumstances are not mediated by language, but language comes in later as an attempt is made to communicate the insight.

Einstein described his realization of the relativistic nature of gravitation as sudden, coming to him in the form of vague visual and tactile sensations. He went on to say that it took him years to find the correct language—the language of tensor analysis—in which to express his insight. Mozart described his discovery of complete, complex new pieces of music in a similar way. And many people who pay attention to their experiences notice similar flashes on a more mundane level. We occasionally experience gaps in the normal flow of our discursive split consciousness, perhaps as brief glimpses of feelings and images to which we cannot put a name, possibly because these feelings and images are altogether fresh or because they occur so rarely that we have not learned names for them. Such anomalous cases would seem to invite another mode of explanation, and we will need to bear them in mind as we proceed.

Buddhist logicians have attempted to elucidate this awareness by pointing to the relation between negation and meaning, to the way negation operates in consciousness. If, for example, someone says the word "dog" to you, you may have a clear and distinct image of a dog. But there is at the same time a vague, felt, quality of not-dog, which forms the background to that clear and distinct image of dog. To put this another way, if someone says "That is a dog," your consciousness may become focused on something that does indeed appear to be a dog. There is a narrowing, or closing, of consciousness. However, if someone says, "That is not a dog," one becomes aware of many vague fleeting images, of all the possibilities for what it could be. There is a broadening and opening, perhaps an awareness of vast potential that is not purely based on going through a list of possible names for the thing that is not a dog. As words actually function in a context of meaning, each word brings with it the shadow of its opposite. And this shadow is felt in awareness, even though it may not be clearly and distinctly present in consciousness. The notion that a concept always contains the seed of its opposite is symbolized in the Chinese Taoist yin-yang symbol and formed an important part of Carl G. Jung's theory of the evolution of human consciousness. The yin-yang symbol was used by Niels Bohr on his family crest, and the idea embodied in it appears to have influenced Bohr in his formulation of his interpretation of quantum mechanics that I discussed in Chapter 2. We will return to these topics later.

SUMMARY: NO SELF IS TO BE FOUND

In this and the previous four chapters I have surveyed fairly extensively some of the data available from the work of the cognitive sciences. I have correlated these data with the psychological constituents of experience elaborated in the lists of dharmas of the early Buddhist schools: sensory input and physical sensation, feelings, emotional and mental process, and consciousness. Nowhere in this survey did we find that a self was needed to explain the phenomena, nor was an explanation of the phenomena made more simple by the assumption that a self exists. I pointed out at the beginning of Chapter 6 that one cannot prove the nonexistence of something directly, one can only search diligently for it, until one is convinced that it is not to be found. This is the method of the abhidharma, and this is what I have attempted to do in the preceding discussions. We might say, in terms of the preceding discussion of negation, that self is a concept that brings along with it the background that is not-self. And it is to this background that our attention is drawn in our search for an entity corresponding to the concept of a self.

As we will see in Chapter 12, the idea of a self affects perception at unconscious levels and distorts it so that our view of *what is* is constantly colored by this idea, and is therefore constantly deceived. In the Buddhist view, understanding this fact, not just at the surface rational level, which we have seen is superficial and deceptive, but at the deep subconscious levels of perceptual processing, is the necessary step to awakening out of this self-deception to perceive things as they are.

11

Where Is a Mind?

IN THE PREVIOUS CHAPTER I suggested that 'self-consciousness,' the divided consciousness that perceives a self and an external world, is generated in the biological and learned language systems of the organism. In talking of the 'external world' and the 'self' that allegedly perceives it as a fabrication of the perceptual process, we might perhaps be misleading the reader into supposing that we are going along with the assumption that the perceptual process somehow belongs to an 'internal world.'

This assumption is as deeply ingrained in the shared conceptual world of modern society and thought as is the assumption that there is a real 'external world.' We conventionally assume that there is indeed an internal world of the mind, the separate private mind of each individual, that we refer to as 'his' or 'her' mind. And we assume that this mind in some way represents the 'external world' to itself, that it is in fact a 'mirror of nature.' Even though we are suggesting that the external world as well as the conscious self-image that arises along with it is a fabrication, we might still be tempted to think that the fabrication is mirrored in our little minds, and that that is how we know it. We might think that, although we have understood the discussion about self-consciousness, there is some unfabricated remainder that can perhaps be the locus of a self. Perhaps my individual little mind that sees as in a mirror is the self? What I would like to convey in this chapter is that this little mirror is an invention, but a few hundred years old, principally by René Descartes and John Locke. To see this we will have to take a short detour into the complex history of the idea of 'mind,' just enough to see some of the threads that led to the invention of the concept of the individual mind as it is commonly conceived now.

MEDIEVAL MIND

During the so-called Dark Ages, outside the monasteries, the civilizing influence and knowledge of the Greek and Roman cultures was altogether lost.[1] Life was barbaric and limited to small groups in villages that did not communicate with each other at all through the dense forests. It is thought that in some areas of Europe even memory of the wheel was lost. The threads of civilization were kept alive in the Christian monasteries by a religion of intense faith and world denial. This faith had combined three influences: the salvation ideas of Christianity, the Platonic ideas of an immortal soul altogether different from the body, and the ideas of a cult known as the Manicheans, for whom the world was a battleground between a good God and an evil God, the body being the creation of evil, the soul the creation of good. Therefore, to attain salvation for the soul, the body had to be denied. Along with denial of the body went denial of the earthly world altogether.

It is somewhat ironic, in this context, to see Buddhism frequently referred to by Western writers as a "world-denying religion." In fact, Buddhism was first taught by a man who lived an apparently joyful life for eighty years, who died a peaceful death among friends, and whose discovery of awakening was preceded by his rejection of asceticism as well as of hedonism. The view of Buddhism as "world-denying" is in part an example of projection of the belief system of Christian scholars of the eighteenth and nineteenth centuries,[2] and the uncritical acceptance of these ideas by popular writers even today. The whole idea of "world-denial" and the fear of it seems to be far more a part of the Western tradition than of the Buddhist traditions.

In the tenth century Europe gradually awakened from its deep slumber, and in the eleventh century, as European Christians became aware of the writings of Aristotle, through Arabic translations, people again discovered the logical empirical method. There was a reawakening to the world of the senses and to a realization that true knowledge can be had by a combination of observation and logic. A bitter conflict arose within the Christian church between the proponents of faith and reason that raged for several centuries. This conflict was also one between those who held to the old view of the earth as evil and those who began to be curious about the world around them. In the cathedral schools, in the newly established universities, and among wandering teachers there was a new excitement and a new interest in the world as workable and conquerable. Knowledge of the world, gained through the senses and understood through reason based on Aristotle's logic, began to threaten faith.

This battle is epitomized by the struggle between St. Bernard, abbot of the great monastery of Clairvaux, and Abelard, a fiery free-lance teacher.[3] Bernard established a new, deeper, and more interior understanding of love and faith as the only way to certain knowledge. Abelard, equally passionate in his proclamation of clarity and reason, who is immortalized in his tragic love for Héloïse, turned the church establishment upside down by applying Aristotle's own logical method to the Scriptures themselves, and pointing out the contradictions that result. Bernard and Abelard both were seen as leaders of the emerging youth. As medieval historian F. Heer says, "Europe was awakening; and its intelligent young manhood roused itself to go in search of teachers, spiritual leaders, masters of the inner life, masters of intellect, philosophers. The grim battle in which Bernard of Clairvaux overthrew Abelard can perhaps only be understood as the confrontation of one *eros* with another." Of this battle Heer says, "Bernard of Clairvaux fought for the primacy of the heart; he was himself in his own day the most powerful and passionate representative of its virtues. Peter Abelard the toughest intellect of his time, fought for the primacy of reason, of the head. The controversy between these two men revealed an abyss; and for centuries afterwards theologians and philosophers were to occupy themselves just as much with widening it as with attempts at bridging, or, indeed, concealing its existence. European thought from this time onwards cannot be understood without taking note of these dialectical efforts to reconcile or separate faith and knowledge, reasons of the heart and rational understanding; the two have finally become so diametrically opposed that Christian believers regard scientists as professional unbelievers."

Since medieval historian Heer so succinctly summarizes the issues involved, I will quote him at some length here:

> The fear of corruption was the most serious motive uniting simple monks, reputable conservative theologians and men such as Bernard in their opposition to Abelard. We may well remind ourselves that Socrates was also accused of seducing the young to godlessness. This little man Abelard . . . appeared to his adversaries as . . . a destructive intellectual, a wicked "progressive," who took pleasure in fuddling the wits of the students and destroying their faith; with his sophistries and conceit he gambled away the certainties of faith, which had seemed fixed for all time.
>
> The much-persecuted Abelard was one of the fathers of scholasticism, or the systematic use of reason in the discovery of truth. . . . Thomas Aquinas and the academic philosophers of the later Middle Ages all rest on Abelard's shoulders. Truth was to be sought and found by posing a rational question,

answered by a much qualified yes and no, *sic et non*, and so, with the help of methodical doubt, the problem could be solved. A dispassionate, honest approach to a question was only possible if faith and knowledge were first (at least for the time being) kept clearly distinct. Faith, so easily confused by emotional excitement, should not be allowed to stand permanently in the path of reason; and reason for its part should not use the intellect as the means of solving the final mysteries of faith, which were inaccessible to reason.[4]

At the same time as all this was going on, another stream of learning had entered Europe via the Arabs. Throughout the Dark and early Middle Ages, the stream of popular paganism and magical beliefs had continued. Now Europe had discovered sophisticated systems of astrology, alchemy, and magic. These interests were reinforced in the fifteenth century by the rediscovery of the hermetic tradition and the unearthing of cabalistic, Pythagorean, and other systems of beliefs and practices dedicated to the spiritual transformation of the human personality. These practices involved the study of sympathetic relationships between the various hierarchical levels of the cosmos: between the solar system, parts of the human body, various metals and plants, and so on. These various levels were thought to be connected in that each of them was a reflection of the same cosmos, giving rise to the well-known principle, "As above, so below." It was thought that by contemplation of various relationships in the natural world one could come to a direct knowledge of relationships on other hierarchical levels. There were contemplative practices in these traditions, particularly connected with visualization, with the art of memory and with alchemy.[5]

According to Carolly Erickson, "Medieval perception was characterized by an all-inclusive awareness of simultaneous realities. The bounds of reality were bent to embrace—and often localize—the unseen, and determining all perception was a mutually held world view which found in religious truths the ultimate logic of existence. This perception, which where it is alien to modern consciousness may be likened to an enchantment, was encouraged by . . . ideas of the power and number of noncorporeal beings, the presence of life in inanimate creation, and the significance of vision as a creative force and as a mode of human understanding. Medieval people lived in a perceptual climate in which noncorporeal beings were a familiar and to some extent a manageable force, recognized alike in theology and popular culture." And according to Erickson it was the practice of visionary imagination that confirmed and nourished this view of reality. Erickson continues, "Visions erased the shear line between the known and the unknowable, the discoverable and the revealed. They interlocked the simultaneous realities; they made visible the unseen; they clarified the hidden shape of truth."[6]

Morris Berman argues that, in the consciousness of the late Middle Ages, two modes of secular knowledge existed side by side, both deriving ultimately from the Greeks: the participatory knowledge coming from active emotional identification with imagery (the *mimetic* tradition), especially the imagery of the poets and of pagan religious ritual; and the newer Platonic tradition, "one that sought to analyze and classify events rather than 'merely' experience or imitate them." Berman remarks that from the time of Plato, "The Greek began to see himself as an autonomous personality apart from his acts; as a separate consciousness rather than a series of moods." But neither of these two modes of knowledge had gained ascendancy in the Middle Ages. For, as Berman says, "Throughout the Middle Ages men and women continued to see the world primarily as a garment they wore rather than a collection of discrete objects they confronted. Yet . . . some form of objectivity was now present; and it was chiefly the alchemical and magical tradition that attempted to demonstrate how limited this objectivity was.

"The 'Hermetic wisdom,' as it has been called, was in effect dedicated to the notion that real knowledge occurred only via the union of subject and object, in a psychic-emotional identification with images rather than a purely intellectual examination of concepts."[7]

The essence of this consciousness is the recognition of resemblances and correspondences between all things: that all things have relationships of sympathy and antipathy to each other. This world view, which did not necessarily distinguish between mental and material events, is the meaning of alchemy. And we can only understand what actually took place in an alchemical laboratory as we recognize participating consciousness. Men and women perceived, in their world, phenomena that we cannot recognize, for we have forgotten participating consciousness.

It was, then, in the Middle Ages that a final split developed between the rational empiricism of intellect and the direct participatory knowledge of intuition. Intuition was included in the Christian idea of 'faith,' and it was also included in the magical practices and belief systems. The primacy of faith was proclaimed by the church, which nevertheless accepted intellect as a steppingstone to faith and a confirmation of it. Faith alone would bring one to God and entry into the Heavenly City, by contrast to which the earth was a place of insignificance and contempt. And the alchemists continued their search for the transformative knowledge that would bring the Kingdom of Heaven about on earth. The primacy of intellect was proclaimed by a new breed of men who set themselves up as professional teachers, separating from the church schools and the church-dominated universities, and proclaimed that the new reason would bring knowledge of the earthly world and, with it, power. For the time being each of these three ways of knowing enjoyed equal status.

The discovery by Newton in the seventeenth century of laws of motion that governed the motion of planets around the sun, as well as of all inanimate objects on earth, paved the way for the final triumph of the inferential knowledge of intellect over the direct participatory knowledge of intuition. Within a century after Newton the common consensus was that the world should be explainable in terms of isolated lumps of fundamentally nonliving matter moving in absolutely empty space according to fixed, mechanical laws. Mind was not necessary for the operation of this mechanical world. Mind therefore became the passive perceiver and the thinker. Furthermore, since lumps of mindless matter cannot possibly have sympathetic correspondences with each other, the principles of magic became 'supernatural,' that is, above or outside of nature. Since mind was no longer an essential part of Newton's mechanical world of mindless matter moving in mindless space, mind's place in and connection with that world now demanded fresh explanation.[8]

DESCARTES SPLITS MIND AND BODY

The founders of the two great contrasting streams of thought that followed Newton, rationalism and empiricism, are usually taken to be Descartes and Locke. In a contemplation that led to perhaps the most popularly known statement in all of philosophy ("I think, therefore I am") Descartes began by doubting. He realized that one can be mistaken about all one's perceptions, all one's memories, and all that one has been taught. One could even doubt that one had a body, since one knew this through sense perceptions, which could be illusory. He came to the conclusion that the only thing one could not doubt was that one was doubting, i.e., thinking.

Since he could not doubt that he was a thinking being, but could doubt that he had a body, Descartes came to the conclusion that thinking was essential to his being while having a body was not. Therefore he concluded that the body and mind were entirely different substances. The mind is a thinking substance, without extension in space. The body is a substance, matter, with extension, but not thinking. So he said, "We must come to the definite conclusion that this proposition 'I am, I exist' is necessarily true each time I pronounce it, or that I mentally conceive it. . . . I do not now admit anything which is not necessarily true: to speak accurately I am not more than a thing which thinks, that is to say a mind or a soul, or an understanding, or a reason . . . I am, however, a real thing and really exist; but what thing? I have answered: a thing which thinks." And this 'I' by which, according to Descartes, "I am what I am" is entirely distinct from the body and can exist without it.[9]

Descartes was fascinated by a mechanical model of people in the gardens of Versailles. The people moved, driven by a system of hydraulics, and Descartes was convinced that all the movements of the body could be explained in this way. He developed a theory similar to the early reflex arc theory of functioning of the nervous-muscular system, that all action of the body eventually reduces to simple components like the knee-jerk reaction. The mind would not be active in this process, and the physical world would go through its motions without the involvement of the mind except as a passive observer. Descartes developed a theory of visual perception that had the mind meeting the mechanical responses from the visual system at the pineal gland. This was therefore the place at which the mind joined the body as passive perceiver.

However, for Descartes, all ideas including ideas of things came from within the mind, innately. Descartes says, "I cannot doubt that there is in me a certain passive faculty of perceiving, that is, of receiving and recognizing the ideas of sensible objects; but it would be valueless to me and I could in no way use it if there were not also in me or in something else, another active faculty capable of forming and producing these ideas."[10] He suggests that our experiences in the world merely serve to stimulate the innate ideas of things that already exist in the mind. We do not know the world directly at all, but only its reflection in the innate ideas of the mind as they are stimulated by experience. This stimulation of ideas by perception happens at the pineal gland, and, apart from this, mind is entirely separate from body.

LOCKE'S CONSCIOUS SELF

The English writer John Locke appeared to take an entirely opposing view to Descartes. He responded to Descartes saying that we can have knowledge of the existence of another thing only by sensation. And he is responsible for the famous analogy of mind as a blank sheet of paper, or more appropriately nowadays, an undeveloped photographic film. "Let us suppose the mind to be, as we say, white paper, void of all characters, without any *ideas;* how comes it to be furnished? Whence comes it by that vast store, which the busy and boundless fancy of man painted on it with an almost endless variety? Whence has it all the materials of reason and knowledge? To this I answer in one word, from experience: in that all our knowledge is founded, and from that it ultimately derives itself."

Locke builds a theory of how complex thoughts arise from these simple ideas placed in the originally blank mind by experience: although there are no innate ideas in mind, mind has an active function of combining and manipulating the simple ideas given to it by experience, and thus creating new ideas. And at the end of it he is led to a person or self able to know these ideas, ". . . a thinking intelligent being, that has reason and reflection and can consider itself as itself, the same thinking thing in different time and places."[11] This is the modern version of ego's fifth skandha, consciousness. For Locke the essential aspect of the self was self-consciousness, that which perceives that it perceives and knows that it knows, but which is otherwise blank.

So in the end both Descartes and Locke have a mind separate from the material world, a mind that perceives that material world without affecting it and that is the locus of personal identity. Although the two have very different ideas about the nature of perception and the origin of knowledge about the world, both agree that at the end of that process there is the thinking, reasoning, nonparticipating self, a self that is not itself altered by the fluctuating contingencies of experience. For Descartes and Locke and all those who followed them, conscious, clear, and distinct ideas that could be manipulated by logical operations were the only basis of certainty. The vague but powerful insights of feeling and bodily sensation, the "responses of the heart," were finally dismissed as sources of true knowledge, relegated and suppressed in a new version of denial of the direct intuitive knowledge that comes from the embodiment of mind and the joint participation or interconnectedness of mind, body, and world.

Morris Berman has demonstrated the suppression of the body that took place at this time, thus removing the rational, conscious reasoning mind from danger of being tainted by the irrational intuitions of bodily participation: the discovery of childhood as a separate type of being and the emphasis on corporal punishment of children and shame of the body and of sexuality, all were directed toward making children feel that their bodies were separate pieces of matter over which their minds should have control. Berman quotes studies that suggest that the personality of Newton himself bordered on the psychotic, yet Newton was hero-worshiped almost to the point of being deified by the society of his own time and of generations to come. As Frank Manuel says, "A structuring of the world in so absolutist a manner that every event, the closest and the most remote, fits neatly into an imaginary system has been called a symptom of illness, especially when others refuse to join in the grand obsessive design. It was Newton's fortune that a large portion of his total system was acceptable to European society as a perfect representation of reality, and his name was attached to the age."[12]

The assumptions that each one of us has an individual mind that passively observes the outer world as in a mirror, and that this mind is in some way either located in the brain or connected to our body via the brain, are nothing other than ideas that were invented at a time when there was an overweening urge to explain all the natural world in terms of lumps of mindless matter floating in empty space. Few people believe now that this is in any way capable of providing a complete explanation of the natural world. In fact many people are beginning to believe that it bears only a very narrow relation to the natural world at all. Yet we cling to the idea of individual 'atomic' minds located in the brain. We tend to take this idea for granted as if it were a self-evident truth that no rational person, but only a fanatic of some kind or another, would question.

However, the belief—and it is no more than a belief—that mind passively mirrors nature in individual heads did not go unchallenged. About thirty years after Locke and Descartes, in the seventeenth century, David Hume effectively argued that the Lockean 'Personal Self' could not be found. His argument was simply to point out that when he actually looked at his own mind and body, Hume found a succession of loosely bound sensations, emotions, and ideas. Nowhere did he find a Self. Hume wrote, "we are nothing but a bundle or collection of different sensations, which succeed each other with an inconceivable rapidity, and are in a perpetual flux and movement."[13] Hume applied a similar argument to the idea of causality generally. All we know of the world is a bundle of sensations, and we have no real reason to suppose that if two sensations frequently appear in succession, such as the appearance of a flame and the sensation of heat, there is any real connection between these two in the outer world. For that matter, if we see a rock one moment and then look away, there is nothing in that original perception of a rock that tells us that we will see it if we look a second time. That we believe in such continuity and in a principle of causality is simply animal faith.

We will recognize this argument from the early Buddhist schools, and we will also recognize the difficulty that it brings: how to account for the apparent logic and continuity of the stream of thoughts and perceptions if this stream is merely discrete, 'atomic' entities strung together. What is the string? Hume himself admitted that this problem was beyond him, but stuck to his assertion that neither a Personal Self nor a principle of causality could be found and therefore, he suggested, in all honesty one must remain skeptical as to their existence. Hume suggested, probably tongue in cheek, that the only way one could be sure of the immortal soul was through divine revelation. But since he himself argued against the existence of God, this did not help him very much. However, Hume's ideas did not really penetrate the dominant pursuit of an empirical basis for knowledge, which depended on the belief in a real external world of objects connected by causality, and an individual mind as the conscious, but passive, observer and logical analyzer of impressions received through the senses.

KANT'S WORLD-CONSTRUCTION

A major criticism of the empiricist view of the passivity of the mind came from the German philosopher Immanuel Kant in the late eighteenth century.[14] Kant's ideas gave rise to the so-called German Idealist school of philosophy and were on the whole dismissed by the scientific community until, in the past few decades, the cognitive psychologists have seen in them much that presages their own 'constructivist' view. Kant believed himself to have finally reconciled the profound difference between the view of Descartes, that all knowledge resides in the mind as 'innate ideas' and is simply called up by the stimulation of the senses, and that of Locke, that the mind is essentially blank and forms knowledge of complex things by manipulation of raw sense impressions.

Kant felt that he was proclaiming a 'Copernican revolution' in the understanding of mind in suggesting that whereas up to then, in empiricism, it had been supposed that our knowledge must conform to the nature of the objective world, he was going to propose that the world of objects must 'conform to our knowledge.' Kant begins by assuming on one side an outside world of 'things in themselves' that a human mind can never know; and on the other side an individual subjective human mind. Kant accepts Hume's criticism of causality, that the appearance of continuity does not come from the outer world. He then asks how it is that we 'know' a coherent workable world. His answer is that the mind already contains, within its own structure, categories that it projects out onto 'things in themselves.' Space, time, causality, objectness, number, affirmation, negation, and possibility are all examples of the categories that are not in the world of 'things in themselves' but that are projected onto that world by a mind. Kant also proposed that the mind contains intermediary concepts, which he called 'schema,' images for concepts that served to coordinate impressions into recognizable objects. These are very similar to the representations of the cognitivists that we met in Chapter 8.

Owen Flanagan speaks of Kant's world thus: "The concepts of logic, causality, substance, space and time are, of course subjective. Other creatures, paramecia for example, probably do not construct their world in terms of these concepts and categories. But these mental structures are subjective in an utterly healthy sense. They are universal species-specific ways in which we organize reality. Without these structures operating as a system of expectations about the world, in anticipation of experience, we would never be able to build up the fantastically complex, adaptive, rule-governed picture of the world we achieve at a very young age."[15]

For Kant there are two faculties. First is the intuitive or sensible, which provides a diversity or manifold of characteristics spread out over space and time, which we interpret as phenomena. The second faculty, the intellect or understanding, relates and synthesizes this diversity, giving it meaning to the 'I.' Both these faculties are projections from the subject of experience, the 'I.' This 'I' and the projecting activity of its two faculties Kant takes to be the foundation of knowledge. But this is not pure idealism, because for Kant while assuming an 'I' we must at the same time assume a world outside it, the world of 'things in themselves.' This is a world that the 'I' can never know, but that nevertheless affirms its validity by the universality of its constructs. The 'I' makes itself known, not directly, but by constituting or projecting an objective reality. For Kant the 'I' can in fact not possibly be known as such, and therefore for him there is no possibility of a 'science of mind.' The human is locked forever in the world of his or her projections, and the hope of knowing a world beyond these projections is a vain one.

Kant is here describing what the Buddhists have termed 'ego.' Locked in a world of its own projecting, the 'I,' which, following Descartes, Kant also referred to as the *Cogito*, or the 'I think,' this 'I' is altogether incapable of knowing either itself or the world of 'things in themselves.' Kant takes as the primary givens the 'I' and the world of 'things in themselves,' and his theory is really about how the world we think we live in is constructed out of the interaction between these two unknowables. Although he thought that he was doing away once and for all with speculative metaphysics, his view is in fact based on the speculation of the existence of these two unknowables. Kant got himself into this difficulty because he too, like Descartes and Locke, assumed that there are individual 'atomic' minds, and that these minds are the loci of the primary fact that there is awareness of something.

The criticism of this, from the point of view of nonduality, is that we have no good reason whatsoever to take these two unknowables as the primary facts. The 'I' and 'things in themselves' arise together along with the very process of projecting; the two are thus mutually fabricating in a reciprocal process in which neither is primary, and in fact neither has any absolute existence beyond the projecting and fabricating process itself. As we will see, the insight gained from the practice of meditation is that the projecting process knows itself, that is all, there is nothing behind it whatsoever, no atomic minds and no unknowable 'things in themselves.' This is hinted at in Flanagan's reference to the paramecium, but the cognitivist psychologists are not in fact consistent in this insight. They too always return to the world as projected by the human perceptual system, of bodies in space and time, as if the world had some validity that transcends this projection.

To summarize, most of us in the modern world bring along many unconscious assumptions when we hear the term 'mind': that mind is located in the head (or the nervous system); that it passively reflects phenomena like a mirror or a camera; that 'clear and distinct ideas,' i.e. 'conscious ideas,' manipulated by intellect, are the only kind of true knowledge it has. These are assumptions behind the belief that computers can eventually simulate all the processes of the human mind, and the growing tendency to equate 'information' with knowledge. The point of this chapter has been to suggest that, while this may form a part of the functioning of the mental processes, the notion that this accounts for all knowledge, or even its most important aspects, was an invention of the seventeenth century. It was an invention that derived from the success of Newton's mechanical explanations of the motion of moving objects, and it was designed to complement these explanations and to do for the mental world what Newton had done for the physical world. Needless to say, these ideas were as narrow in scope as we now know Newton's ideas were. There is no grounds for believing that such 'minds' actually, ultimately exist, or for thinking personally that we have such minds and that these minds could be the loci of a really existing self. In Chapter 13 we will see, as we might expect, that this narrow concept of the individual mind is at last beginning to show its inherent contradictions, and to become fuzzy at the boundaries. In the next chapter we will draw back together all the elements of experience into a description of the way these elements appear to be synthesized in a temporal process in the experiential moment.

12

The Process of Perception

IN THIS CHAPTER I will suggest that Buddhism and science meet at the level of perception. As I hope the reader has by now begun to understand, by 'perception' I mean a process far more profound than merely taking in 'information' about the 'outside world.' I will first describe the process of perception according to the Buddhist discoveries, and then I will present the experiments in cognition that seem to corroborate these discoveries. We must be very cautious here because what consciousness infers about what it is experiencing may be quite different from what the organism as a whole *is* experiencing. This is not to say that consciousness is not experiencing what it seems to be experiencing. That is necessarily true, since consciousness is consciousness just of what seems, and nothing else. But it is saying that the conclusions consciousness jumps to may be wrong: I may be hallucinating, I may be deceiving myself or simply misinterpreting. This is why it is important to develop methods that to some extent bypass consciousness, and this is precisely what the methods of cognitive science and of the practice of mindfulness-awareness are designed to do.

THE FIVE SKANDHAS REVISITED

The Buddhist description is based on the dharma analysis of Chapter 5. Dharma analysis of experience breaks down each moment of experience into its component dharmas. Having done this, of course it is desirable to understand how these dharmas combine into the apparent unity of that moment. The development of a moment of experience is not instantaneous but develops over a very brief period of time. During this period dharmas enter into combination sequentially, in five stages corresponding to the five skandhas, culminating in a conscious experience. The duration of an experiential moment has been variously estimated by Buddhists, a fairly common estimate being approximately ⅟75 second, or about 13 milliseconds.[1] This agrees fairly well with estimates of experimental psychology, although it is perhaps a little low.[2] Joining in a natural, automatic, causal process, abiding momentarily, and then separating again, the constant turmoil of dharmas gives the appearance of the world as we know it. Let us briefly review the five skandhas, this time from the point of view not so much of the general analysis of experience, but of the direct perception of the arising and decaying of each moment as that arising and decaying has been reported by master practitioners of meditation. This way of making use of the skandha classification comes particularly from the contemplative vajrayana tradition of Tibetan Buddhism.[3]

The dharmas arise within the gap in which there is no sense of self or of separateness from nonduality. This stage is, of course inaccessible to the methods of dualistic science, to dualistic observation. But, as we will see when we come to discuss the details of mindfulness-awareness practice, it *is* accessible to direct experience. It is felt as spacious, open, and vast, with a quality of peacefulness and brilliance. Within that openness there is primordial nondual intelligent insight, known as *vidya* in Sanskrit; the Tibetan is *rigpa*. *Avidya*, primordial ignorance, is thus the opposite of the intelligent insight at the basis of perception, before the skandhas arise. Sparks, or flashes, of primordial intelligence continually arise from moment to moment. Such a flash may recognize the nondual openness within which it arose, and rest back into that. Alternatively there may be a clinging to the feeling of separate existence, which leads to panic. With the panic the energy becomes frozen into a first, primitive distinction between self and other. This is the beginning of the first skandha, the skandha of *form*. This first stage may be a little difficult for the reader to grasp conceptually until it is understood that perception arises before the distinction has been made between the outside world and the inside world. That is, perception arises within the whole field which a third-party observer divides into organism and environment; perception is not initiated purely from within the organism.

Form is the first activation of the five senses and the six consciousnesses. This is a primitive stage, not by any means 'conscious' in the sense we usually mean it. It is a preconscious recognition, or apperception, of patterning. It is without interpretation other than the distinction between 'outside' and 'inside,' between 'that' and 'this.' The sixth sense consciousness, mind, is felt as 'this,' or 'inside.' The patternings in the five sense consciousnesses, arising from the first contact between the sense organs and sense fields, are felt as 'outside.' This includes the 'proprioceptive' sense of neurology, which is the inner sensation of owning a body. For 'mind,' even the body perceived through this inner sense, is 'other' or 'outside.'

The basic quality of form is ignorance or bewilderment, since form is built on ignoring the first split between inside and outside. Ignorance is termed *avidya,* the opposite of *vidya.* Each succeeding moment of experience is conditioned by the pattern of dharmas occurring in the immediately preceding moment. Thus there is the appearance of continuity—a continuous 'outside world' and a continuous 'self.' This gives rise to further levels of ignorance characterized by ignoring the fundamentally changing quality of perception and by ignoring the profound anxiety that arises from this belief in permanence of the 'objects' and 'subject' of perception. There is profound anxiety because the belief in permanence is continually contradicted by the actuality of change.

This anxiety, of course, is normally deeply below consciousness. But because we ignore it we are driven by it, both individually and socially, as every psychiatrist knows. Anxiety is said to be the scourge of our modern world. But trying to hide from it, by patching up the ego in 'therapy,' trying to constantly crank up a stronger sense of self-importance, at the individual or national level, or to smooth it over with Valium, only deepens the wound. From the present analysis we can see that the wound occurs at a basic level of perception. It can be healed only by a precise and finely detailed knowledge of the process of perception. Without this understanding, philosophies, sciences, paradigms, religions, and social actions, new or old, are bound to create only further ignorance and deeper anxiety. As Buddhist scholar David Kalupahana describes it, "Ignorance is said to determine the dispositions in the sense that in the absence of correct knowledge about the nature and destiny of the individual, one's dispositions are determined in a way detrimental to one's future. These dispositions give shape to one's consciousness which in turn tends to determine one's current psychophysical personality."[4]

The second stage of perception is the skandha of *feeling.* Having made the first basic split between 'inside' and 'outside' and having acknowledged, apperceptively, the sensory patternings in the 'outside,' there is a reaction of feeling toward these patternings. Feelings are relative to the survival of the primitive sense of ego that has already appeared at the level of form, determining what sensory dharmas are attended to. Thus feelings are positive, negative, or neutral, depending on whether the 'outside' patternings are apprehended as supportive, threatening, or neither supportive nor threatening to ego.

In the third stage, the skandha of *perception,* feelings refer back to the inside, which then reaffirms itself and tries to take charge as a kind of switchboard or central processor, to use the analogy of computers. This is the first actual cognition of a separate sense of self, the first cognition that a perception of a specific object with specific characteristics is taking place, and a grasping onto that object as meaningful. There are primitive judgments involved at this level, judgments of near or far, large or small, strange or familiar, looming or receding, frightening or relieving. All these judgments are in reference to the 'inside,' now apprehended as a distinct self, and the 'outside' grasped onto as distinct 'objects' or 'things.'

The fourth skandha is the stage at which intellect, as naming and meaning interpretation, comes in. It is the level at which complexes or *formations* of concepts with affects are projected onto the 'outside' together with names. There is recognition of actual objects. A chair is recognized as a chair, with all the connotations of chairness. A chair is a thing to sit on; it is also the thing we first stood on to wash dishes as a proud little boy, it is also an example of a seat, something we offer to our guests, and so on. A face is the face of my friend, Nicholas, whom I knew at college, and who first taught me the meaning of emptiness, and so on. That voice is the sound of a Russian, a Russian is a communist, and so on. All the belief systems we have—philosophical, religious, economic, political, personal and so on—are stored and ready to be applied to a developing perception at the level of formation. Formation therefore takes its name because it is at this level that the perception is unified into a coherent recognizable thing, a form with a name.

At the stage of the skandha of *consciousness* we are conscious of a thought or a perception. Consciousness is a narrative that gives the formations a context. It is like a constantly circulating radar beacon that checks out the coherence and meaningfulness of the entire scene. It fills in any gaps it finds with its projections or reasonable hypotheses as to what is there, so that there are no uncertainties. We know we are here in this familiar and recognizable world. Anything that does not fit in is finally excluded at the level of consciousness. Consciousness keeps up a story line as to what is going on to provide continuity from moment to moment. Our conscious life follows this story line as far as it is able and so long as no incoherence is able to break through it. What we normally think of as 'waking consciousness' or 'self-consciousness' is a combination of the fourth and fifth skandhas. All five skandhas are occurring in every moment of experience, but attention is normally of such a coarse grade that we experience the skandhas lumped together in a continuous 'stream of consciousness.'

This then is the process of perception in five stages as discovered in the practice of mindfulness-awareness meditation. Concept is present in the sense of the involvement of images projected by the developing sense of self all the way from the stage of *form* to that of *consciousness*. From this point of view, so long as the five skandhas are all stuck together as I have presented them, and experienced as one stream of consciousness, then that stream of consciousness is the end of a long train of inferential perceptions. 'Inferential perception' refers to perception mediated by concept, image, or word. It is perception of an symbol, a representation of the situation rather than the situation itself. In other words, so long as our awareness dwells in the fifth skandha, consciousness, then that consciousness itself is the object of each successive moment of perception. We perceive only our narrative of the world and never perceive the world as it is. Under these circumstances, even form is experienced inferentially, mediated by concept. And as we saw in the chapter on form, this is corroborated by cognitive science studies of the initial sensory input.

PERCEPTION AND TIME

Let us turn back to take a final look to see how far cognitive science might go along with the Buddhist insight into perceptual processing. Some general characteristics of preconscious perceptual processing are now fairly widely accepted:

1. Perception is not immediate; there is a finite time interval between the first receipt of sensory input and the final, conscious awareness of a perception.
2. Preconscious perception is an inferential process closely akin to thinking.
3. This inferential process is strongly affected by preconscious emotional arousal, much more so than it can be affected by conscious effort.
4. Emotional arousal from sources other than the immediate perception can affect that perception at the earliest stage of extraction of bare sensory data.
5. Consciousness may not necessarily enter the process at

all. It is probable that in the vast majority of situations in which the organism receives a sensory stimulus and even *acts* in response to that stimulus, consciousness is not an intermediary. Thus consciousness plays an occasional and relatively small part in the total perceptual life of the organism.

6. Perception occurs in stages involving extraction of form with preverbal judgment of meaning, affective response, recognition of objectness, and at times, conscious awareness. We can recognize here the first, the second, a combination of the third and fourth, and the fifth skandhas.

That perception takes time was shown very directly by Benjamin Libet for the sense of touch.[5] Libet performed experiments on subjects undergoing brain surgery who were conscious and who consented to take part in them. He found the following results:

1. A single, brief electrical impulse, lasting for one-half millisecond, applied to the skin can be detected consciously *one-half* second after it is applied, although the subject is not aware of this perceptual time lag. That same impulse causes a measurable electrical response at the cortex only *one one-hundredth* of a second after the impulse is applied to the skin.

2. A single impulse of one-half millisecond applied directly to the exposed cortex cannot be detected consciously. However, a series of such impulses applied ¹⁄₂₀ second apart and lasting for at least one-half second can be detected consciously.

3. A single impulse applied to the skin was not detected if the cortex was directly stimulated by a series of impulses beginning less than one-half second after the first impulse. Thus the train of cortical impulses was masking out the skin stimulus as if the process required for that impulse to become conscious had not been completed within this half second.

Libet concluded that although a single impulse to the skin can reach the cortex in less than one one-hundredth of a second, this impulse had to be somehow repeated and elaborated at the cortex for at least a half second for the conscious perception of it to be completed.

Similar results have been shown less directly with the visual system in experiments in which subjects were shown words for too short a duration to be detected on one showing (a 'tachistoscopic exposure'). As reported by Norman Dixon, one of the foremost workers in preconscious processing, ". . . repeated tachistoscopic exposures, at constant durations, of an initially subliminal word eventuate in accurate reporting of the individual letters contained therein. Since the effect has been found for exposure durations of from 15 to 30 microseconds, for meaningless as well as for meaningful words, for familiar and unfamiliar words, whether or not the subject knew which word was to be presented and even when other stimuli were interpolated between the critical repetitions and there was a set not to see the same word again, we can conclude that the data from these various researches constitute a robust demonstration of the fact that conscious perception of visual stimuli may result from the progressive summation of repeated subliminal presentations."[6]

Numerous masking experiments in which an interfering stimulus, the mask, was presented after a stimulus to be identified have shown similar timing. If the mask was presented within a hundredth of a second after the stimulus, complete obliteration of the stimulus resulted; if the mask was presented later, up to one-half second after the stimulus, some difficulty in identification of the stimulus was reported. A variety of more direct experiments on the discrimination of stimuli separated by short intervals have been reported. For example, if two lights are shown successively with an interval of less than about $\frac{1}{10}$ second they will be seen as simultaneous, at least by untrained subjects. If this interval is slightly increased, then the stimuli will appear to be in rapid motion, and a slight further increase enables the subjects to discriminate sequential motion. As we will see in the next chapter the results appear to be different for trained meditators. Summarizing similar experiments with nonvisual phenomena, M. R. Harter concludes, ". . . the critical periods of time at which the above phenomena occurred ranged from 50 to 250 millisec., the most common value being 100 millisec."[7] Experiments by Francisco Varela and his colleagues strongly suggest a correlation between this 'perceptual framing' and the alpha rhythms of the brain detectable in the electroencephalogram (EEG). These rhythms, which are the most prominent in the electrical activity of brain of the normal resting adult, have a frequency of 7 to 13 cycles per second, corresponding to time intervals of 150 to 75 milliseconds.[8]

These experiments and others like them indicate that perception takes time, an extremely significant observation that was ignored by many experimental psychologists only ten years ago. But beyond this they suggest the disturbing fact that we live our conscious lives one-tenth to one-half of a second behind the 'reality' we are supposedly being conscious of. During this perceptual moment a complex creative process is occurring, involving all the elements that we have examined in the previous chapters and collected under the scheme of the five skandhas. This is the creative process that gives rise, moment by moment, to the perceived world and the self that perceives it.

CONSCIOUSNESS IS UNNECESSARY

Now let us look at some experiments and data that have attempted to separate out the various stages of perception. First, numerous studies have shown that there can be intelligent action based on perception without consciousness, action in which there must have been recognition of the meaning of objects to the organism even though no meaning was reported. Human subjects with cortical damage leading to reported blindness are able to catch a ball thrown to them. If asked to "guess" where an object is and point to it, they are able to do so with accuracy far greater than chance, a phenomenon named 'blindsight.'[9] And the work on split-brain patients reported in Chapter 10 supplements these findings.

Beyond these artificial situations we have, of course, numerous situations in which complex actions are performed without conscious knowledge of the operations involved, from bicycle riding to higher mathematics. In fact it is clear that in almost all circumstances, while we may or may not be conscious of the final result of perceptual processing, we certainly are not conscious of the processing itself. Indeed the processing is able to carry on quite nicely without us, and is even inhibited if we try to become conscious of it.

Much more necessary than consciousness are the stages of the process that precedes it. In approaching the problem of delineating stages, according to John Wilding, "[one approach] is to attempt to halt or tap the process before it is completed. Early experiments simply varied the input duration and asked for reports. There was surprisingly good agreement by observers on what was experienced as the input duration increased."

According to Wilding, the evidence suggests four stages: "1) a vague awareness of something present or an indefinite object, 2) awareness of a generic object belonging to some general category,

3) awareness of a specific object, and finally 4) understanding of meaning." In masking experiments, results very similar to these were obtained. Subjects reported a shift, with increasing interval between stimulus and mask "from reporting little or no evidence of the target letter to an intermediate state of noting its presence, and finally reporting not only that it was present but that its form was clear and that the problem was to identify it before it was replaced by the pattern mask."

THE INITIAL INPUT

As we saw in Chapter 6, a great deal of work has been done on the initial input, the "vague awareness of something." There has been extensive debate on whether this initial sensory input must be first analyzed into very simple uninterpreted elements such as points of colored light, separate tones, and simple features such as lines, curves, shadows, and so on, or whether even at this first stage there is some conceptual, interpretive component. On the whole the latter point of view is becoming dominant. As Wilding summarizes it, "the assumption that complex stimuli are analysed into component features has proved a very useful one and increased our understanding of many areas of perception. However it is quite clear that no simple version of such an approach is adequate, which postulates simply sets of independent detectors, each looking for one easily defined aspect of the input. More sophisticated versions are needed incorporating complex features and sensitivity to task demands, current context and past experience in the type of features used and the level of identification achieved."[10]

Irving Rock suggests that this first level of perception, which he calls the 'literal perception,' depends on at least some level of cognitive processing. He points out, "The fact is that the light rays from two separate points within an object have no more connection with one another than the rays from one such point with those from a point outside the object. Therefore it is a problem why we usually group together into one phenomenal thing all the proximal stimuli related to one object rather than group some stimuli from the object with others from the surfaces between objects, or for that matter, it is a problem why such organizations occur at all. The problem is easier to grasp when the pattern of stimulation is ambiguous in the sense that it can be organized in different ways. But it is worth emphasizing that, logically, the problem is no different when the pattern of stimulation is more typically not of this kind, as in daily life."[11]

Furthermore, as Wilding says, "the appropriate description for a given input is highly dependent on the way the perceiver chooses to process it, which may vary qualitatively in the way information is interpreted and the degree to which information in memory is tapped, and quantitatively in the number of features extracted from the stimulus and from information in memory associated with it . . ."[12]

We may conclude, then that even at this preliminary stage, of awareness of a vague something there, which Rock calls the 'literal perception,' there is a *selective* patterning at the boundary between sense organ and sense field. The nature of the selectivity depends to some extent on the present *intentions* of the organism and on the history of its interactions with the environment. This is in accord with the skandha of form.

TO THE FINAL IMAGE

Rock argues that the process leading from the 'literal perception' to the final perception of an external scene with meaning is one so close to thinking that it may as well be considered a form of thinking. Through analysis of visual illusions and experiments, he proposes that "the basis of form perceptions, i.e. of the subjective experience of specific shape or, otherwise expressed, of the phenomenal similarities and differences among shapes, is a nonconscious nonverbal structural description of the shape. The description is given by the executive agency that is outside the sensory domain (the sixth consciousness?) based on the inspection of the proximal (initial) input. . . . The process is hierarchical, with properties emerging at higher levels that can have no reality at lower levels. The final step is a description of the category to which the object belongs, if it is known, and this can even affect the very description of the form under some conditions."[13]

The object is also stored in memory as a description, to be compared later to other objects, description with description. Rock's arguments for a descriptive basis for this storage are based on extensive analysis of a variety of perceptual phenomena: the perception of the path of a moving spot of light; the fact that an outline changes its shape according to which directions are designated up, down, etc.; the way in which complexity is recalled and the role of attention in this; the phenomenon of ambiguous figures.

I will not go into the details here, but all imply the involvement of high-level conceptual processing of the nature of a description. Obviously the language in which the organism describes scenes to itself cannot be natural language. This is clear first because the process of perceiving and storing objects is presumably well along the way in infants who have not yet learned a natural language, and second because a similar process presumably also takes place in animals. Rock suggests that the language may be the same as Fodor's 'language of thought,' the biologically based language-like system that is logically necessary in order for the learning of a natural language to be possible at all. And, as we saw in Chapter 8, there also appears to be capacity for pictorial storage and manipulation.

Rock now goes on to show that the way in which the final form is arrived at is highly analagous to problem solving and inference. Fundamentally the idea is that the initial 'literal' input is insufficient to determine the scene unambiguously. The perceptual process compares its description of this initial input with stored descriptions of objects provided from past experience in a process analogous to making and testing hypotheses to find the 'best fit.' This 'best fit' is the category of object finally settled on by the perceptual process to describe what is 'out there.' All this is taking place at the preconscious level.

The description of perception as a process of hypothesis formation and testing has also been extensively demonstrated by Richard Gregory among others and is quite widely accepted now. Gregory has given many examples based on a study of visual illusion. For example, in the old woman/young woman illusion of Figure 12-1 we can adopt either of the interpretations at will, once we have recognized

Figure 12-1

both. Gregory suggests that it is at the higher conceptual levels that this alternation back and forth takes place. In the case of Figure 12-2 in which we "see" a white triangle connecting the black figures, or of Figure 12-3 in which most people are able to "see" a spotted dog, the visual data are insufficient to determine the final image and we fill in the gaps with our projections.[14] Gregory and Rock, on the basis of many examples such as this, propose that all ordinary apparently unambiguous perception proceeds in this way. We are not normally aware of this process simply because it happens so fast.

In some ways this view of perception goes back to the suggestion of unconscious inference from sensation to judgment suggested by Helmholtz more than a century ago and elaborated by Wundt at the turn of this century. However, Rock points out some differences between the modern version and that of Wundt, principally that Wundt's first stage did not involve concept at all but was a direct manifestation in consciousness of the neurally encoded representation of the stimulus, the old 'raw sense data,' and his last stage was not one of perception of a final image but was more akin to rational judgment. The change in view is, then, that concept is now thought to enter significantly into the process all the way through from the earliest stages, and this whole process must now be regarded as 'perception.'

PATTERNS OF ASSOCIATION

We can presume that Rock's and Gregory's final perception is a combination of the fourth and fifth skandhas—formations and consciousness. We have already shown that the fifth skandha can be

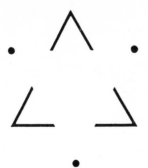

Figure 12-2

separated from the first four on the basis of various phenomena like "blindsight." The fourth skandha can also be separated from the fifth on the basis of the large amount of data of Freud, Jung, and their followers. The relevant finding here is the presence of various complex association patterns of concepts at a level below normal consciousness.

These association patterns have also been demonstrated experimentally. In the words of Norman Dixon, "Taking the view that preconscious thinking follows associative pathways, Spence and Holland have tested the hypothesis that the number of associations evoked by a stimulus of which the recipient is unaware would exceed that elicited by the same stimulus above the awareness threshold. . . . Spence concluded that, while at preconscious stages of perceptual development, verbal stimuli fan out to activate a wider range of associates, these become severely restricted as soon as the subject becomes aware of the stimulus." Dixon concludes that "being conscious of a stimulus in some way restricts such related cognitive processes as it might have set in motion . . . [and] there are many

Figure 12-3

other phenomena of a like kind which suggest that this restrictive effect may well be a general principle of cerebral functioning."[15] Spence's fanning out to "activate a wider range of associates" is the fourth skandha, formations, and is the beginning of conceptual proliferation.

EARLY AFFECTIVE REACTIONS

Based on the skandha description, we might now ask, Is there any evidence of a stage, akin to the skandha of feeling, interposed between the initial perception and the final conscious image? The answer is yes, there is evidence indicating that there is affective reaction at an early stage in the perceptual process, certainly prior to the stage of natural language labeling, the fourth skandha. First, of course, the fact that animals and preverbal infants experience emotional response to stimuli without verbal meaning analysis is a powerful statement to this.

In one type of experiment, reported by Dixon, unpleasant words, such as taboo words (penis, fuck, whore, etc.), presented subliminally produce galvanic skin responses (GSRs), which are evidence of emotional arousal, before the meaning of the word is detected. Further, nonsense syllables previously conditioned to be associated with unpleasant electric shocks can evoke GSRs even when they are presented too briefly for conscious recognition.

In another type of experiment, the word "Beef" was flashed for 1/200 second at 7-second intervals during the showing of a film. After the showing, subjects were required to rate themselves for hunger and encouraged to choose from an assortment of sandwiches. The subjects rated themselves significantly higher on hunger than did a control group. But their choice of type of sandwich was not affected. These results showed that whereas the below-threshold stimuli had a significant effect upon hunger ratings, they did not influence subsequent choice behavior. Dixon comments, "Evidently the feeling tone of hunger came into awareness but, presumably because it was unaccompanied by consciously perceived meaning, did not affect existing food preferences." Dixon summarizes the results of a number of experiments thus: "All in all, the findings . . . suggest that the meaning of a stimulus which does not enter awareness may nevertheless be analysed unconsciously and yet evoke consciously experienced feeling tone. . . . the absence of any conscious representation of stimulus meaning appears to restrict (presumably through non-labelling) certain behaviours or somatic outcomes of the unconsciously registered stimulus."[16]

In order for emotional response at this level, there must be some extraction of meaning at a level prior to verbal labeling. That this is the case has been indicated in other experiments. A. J. Marcel in particular argues that as we learn to interpret the significance of a set of cues, "we are aware of that significance instead of or before we are aware of the cues."[17] Marcel and others have shown that under some conditions there is evidence that people "know" to which category a specific event belongs (e.g., furniture, landscape) without being able to identify which particular item they had witnessed. And unidentifiable words still significantly affect the interpretation of material presented later. For example, Marcel presented single words at the point where subjects were fixating, and masked them by a random pattern so that subjects could not tell whether a word had preceded or not.[18] They were offered a choice between (1) whether a word had been present or not; (2) whether that word was visually more similar to one or the other of two possible words, or (3) whether it was more similar in meaning to one or the other or two possible words.

Some subjects were persuaded to continue guessing as the words were presented more and more briefly. Performance fell to a chance level first on (1), then on (2), then on (3), implying that meaning is extracted at energy levels lower than physical form. This result is not restricted to words; similar results have been found with pictures. Notice that the extraction of physical form to which Marcel is referring here is form that can be named. Thus these results indicate that meaning may be extracted, and presumably responded to affectively, before the form is named.

There are debates about the interpretation of some of these results. However, as Dixon, Mandler, and others point out, in addition to these experimental indications, there are good evolutionary grounds for the possibility of affective response without full cognitive processing. First, any given affect may accompany a wide range of conscious perceptual experiences; second, affects signal merely the threat value or need relatedness of an external stimulus. They may therefore interrupt a conscious experience and signal an alarm prior to a full cognitive analysis of their cause. Affective signals thus may fulfill three different roles at the same time—that of an alarm signal, that of directing attention to the underlying need or threat, and that of a motive toward behavior that will meet the need (the reduction of unpleasant feeling tone), all without the presence of conscious meaning analysis.

AGREEMENT BETWEEN BUDDHISM
AND THE SCIENCES OF MIND

I have shown in this chapter that there is a significant amount of work in experimental psychology that can confirm aspects of the process of perception discovered in the practice of meditation: that perception takes a finite time; that it occurs in stages involving an initial perception with some conceptual content, an emotional response, a verbal meaning analysis, and finally consciousness. This potential area of agreement between Buddhist meditative insight and experimental psychology is related to specific details of a directly observable process, and it provides suggestions for further research: the third skandha, perception, has so far not been separated at all by experimental psychology, although the role of perceptual grasping of the object has been recognized by emotion theorists such as Magda Arnold.[18] Furthermore the enrichment is not one-directional. The experimental investigations are able to enrich the Buddhist insights by their detailed elaboration of the causal mechanisms involved. Finally, Buddhism and experimental psychology agree that our conscious perception and action are affected by profound prejudices beyond our conscious control, as demonstrated in the work on perceptual defense and on decision-making. The two also agree that, whatever we may believe for religious, philosophical, or political reasons, consciousness (the fifth skandha) plays only a limited role in the perceptions and actions of everyday life. Most important of all, Buddhism and the sciences of mind agree that perception is an active process in which what we think of as the 'outside world' is, like the 'self,' a conceptual, symbolic fabrication.

The reader will not, however, have found any reference to the unconditioned dharma in the account of the sciences. I introduced the 'unconditional dharma' in Chapter 5 as a momentary gap in the flow of perceptual moments that brings with it a sense of freedom from habitual patterning. That cognitive science remains unaware of this gap is probably for at least two reasons. First the sciences have not yet realized the need to train attention to fine time intervals and have not fully acknowledged the importance of the discontinuity of that process. This does not seem to be an insurmountable problem. Second, the unconditioned dharma can be only pointed to, but not literally described, by symbolic means, such as language. We will examine this point very thoroughly when we discuss the role of language in the world-fabricating process. Since objective science deals essentially in the symbolic representation of phenomena, this is a very serious problem. We might expect that the sciences of mind will be able to clearly delimit the *boundaries* of the discontinuity of perception, perhaps to the point of the origin of self and world, as the analysis of Maturana and Varela has begun to do. But we would not expect that the cognitive sciences will be able to penetrate beyond those boundaries with present dualistic methods.

There is another point of view from which we can begin to understand the unconditioned dharmas, the gaps in the perceptual process. Our discussion has suggested that the appearance of continuity in our everyday perceptual world is brought about by the patching job of the fifth skandha, divided self-consciousness. Self-consciousness, as we have seen, dwells in the language web that goes to the root of our dualistic being. The continuity of the world of everyday perceptions can also be expressed as the continuity of the perceived sense of time. And we might wonder at this point about this perceived continuity in time. If the continuity of our perceptual world is open to question, is this not also true of the continuity of our perceived time? We will take up this question in the next chapter.

13

Time and Nowness

•

NOW LET US LOOK from a different viewpoint at what is obscured by obsession with the belief in the continuity of the 'external world,' as well as the corresponding 'internal world.' One of the boundary conditions of the conventional world is time. We feel that time bounds our world, that our world is contained within time. We have seen that being caught up in the conceptual discriminations of divided self-consciousness provides a sense of continuity of our present, but that even the ordinarily experienced present comes from the projections of memory, which is the past. Therefore if, through the practice of mindfulness or otherwise, we become aware of this whole process, then we become aware of this process happening at this very moment, which cannot be in the past, the future, *or the conventional present*. This moment is sometimes referred to in Buddhist traditions as the fourth moment, or *nowness*, to distinguish it from the imagined, or conceptualized present, the conventional present of the 'external/internal world.'[1]

There is a sense in which we are going beyond science as it is currently practiced, which assumes a one-faceted view of time, an abstract universal entity independent of human mind and observation. Science does not speak of what *now* is, but assumes it in all of its activities and theories. There is no place for the fourth moment in the 'normal' science of today, from two points of view. First, each such moment is entirely unique. This actual moment never happens again. This is not a philosophical point, it is a very obvious point. Yet science in its very nature deals only with events that are reproducible, following general laws or describable patterns. It deals only with the general characteristics of moments, never with the actuality of *this* moment. It can deal with red in general, or aggression in general, but it cannot deal with this red that I am now seeing, or this aggression that I am now expressing. Yet if any transformation of human perception is possible it is possible only now. Only this

165

particular moment of aggression can be transformed, not some generalized idea of anger, but the living energy of this particular anger that is felt right now.

The second reason that science does not accommodate the fourth moment is that for science time is outside of observation, but assumed in all observation, and is a measure of the passing of something relative to another thing: the apparent daily passing of the sun around the earth, of the earth around the sun, of sand in a sandtimer, of electrons around a nucleus in an atomic clock. The time assumed by science is thus the relative measurement of the separation between two moments neither of which is *now*, both of which have already past by the time science measures them.

This universal linear time, given the label '*t*' in all the equations of physics and chemistry, is supposed to form, together with space, a kind of framework within which events happen, while itself being outside of those events. And this one-faceted time dominates our modern way of life entirely. We believe that such a 'time' is real, that it exists, that it is what we measure on our watches, and the scientists measure on their atomic clocks, that it bounds our births and deaths and goes on beyond both.

Yet this abstract universal time is an invention. In our own culture prior to the late Middle Ages, time was an expression of the fact that appearances change. Time was not separate from changing appearances. Plato and Aristotle, the two most influential Greek natural philosophers, who disagreed at many points, both described no time outside of change. For those who, like Plato, held that true reality is unchanging, this true reality is outside of time, and therefore beyond appearances. But there was no time other than in phenomena. And this view of time held throughout the discussions of the ancient and medieval philosophers. It is the way time is thought of in most nonscientific societies, from the great Chinese and Indian civilizations to the Native American and Balinese societies.

However, as physicist and historian Geza Szamosi has shown, in the late Middle Ages a number of factors combined to give rise to a new concept, the concept of mathematical time outside of changing things.[2] This concept was used by Galileo in his experiments on motion, and finally articulated in the form it came down to us by Isaac Newton. Newton, in one of his most famous and profoundly influential proclamations, said, "Absolute, true and mathematical time, of itself, and from its own nature, flows equably without relation to anything external." Useful as it was for his calculations to assume such a 'thing,' this was pure invention. Yet we now believe in this 'thing' called 'time' so deeply that we are willing to fight and die for it. And it is no accident that this abstract 'time' was invented just shortly before Descartes came up with his brilliant invention of the individual little minds mirroring nature. For Descartes, body or matter was that which was extended in space while mind was that which was extended in time. And as time was now "absolute, of itself, and from its own nature, . . . without relation to anything external," so too was mind.

THREE LEVELS OF 'TIME'

Yet reflective scientists know very well that this one-faceted view of time is simply inadequate to account for the richness of the natural world, which includes life and consciousness. In the past fifteen years a series of conferences organized by the International Society for the Study of Time have at least begun to clarify the complexity and richness of those aspects of phenomena to which we give the name 'time.'[3] Two things stand out at the beginning of such discussions and reflections. The first is that 'time' cannot be said to 'exist.' Because to say something *is* is to say that it *is* in time. It is simply logical nonsense to say 'time' is in time. Likewise the commonplace idea that "time passes" is nonsense. Time passes relative to what? The first point, then is that 'time' is not a 'thing,' nor does it pass.

Second, 'time' is not at all a unitary concept referring to one single real thing. It is a multitiered or multifaceted concept. This multitiered nature of the time concept has been very clearly analyzed by Kenneth Denbigh, a chemist and Fellow of the Royal Society, in *Three Concepts of Time*.[4] At least three clearly distinct concepts can be separated out under the label 'time.' First there is the abstract time of physicists, invented by Newton and essentially carried over into relativity and quantum theory. Second is the time of living organisms and biochemical processes, and third the time of ordinary conscious experience.

When we ignore the role of conceptual fabrication in the construction of the conscious present, then we see a world 'out there,' and in that world we see change. In this way we come to the time of Plato and Aristotle, to the time of the biologists, and perhaps closest to the ordinary experience of a changing world. In this world there appear to be 'things,' and these things appear to change; this change occurs in time. And the most important characteristic of this change is that it is irreversible: if we drop an egg it breaks, trees grow from seeds, humans develop from the fetus through birth, old age, and death. None of these changes occurs in the reverse order; we never see a tree becoming a seedling and then a seed. In fact if we were to see a film of the everyday world run backwards we would immediately know that this was the case. The irreversibility of all natural phenomena has been the greatest thorn in the sides of scientists since the time of Newton, because in the abstract time of physics all physical processes are reversible, including the processes described by relativity and quantum mechanics. The only kind of film that we would not be able to detect running backwards would be a film of planetary motion or one of billiard balls bouncing around on a billiard table. This is the closest approximation we have in the ordinary world of anything like a classical physical system. And even here, if the film ran long enough we would eventually notice that the balls were slowing down (or speeding up) in which case we would know that it was being run forwards (or backwards.)

In recent decades some theoreticians have been able to show that the irreversible time of everyday appearance can be derived from the reversible time of physics. In particular Ilya Prigogine in developing the thermodynamics of open systems, which I describe in Chapter 17, showed that each system has its own time and each of these system times is irreversible.[5] The unique time line associated with each system describes the pathway that that system has taken in developing increasing complexity and higher energy levels. This begins to approach biological time, in which each organism has its own internal clock that measures its personal constitution and history. The importance of this work has led Prigogine to title one of his books *The Birth of Time,* by which he refers of course to the possibility at last of including a more real understanding of time in the conceptual world of science.[6] Nevertheless even this is a strange twist on the logic of experience, which begins with the ever-changing creativity of the conscious moment and generalizes from that point to the constant change of appearances and only from there derives, in thought, the abstract, reversible time of physics.

As we have seen, conscious experience and its unconscious supporting processes occur as a series of moments of finite duration. Estimates of the duration of an experiential moment vary from one-tenth to one one-hundredth of a second depending on the type of test and the sensory channel being tested. We experience a continuous world because we normally do not attend to the transitions between moments and because each moment contains not just present perceptions but also memories of past moments and anticipations of the future. That is to say, our conscious present moments appear to overlap. That our conscious experience is discontinuous but overlapping in this way has been known in the West since the experimental psychology of the nineteenth century. William James adopted the label 'specious present' for this experiential moment, because he thought that it was simply a construction of subjective neurological processes while the 'true present' must be that of the physicists. With the coming of behaviorism the 'specious present' was ignored and it is only in the past few decades, with the rediscovery of the temporal duration of the basic perceptual processes, that attention has again turned to it. I have shown in detail in the first part of this book that the experiential present is a conceptual fabrication in which the world experienced as 'outside,' as well as the 'inner' self that experiences it, arise together within emptiness, become conscious, and decay together. Thus this time, like the other two, the physical and biological times, is a conceptual fabrication.

What we ordinarily refer to as 'time' is a confused conglomeration of all three concepts, the time of consciousness, the time of 'external' phenomena, and the abstract time of physics. It is, Denbigh suggests, complex and multitiered, the three concepts forming a series of increasing abstraction and decreasing richness. From the time of appearances, the abstract mathematical time of physical processes deletes the sense of past, present, and future, of 'ongoingness' and of irreversibility, as well as the presence of the experiencer. Biological time replaces irreversibility but still omits the observer. In this series the time of consciousness is logically as well as experientially primary, the other two concepts being constructed through verbal and other symbols. But even our conscious sense of time is a product of language. The life that I watch flowing past me, 'inside' or 'outside,' is the conceptual life of my inner language, my discursive self-consciousness. Similarly the world that science describes is one that flows past some imaginary observer in linguistic or some other symbolic representation. As G. J. Whitrow, Professor of History and Application of Mathematics at the University of London and another scientist who has made a lifetime's study of time, says, *"Our 'sense' of time is neither a necessary condition of our experience, as Kant thought, nor a simple sensation, as Mach believed, but an intellectual construction. It depends on processes of mental organization uniting thought and action. It is a late product of human evolution, in all probability closely related to the development of language."*[7] And indeed studies have shown that the gradual acquirement of particular temporal conceptions can be closely correlated with the child's acquisition and use of language.

William James, one of the few American psychologists to make any contribution to understanding consciousness before it was engorged by behaviorism, made a beginning at understanding this linear flow of consciousness. In one of his most well-known passages, James said, "Like a bird's life, [the stream of consciousness] seems to be made of an alternation of flights and perchings. The rhythm of language expresses this, where every thought is expressed in a sentence, and every sentence closed by a period. The resting-places are usually occupied by sensorial imaginations of some sort, whose peculiarity is that they can be held before the mind for an indefinite time, and contemplated without changing; the places of flight are filled with thoughts of relations, static or dynamic, that for the most part obtain between the matters contemplated in the periods of comparative rest. *Let us call the resting-places the 'substantive parts' and the places of flight the 'transitive parts,' of the stream of thought.* It then appears that the main end of our thinking is at all times the attainment of some other substantive part than the one from which we have just left. And we may say that the main use of the transitive parts is to lead us from one substantive part to another."[8]

James delightfully catches the rhythm of thought here, its fickleness, its alternation between slow contemplation and rapid movement. Yet for us the more interesting points are the moments of transition between thoughts, between and within the substantive parts and the transitive parts. Later in this passage James remarks on how difficult it is to catch the "transitive" parts. How much more difficult it is to see what is taking place at the very moment of change from a substantive part to a transitive part, or from a transitive part to a substantive part. Apparently, James did not realize that even in the "resting places" the mind moves: the "contemplation" of "sensorial imaginations" he speaks of is expressed in language. It is only at the breaks between thoughts, which are so swift as to be almost imperceptible to untrained attention, that there is any freedom from the domination of language and from the movement of thought.

From all of this discussion we can begin to see that when *nowness* as awareness beyond past, present, and future is spoken of, it is synonymous with awareness beyond conceptualization, beyond divided self-consciousness. The conceptualized 'times' of physics and of the rational world are all embedded in and derived by abstraction from the time of conscious experience.

TIME IS MULTIFACETED

Understanding that the time of conscious experience is primary, in order to appreciate its richness and to try to see where gaps might arise in the linear view, we must examine all the data available on the experience of time, and particularly the data that are excluded by the strongest adherents to the one-dimensional, one-faceted view: I refer specifically to data on precognition and meaningful coincidence. Although it is of course important to be as careful in gathering such data as in any field of investigation, the irrational and sometimes fanatical attempts to deny these data would seem to be a symptom of the very powerful grip that the linear view of time has on conventional science and commonsense belief. Carl Sargent, the coauthor of a book on these phenomena with a respected elder of statistical psychology, Hans Eysenck, reports that a colleague of his at the University of London said to him after a presentation of his research on precognition, "The results you presented would convince me of anything else, but this: I just *cannot* believe it and I don't know why."[9]

On precognition there are of course innumerable anecdotal reports many of which are hard to verify, but some of which—for example those relating to a mining disaster in the Aberfan Valley in Wales in 1966—have been verified beyond reasonable doubt. About twenty years ago British poet laureate J. B. Priestley announced on BBC-TV that he was conducting an investigation into unusual experiences in regard to time. He invited viewers to write to him and received thousands of letters. These were investigated by a team of scientifically trained and avowedly skeptical investigators, whose job was to eliminate fraud and obvious error and reports that could be explained in a 'normal' way. Priestley was left with several dozen reports of precognition that could not be explained away.[10]

Psychiatrists such as Carl Jung and Alex Comfort have pointed out that precognition is reported especially in situations of psychological counseling, when people are perhaps less afraid of being considered silly and more willing to notice fleeting images.[11] Hundreds of such well-documented anecdotes have been reported, and perhaps thousands more have gone unreported. They occur by chance, we cannot manipulate them, and they have no particular importance, and for just this reason we might have even less reason to doubt them than we have to doubt the more dramatic instances.

On the experimental work done on precognition, the early work in the laboratory of J. B. Rhine was open to the criticisms of sloppiness and of not demonstrating adequate precaution against fraud.[12] But in the past two decades much more careful work has been done that, according to all the standards of careful science, demonstrates seemingly strong evidence for precognitive events. One example of such experimental work is that of Helmut Schmidt, a physicist working for Boeing Research Laboratories in Seattle, who built a machine that tests precognition without any intervention of a human recorder. This work is reported in *Explaining the Unexplained*, by Sargent and Eysenck. Hans Eysenck has been for decades one of the leaders in the statistical analysis and assessment of personality traits.

Ray Hyman, a distinguished critic of parapsychology, says of Schmidt's work, "By almost any standard, Schmidt's work is the most challenging ever to confront critics such as myself. His approach makes many of the earlier criticisms of parapsychological research obsolete. [I am] convinced that he was sincere, honest and dedicated to being as scientific as possible . . . the most sophisticated parapsychologist that I have encountered. If there are flaws in his work, they are not the more obvious or common ones." Sargent and Eysenck estimate that if the odds against Schmidt's work's being due to chance were written down, the "millions" would cover quite a few lines; in other words, they are astronomical. They add that the only possible alternative explanation for Schmidt's work, other than some under-standing of time beyond the common linear one, seems to be whole-sale fraud.[13] However, everyone who has met Schmidt, including skeptics such as Hyman, finds this extremely unlikely. Furthermore, his work has been reproduced independently by several people.

Perhaps of all the kinds of events that point beyond the linear, one-faceted view of time, the one we are most familiar with is that of meaningful coincidences. A meaningful coincidence consists of two simultaneous events that appear to be interconnected, though not by the separate causes that gave rise to them individually. For example, probably many of us have experienced something like speaking to someone about a mutual friend, whom neither of us has heard from in five years, when just at that moment the phone rings and it is that friend calling. Several well-known authors have described desperately searching, sometimes for hours, for an obscure piece of information, when a book falls open at the very page they needed. For example, Rebecca West reports that as she was searching for a record of an incident in the Nuremberg trials, "I looked up the trials in the library and was horrified to find they are published in a form almost useless to the researcher. They are abstracts, and are catalogued under arbitrary headings. After hours of search I went along the line of shelves to an assistant librarian and said: 'I can't find it, there's no clue, it may be in any of these volumes.' (There are shelves of them.) I put my hand on one volume and took it out and carelessly looked at it, and it was not only the right volume, but I had opened it at the right page."[14]

Just as with precognition, we have no more reason to doubt the veracity of these stories than we have to doubt the veracity of a scientist's report of his work, so long of course as we open ourselves to a broader view of time and causality. Unlike precognition, meaningful coincidences occur quite frequently in the lives of many people, and often provide a sense of direction for one's life. As I was finishing my Ph.D. thesis in physics in 1964, the possibility of a change in fields came up. I spent several weeks thinking over whether to make the rather big leap from theoretical physics to experimental biology, and finally the day arrived when I had to make the decision. Walking along the street, still uncertain, I came across a traffic jam, and there right in front of me was the bus leading directly to the biology laboratory. I climbed on the bus and reported to the director of the laboratory that I would like to go and work there. That is how the decision was made that led to a tremendous expansion of possibilities in my life, in more directions than biology. Similar incidents are almost commonplace and have probably occurred in the lives of many readers.

There is much more general willingness to acknowledge that such coincidences happen than is the case with precognition, probably because such events can more easily be incorporated, as 'pure chance,' into a conventional view of time. The issue here, though, is whether they are *meaningful*. The key point is the lack of apparent causality in such events, and it is this acausality in the linear, deterministic sense that causes most 'normal' scientists to reject them. Yet the simplistic ideas of rigid causality and determinism carried over from nineteenth-century determinism are widely questioned by many reflecting scientists today. Most philosophers of science adopt a view that, in its balance between determinism and indeterminism, chance and necessity, is very similar to the Buddhist view of pratitya samudpada, dependent co-origination or situational patterning, that I introduced in Chapter 5. The Tibetan term for this is *tendrel*, which has been translated as 'auspicious coincidence.'

Astrophysicist Michael Shallis suggests that in order to accommodate precognition and meaningful coincidence into our understanding of time we need to regard the time of consciousness, too, as multifaceted. "Coincidence as a temporal phenomenon is a wonderful example of time's duality. If the concept of the dual nature of light as both wave and particle is acceptable . . . then coincidences should help in the no more strange idea that time displays the duality of the connected, linear causal side of its nature and its acausal, interconnected aspect. The experience of time through coincidence points to a much more complex, much more bewildering and awesome aspect of nature that was overlooked in the more familiar descriptions of the apparently explicable and controllable world given by instructional [normal] science." [15]

This other aspect of time has been recognized in the Western alchemical and hermetic traditions as well as in the Chinese Confucian and Taoist traditions, in the Javanese shadow theatre, in the Native American rain dances, and in just about every culture not dominated by the scientific concept of objective linear time. In many of these traditions it is connected with the recognition of correspondences between various realms of existence: inanimate, plant, animal, human, and heavenly. What appear to be "chance" coincidences when we consider only a narrow realm of experience are recognized to be dependent on multifaceted causes when a larger realm is included. In many traditions also, such as the Greek, these larger realms of existence were symbolized by the gods, who, while conducting their own affairs independently of people, could also at times enter into and affect the affairs of people—such times being turning points in the lives of those affected.

Assuming that time is only of the linear type measured by clocks, there can be no place for precognition or meaningful coincidence in the natural world. We can respond to this in one of three ways. We can discount all the observations, or we can accept the observations and claim that they provide evidence for a 'supernatural' or 'paranormal' realm, or we can accept carefully documented evidence and suggest that our idea of time, as well as of what is 'normal,' needs to be expanded. It would seem that, of the three, the third alternative is by far the most 'rational' and in keeping with the scientific tradition. That is, we could suggest not that the common view of time, and of nature, is wrong, but only that it is too limited.

There is no reason to dismiss honest and carefully gathered data merely because they go against the authority of the times. There is good reason not to cling to the narrowly defined and altogether incoherent idea of time as an abstract, linear 'something' that flows evenly outside of us. As Shallis says in summarizing his researches: "Objective time has gone. It has gone in relativity, gone from the quantum world, gone in cosmology, where scales and redefinitions of time are arbitrary. Objective time has vanished in the paranormal. Only in the 'normal' world, which has been impoverished by our definitions and explanations which define poorly and explain little, does objective time still hold sway. One thing seen in this journey is that the time we think we inhabit is neither simple, linear nor objective. We are immersed in pools of time and timelessness, in a sea of causality and acausal connections."[16]

NOWNESS

We find then that the concept of time is far more rich, complex, and multifaceted than the impoverished commonsense or scientific view of it. Yet when we join all these various facets, the situation again seems to be simple: we experience a 'stream of consciousness,' by which is meant divided self-consciousness in which the experiencer separates himself or herself off from what is being experienced. This 'stream of consciousness' is experienced as having components of past, present, and future. When consciousness ceases to divide itself, then, for however brief a moment, time ceases. That is nowness.

The perception of nowness is described in the vivid words of Chögyam Trungpa, Rinpoche:

> Sometimes when we perceive the world, we perceive without language. We perceive spontaneously with a pre-language system. But sometimes when we perceive the world we think a word first, and then we perceive. In other words, the first instance is directly feeling or perceiving the universe, the second instance is talking ourselves into seeing our universe. So either you see the world through the filter of your thoughts, by talking to yourself, or you look and see beyond language—as first perception. . . . When you feel that you can afford to relax and perceive the world directly, then your vision can expand. You can see on the spot with wakefulness. Your eyes begin to open, wider and wider, and you see that the world is colorful and fresh and so precise; every angle is fantastic.

In a later passage Trungpa explains further: "Your sense faculties give you access to possibilities of deeper perception. Beyond ordinary perception, there is super-sound, super-smell and super-feeling existing in your state of being. These can be experienced only by training yourself in the depth of meditation practice, which clarifies confusion or cloudiness and brings out the precision, sharpness, and wisdom of perception—the nowness of your world. . . . Normally we limit the meaning of perception. Food reminds us of eating; dirt reminds us to clean the house. . . . In other words we fit what we see into a comfortable or familiar scheme. We shut any vastness or possibilities of deeper perceptions out of our hearts by fixating on our own interpretations of phenomena. But it is possible to go beyond personal interpretation, to let vastness into our hearts through the medium of perception. We always have a choice: we can limit our perception so that we close off vastness, or we can allow vastness to touch us."[17]

Krishnamurti, who was hailed in his youth as the expected great world spiritual teacher, and then shocked all his followers by renouncing all tradition, authority, and 'isms' of every kind, traveled the world speaking of "Freedom from the Known" for fifty years until his death in 1986. He describes the experience of nowness, or 'freedom from thought' in this way: "Words and theories become amazingly important. . . . The brain and its thought functions at a very superficial level, however deeply thought may have hoped it has journeyed. The brain and its activities are a fragment of the whole totality of life; the fragment has become completely important to itself. . . . Thought can never formulate the whole of life. Only when the brain and its thought are completely still, not asleep or drugged by discipline, compulsion or hypnosis, then only is there the awareness of the whole. . . . The complete stillness of the brain is an extraordinary thing; it is highly sensitive, vigorous, fully alive, aware of every outward movement but utterly still. It is as still as it is completely open, without any hindrance, without any secret wants and pursuits. It is even without a center, without a border.[18]

Over and over again in his conversations, Krishnamurti stresses that awareness beyond thought is neither dull nor inactive, but is fully alive. He says, "When the whole pattern, when this whole structure [of observer and observed] has been understood, conflict has come to an end; and therefore the mind—because the mind *is* this awareness—has become extraordinarily sensitive, highly intelligent. In this awareness, because it has exposed everything very clearly . . . there is clarity. And this clarity is attention. When there is this attention, in which there is no observer nor observed, this attention is intelligence. . . . And, this attention has its own activity, its own action. So there is an action which is not born out of the observer. When the observer acts, his action is always separate. We cannot go further into this matter unless you actually *do* it. Then you will find that attention being intelligence, is beauty and love—which the observer, separate, tries to imitate—then the mind has no limit."[19]

For Buddhist teacher Trungpa Rinpoche, as well as for the renegade from tradition, Krishnamurti, nowness is not 'world-denying.' It is actually, for however brief a moment, living fully in the world, free from the barrier of preconception; free from the 'known,' which is imagination, memory, and the past; and free from the 'unknown,' which is the future and projection of the past into the future. Nor does 'freedom from thought' mean that rational mind is abandoned. On the contrary, because it is seen clearly rational mind can be used as a tool, rather than a drug that numbs against the brilliance of perception. For both Trungpa Rinpoche and Krishnamurti, perception of that nowness brings with it freshness as well as tremendous energy. This is powerful energy that does not have to be cranked up within one's self but that already exists within phenomena as they are, and that one can connect with further and further as the self is less and less involved. In later chapters we will examine further the quality of awareness within nowness.

In Chapter 15 I will present the method by which Buddhist practitioners of meditation have unravelled the perceptual process into temporal stages which, as I have shown, are quite well confirmed by some of the data of modern science. Before we do this we will, in the next chapter, take a look at some other facets of the idea of mind so that we can discuss meditation from a broader point of view than the narrow idea of the little mirror in the head, forever separated from everyone and everything. For there still remains the question of how is it that the perceptual process culminating in self-consciousness can be known at all? What is the nature of the awareness that directly knows this whole process? Is it anything at all?

14

Joining Intellect and Intuition

IN CHAPTER 11 I suggested that it is no more than an act of faith to postulate that there are individual minds that, passively or actively, mirror nature, are localized in individual bodies, and are forever separate from other similar minds. Nowadays this belief is being challenged from within science rather than merely from the streams of thought that have stood outside of science and berated it from afar. To some extent the problem with the views that we have been discussing is that these views are based on inattention to the subtle details of what it is that we do or can perceive, and an overemphasis on the gross aspects of perception as it is similar to thought. It is taken for granted that what we do in fact perceive is a solid continuous world full of objects. It is very much a thinker's world, the world of the rational man, the businessman and the practical man, in which the subtleties of perception long known to women, artists, and psychotics is largely ignored.

INTUITION REAPPEARS

There has however always been available evidence that suggests that the human organism is able to experience nonseparateness in a direct way, not mediated by thought. This experiencing, which seems to occur suddenly and perhaps very briefly, has been referred to as "flashes of insight," "sudden intuition," "hunches," or "creative moments." These were ignored or even ridiculed by many generations of scientists and by an educational system that recognized only the systematic analysis of intellect as a valid form of knowledge. The description of "The Scientific Method" in school books usually makes very little mention of this experiencing, if any.

Artists have always acknowledged such moments, but art has not been regarded as a valid means of knowledge in a society dominated by the standard view of science. Art has been thought of more as recreation, a relic of less enlightened times, or as therapy. Such moments are, of course, also reported by the mystical writers. But the dualistic religious context in which these moments have occurred and the corresponding language in which they have been reported have given the impression that these writers are reporting 'otherworldly' phenomena. This is an impression quite the contrary of what contemplatives have actually said about their experience. In any case, the traditional wars between science and religion, as well as between conventional religion and mysticism, have made these reports unacceptable all around.

However, in recent decades scientists themselves have begun to admit that without such moments there would *be* no science. So at least now there is a body of anecdotal evidence that such moments happen, even to scientists, and that often the quality of experience at such moments is quite different from that at moments of mundane experience. There is a sense of fullness and totality, and a discovery of insight that often takes many days or even years to formulate in the language of intellect. There are several well-known cases in which these insightful moments have led to major scientific breakthroughs: the chemist Kekule discovering the structure of the benzene ring as he gazed into a fire; mathematician Henri Poincare, who describes solving a problem he had been working on for months as he stepped onto a bus; and Albert Einstein describes his realization of the principles of general relativity as arriving suddenly and completely after which it took him years to find an appropriate language in which to express these insights. In each of these cases, and there are many others, a complete and radical break with conventional patterns of thought was needed and was found.[1]

It is not necessarily the whole that is being experienced under these circumstances. And indeed the idea of 'the whole' would seem to be itself a trap given the openness and non-thing-thinking that we have been pointing to all along. The point is that whatever is experienced, it is experienced as a whole and not as fragmented. It is, in particular, not experienced as fragmented into observer and object. Thus it is not experienced as conventional perception or thought, and there is, therefore, often some difficulty in describing the experience later. In fact it is often the aftereffect of such a flash that is described, the flash itself being too brief, and the experiencer not having the language available to describe it. Unfortunately it is very difficult to do systematic, repeatable experiments on such experience because one of their characteristics seems to be that such moments are, as they occur naturally, not systematic, repeatable or predictable.

These questions are important because if our analysis is correct in pointing to an active process of perception that fabricates our world, and to an undivided ground for experience in which there is not a distinction between the experience and the subject of experience, then we would certainly like to be able to connect our awareness with such a fundamental aspect of our being. Fragmentation in thought and perception naturally results in fragmentation of our projections, that which we believe thought to be about (whether there is or is not a 'that' that thought is about). Thus our minds become fragmented from our bodies, each of us becomes separated from each other, we feel ourselves to be separated from nature and from our society, nation is separated from nation—all this in large part the result of fragmented thinking and perceiving, of 'thing-thinking.' If our perception and thought are indeed based on undividedness, as this analysis has suggested and as moments of insight also suggest, then to connect conscious rational discrimination with insight arising directly from undividedness, that is to join intellect and intuition, may heal such fragmentation.

These questions may be important to scientists apart from the fact that scientists, too, are experiencing humans. For if the new context for science has some validity, and if reliable means can be found for testing it, then it may be possible for science to expand its scope to contribute to the inevitable change of society resulting from the discovery, or rather recovery, of nonduality. The only alternative would be for science to constitute a major obstacle to this change and eventually lose its authority altogether. Science in our society has become the major custodian of intellect and analytical 'reality' testing. It is therefore important that science does not lose its authority entirely, for if it does, the growing interest in intuition and 'holism' may result in a resurgence of blind faith in any magical and occult practices that anyone comes up with. This would be a disastrous step backward.

We see this happening already, with people flocking to southern California to live near a middle-class housewife claiming to be the reincarnation of a 35,000-year-old man; with young people getting trapped in all kinds of cults that tighten the grip of concept rather than free it; with millions of people, looking for a "quick fix," attending training programs proclaimed to change one's life in one weekend. A major factor contributing to this may well be that the authority of science has, generally speaking, refused so far to recognize the actuality of intuitive insight or any validity to the insights of intuition.

In recent decades there have been a few scientists who, reflecting on the foundations and activity of science, have realized the need for broadening our view of the relationship between mind and nature and of the nature and source of knowledge. Particularly articulate have been mathematician and philosopher Alfred North Whitehead, chemist Michael Polanyi, and anthropologist and biologist Gregory Bateson.

WHITEHEAD'S CAUSAL EFFICACY

Alfred North Whitehead began his professional life as a mathematician and logician and wrote, with Bertrand Russell, a groundbreaking work on the foundations of mathematics. In his middle life he wrote extensively on the foundations of physics, while having an active career as an educational administrator. In the final twenty years of his life Whitehead developed the 'philosophy of process,' which is regarded by many as the most profound and far-reaching philosophical system since that of Plato. It should be added in fairness that it was also regarded as very muddle-headed by behaviorists and analytic philosophers. Process philosophy is grounded in nonduality, but provides a very extensive understanding of how dualistic phenomena, particularly in the scientific realm, arise from this ground. Although Whitehead had very little knowledge of Buddhism, process philosophy is widely regarded as being very close to Buddhism. Whitehead's account of perception is strikingly close to the one I have developed here, based on Buddhism and the findings of modern psychology. Whitehead, too, recognized that perception occurs in temporal stages and recognized the importance of the preconscious stages. He recognized especially the importance of the role of feeling and valuation at the earliest stages.

For Whitehead the conscious perceptual process, the 'sense perception' isolated by Descartes, Locke, and Hume that forms the empiricist basis for science, was only one side of the story. Whitehead called this perceptual process 'presentational immediacy;—"our immediate perception of the contemporary external world, appearing as an element constitutive of our own experience. In this appearance the world discloses itself to be a community of actual things, which are actual in the same sense as we are."[2] In pure presentational immediacy there is no sense of causality, no connection with preceding moments of experience, therefore no symbolism and no meaning. This is in fact the problem that David Hume met, as well as all the behavioral philosophers and linguists of the present time: if perception is merely the reception into the organism of bare sensory data, how does meaning arise and how is the discovery of causal connections possible?

Whitehead pointed to another mode of perception, which he called 'causal efficacy'—the feeling of the relationship between the present moment and the immediate past moment, the felt continuity of the world as we perceive it. It is the causal 'weight' of the world impressing itself on this moment so that this moment conforms to some degree to the past moment. It occurs in all grades of organism from the lowest sentient organism to people, unlike presentational immediacy, which occurs only in complex organisms. In all organisms it is the felt presence of the body, it is the recognition of the body as the basis of feeling. Whitehead says, "sense perception of the contemporary world is accompanied by perception of the 'withness' of the body. It is this 'withness' that makes the body the starting point for our knowledge of the circumambient world. We find here our direct knowledge of 'causal efficacy.' Hume and Descartes in their theory of direct perceptive knowledge dropped out this withness of the body; and thus confined perception to presentational immediacy."

Presentational immediacy is clear and distinct, is comprised of the elements of experience that we can consciously select out and is relatively trivial. Causal efficacy is vague and imprecise, and is the interconnection between the immediately perceived present and the felt totality of the immediately preceding moment. For this reason, as Whitehead says, "It is evident that 'perception in the mode of causal efficacy' is not that sort of perception which has received chief attention in the philosophical tradition. Philosophers have disdained the information about the universe obtained through their visceral feelings, and have concentrated on visual feelings."[3]

For Whitehead, meaning comes not from the relations between linguistic symbols, but only from the connection between the two modes of perception. Both modes of perception are always necessarily present at any moment, but since we have so much emphasized presentational immediacy in our theories of perception we have actually begun to lose awareness of causal efficacy. Thus our perceptions gradually become shallow and meaningless. And the society built on these perceptions reflects their shallowness and meaninglessness.

POLANYI'S TACIT KNOWING

Michael Polanyi has made a very similar distinction between two kinds of knowing, which he calls 'focal awareness' and 'tacit' or 'subsidiary awareness.' Focal awareness is fully conscious awareness of the focus of attention. Tacit awareness is awareness that arises from subsidiary facts bearing on the focus to which we are attending. In other words, says Polanyi, "the functional structure of from-to [tacit] knowing includes jointly a subsidiary 'from' and a focal 'to.' But this pair is not linked together of its own accord. The relation of a subsidiary to a focus is formed by the *act of a person* who integrates one to the other. The from-to relation lasts only so long as a person, the knower, sustains this integration."[4] Polanyi gives the example of driving a nail with a hammer. The focal awareness is watching the strokes of the hammer as they hit the nail. The pressure of the hammer on the hand is subsidiary, it is known indirectly in that we rely on it to hit the nail even though we do not attend to it directly.

'Tacit,' of course, means "assumed" or "taken for granted." And Polanyi's point is that any act of focal knowing assumes a vast range of tacit knowledge ranging from the subliminally conscious to awareness of functions deep inside the body that are normally inaccessible through direct experience. Tacit knowledge may have been learned consciously in the first place; for example, all the tacit knowledge needed to drive a car is later not conscious when we carry on a conversation as we drive. Polanyi's story of the medical student learning to read x-rays, quoted in Chapter 1, is another example. But tacit knowledge may also be innate, for example, the knowledge used by the visual system in estimating relative distances. Further, focal knowledge and tacit knowledge are always linked through a person: it is the tacit knowledge that gives the focus meaning.

Recognition of the tacit component brings personal knowledge, which for Polanyi is beyond the dichotomy of subjective and objective. "I think we may distinguish between the personal in us, which actively enters into our commitments, and our subjective states, in which we merely endure our feelings. This distinction establishes the conception of the *personal*, which is neither subjective nor objective. In so far as the personal submits to requirements acknowledged by itself as independent of itself, it is not subjective; but in so far as it is an action guided by individual passions, it is not objective either. It transcends the disjunction between subjective and objective."[5]

BATESON'S CIRCUITS OF MENTAL PROCESS

Gregory Bateson suggests that we should consider circuits of mental process reaching out from the body to the center of attention and back to the body. He gives the example of a man using an axe to cut a tree. Although the man is attending to the tree, the circuit of mental process actually connects the axe handle to his hands and arms, through his nervous and muscular system to his eyes and from there to the head of the axe as it hits the tree. It makes no sense to localize awareness in one part of this circuit, some particular spot of the man's brain, and exclude the remainder.

Bateson suggests, "The total self-corrective unit which processes information, or, as I say, 'thinks' and 'acts' and 'decides' is a *system* whose boundaries do not at all coincide with the boundaries either of the body or of what is popularly called the 'self' or 'consciousness'; and it is important to notice that there are *multiple* differences between the thinking system and the self as popularly conceived. . . . The individual mind is immanent but not only in the body. It is immanent also in the pathways and messages outside the body; and there is a larger Mind of which the individual mind is only a subsystem . . . [that] is still immanent in the total interconnected social system and planetary ecology."[6]

Thus, like Whitehead and Polanyi, Bateson is pointing out the importance of the links in awareness that are not the focus of consciousness and that may not even be available to consciousness. For all three of these scientists, the embodiment of awareness in nature is the factor that has been forgotten in our emphasis on conscious perception. And this brings us back to the notion of participatory consciousness.

In *The Reenchantment of the World*, Morris Berman describes the "disenchantment of the world" that occurred with the establishment of Newton's universe in people's minds. With the appearance of this universe, participatory consciousness was finally pushed from awareness. Mind was removed from nature, and at the same time there was a repression into the unconscious of bodily feeling, sexuality, and the 'irrational' aspects of thought, that is, the aspects of thought that do not conform to one-dimensional, Aristotelian logic. Berman argues, "Modern science and technology are based not only on a hostile attitude toward the environment, but on the repression of the body and the unconscious; and unless these can be recovered, unless participating consciousness can be restored in a way that is scientifically (or at least rationally) credible and not merely a relapse into naive animism, then what it means to be a human being will forever be lost."[7]

All the writers we have been considering have in their own ways been pointing to the mode of knowing that directly feels interconnectedness and the totality in which any particular conscious discrimination is embedded. They have also pointed to the need to join this intuitive insight with the analytical discriminations of intellect.

In Chapter 11 I reviewed how the idea of 'a mind' arose, as a reasoning intellect manipulating thoughts as symbols of the world, and how this intellect became split off from a direct, intuitive way of knowing to become the only locus of valid knowledge. We are nowadays, perhaps, in a certain sense coming full circle: through stages of withdrawal of mind from nature and the discovery, or perhaps we can now say invention, of individual 'minds' and separate mindless nature; to realizing the lack of substantiality, or inherent existence, of individual minds and to the discovery that the individual mind and the nature it is supposed to mirror are, after all, our own inventions, emerging together as concepts that have dominated modern society until now. We have seen that in the view of at least Whitehead, Polanyi, Bateson, and Berman, there is a need for the rediscovery of the participatory, intuitive knowing, and the joining of this with the analytical and representational knowledge of intellect.

JOINING INTELLECT AND INTUITION

The various Buddhist traditions have a variety of ways of analyzing the modes of functioning of the five-skandha setup in terms of the organism's gaining knowledge of the world of its projections, the 'external world.' One way this has been done, in the Tibetan tradition, is in terms of intellect, *shepa* (Sanskrit, *jna*), and intuitive insight, *rikpa* (Sanskrit, *vidya*).

Shepa is variously translated as 'knowing,' 'comprehending,' or 'intellect.' It is that which has an intelligent and knowledgeable attitude to the world, knowing the basic regularities and causal relationships that operate in all the various aspects of life: automechanics, home economics, musical harmony, politics and government, and so on. It is the function of mind that makes distinctions and discriminates between things, and is knowledge of the conscious discriminations of sense perceptions.

Rikpa means 'able to be touched by a situation,' having a 'visceral feeling' for the qualitative tone of a situation. If, for example someone were to walk into a doctor's office, the doctor might immediately know that that person was sick and might even know quite clearly what the problem was. This intuitive knowing would be rikpa. The doctor would then have to examine the patient carefully, note the symptoms, and analyze them according to his wealth of knowledge about the various diseases. This is the activity of shepa, intellect.[8]

To give a simple example of how these might work together, suppose you decide to go somewhere in a car on a wintry day. Shepa knows where to go, the reasons for going, and how long it will take;

it reads the map and watches out for road signs. Rikpa drives the car "by the seat of its pants," knows how fast to go around sharp corners, gets you out of an icy skid, and so on. If you are stopped by a police officer, shepa understands (or does not understand) why you were stopped, what the consequences will be, what excuses you might make, and so on; rikpa shows how to behave, without panic and with ordinary courtesies of human communication, and the right timing of when to smile and when to say "sir." We can perhaps see, in the two ways of knowing toward which Whitehead, Polanyi, and Bateson are groping, similarities to shepa and rikpa. Each of these pioneers had to develop fresh language to express his insights, and these insights arose in different contexts. Nevertheless there is a common thread: the way overemphasis on the clarity and distinctness of perception and thought can obscure the felt quality of interconnectedness, which is knowable in a different way, intuitively.

Just as the whole process of perception is normally based on ego, directed toward survival of the self-sense, but need not be so directed when this entire self-deception is seen through, in a similar way, shepa and rikpa have both ego-oriented aspects and aspects that go beyond, or 'transcend' ego. These 'transcendent' aspects can be discovered within the mundane with appropriate training, just as absence of the ego viewpoint is already the basis of mundane perception. The transcendent aspect of shepa is sherap. The suffix -rap, means 'highest' or 'best,' so that sherap is the 'highest' knowledge. It is better known by its Sanskrit name, *prajna*. We will discuss these aspects of intellect and intuition in later chapters, after we have looked more closely at the nature of nonduality.

The most important point of all this from the Buddhist perspective is that there is a training process by which sherap, or prajna, and rikpa may be realized and joined. The term for 'education' in the Tibetan Buddhist tradition is *sherik*, a combination of *shepa* and *rikpa*, implying that education *is* the joining of intellect and intuition. A major element in the training of intellect and intuition is the practice of mindfulness and awareness meditation, which I describe in the next chapter. Through the practice of mindfulness, one experiences the underlying sense of peace or nonseparateness from which discriminating thoughts arise, at first in the briefest of glimpses. These glimpses are rikpa, and if they are acknowledged, rather than ignored as is usually the case in everyday life, then rikpa is able to develop in our state of mind. Through the training of the awareness aspect of meditation, discriminating insight of sherap is sharpened. Conceptual discriminations are seen more clearly, and deeper and deeper layers of conceptual presuppositions are discovered until the entire projection process of perception is directly seen through. Joining mindfulness and awareness in the practice brings about the joining of rikpa and shepa, intuition and intellect.

When intellect and intuition are joined, then, in Whitehead's terms, the representations of presentational immediacy and the interconnectedness of causal efficacy are in harmony. The symbol, the 'external object,' is not separate from the totality within which it arises as a symbol and therefore is not taken to have, itself, independent isolated existence. The symbol is not separate from that which gives it meaning—it is authentic. In Polanyi's terms, again, the focus of knowledge is felt to arise within the unbounded field of tacit knowledge that gives it meaning. Knowledge is then personal, and, in Polanyi's evocative words, "The personal participation of the knower in the knowledge he believes himself to possess takes place within the flow of passion. We recognize intellectual beauty as a guide to discovery and as a mark of truth."⁹ And in Bateson's terms, the conscious self-process experiences itself as not separate from the larger circuits of mental process of which it is a part, and which themselves are parts of still larger circuits in continually expanding horizons of mind/body unity.

It is important to emphasize that this does not mean the loss of rational thought or of dualistic perception, returning to some vague, 'oceanic' feeling. It is the fear of this loss, and the misunderstanding of the nature of nonduality that sometimes inhibits people from beginning to practice meditation. On the contrary, dualistic thought and perception continue, but they are seen within the context of nonduality, and therefore lose their grip on us as we cease to believe in the *ultimate* reality of the world that they project.

Ken Wilber has made a very useful distinction, from this point of view, between what he calls 'prerational' and 'transrational' knowledge and understanding. He says, "The point is that, since prerational and transrational are both in their own way nonrational, then they appear quite similar or even identical to the untutored eye."⁹ Wilber elucidates this in terms of what he calls the spectrum of consciousness, which is his way of separating out the various concepts that are conventionally all squashed together under the virtually meaningless term 'consciousness.' It is necessary to realize that the conventional term 'consciousness' is a complex concept containing a range of different meanings, and not to confuse these meanings. The confusion produces the rather absurd idea that any insight that cannot be precisely and literally converted into words has to come from the prerational mind, or the pre-adult phase of the child. This absurdity Wilber has referred to as the pre/trans fallacy. In the terms of this chapter it simply means that the state of being in which intellect and intuition are joined should not be confused with a state in which intellect is denied and there is a return to the wishful thinking and vague beliefs that often go under the name of 'intuition.' On the contrary, because intellect has reached its sharpest point, there is no need for reliance on unexamined beliefs, and therefore genuine intuition is possible.

15

The Method of Mindfulness-Awareness

LET US NOW DISCUSS the method used by Buddhists to gain insights into the nature of perception, the practice of meditation. The practice of meditation in the Buddhist tradition has nothing to do with escaping this world by getting into trance states or "altered states of consciousness." On the contrary, it has the aim of joining mind and body, awareness and perceptions, so that one is fully *in* this world. In fact there is no word in the Buddhist traditional languages that is really equivalent to 'meditation.' The Sanskrit term *bhavana* and the Tibetan term 'samten,' which are often translated as 'meditation,' are more accurately translated as "attending" or "cultivating knowledge." Another related term, *darshana*, can be translated as "seeing." Thus the "practice of meditation" is more accurately the "path of attending, cultivating knowledge, or seeing."[1]

The practice has two aspects, known as mindfulness and awareness.[2] 'Mindfulness' refers to attending precisely, almost deliberately, to the details of one's bodily sensations, feelings, perceptions, thoughts, and overall state of mind, one's 'mood,' or 'state of consciousness.' 'Awareness' refers to attending to the environment of those details, the space around them, their interdependence, their arising, dwelling, and ceasing. This attending is done without preconceptions as to what one will find and without judgment of what one in fact finds. Therefore the mindfulness aspect of the practice is sometimes known as 'bare attention.' The awareness aspect is also known as 'insight' because it is direct seeing into the causal nature of thought, emotion, perception, and environment.

THE METHOD OF JOINING MINDFULNESS
AND AWARENESS

Although mindfulness and awareness can be done at any moment in one's life, in order to practice and to develop the skill, one usually

189

does it in a situation in which one's life and environment has been temporarily simplified. One would do it in a relatively quiet place, at a prearranged time, for a prearranged length of time. One would sit in a simple posture, such as crosslegged on the floor, or on a stool without leaning on a backrest for support. The outgoing breath provides a focus of attention by which one can bring mind back again and again as mind tends to wander and get lost in its own processes of thought, emotionality, and fantasy. One simply acknowledges what arises into consciousness, without holding onto it or trying to suppress it or hastily remove it. In this way one's mind begins to relax and one begins to directly identify with the mental process in operation at each moment.

Mindfulness is that state in which mind is fully present with whatever action we are executing: placing a flower, wiping a teacup, washing the car, programming a computer. It is attention to detail, careful and almost deliberate. It is identifying fully with one's body, thoughts, and actions so that there is nothing left over, no self-consciousness, no watcher, no split mind. It is not watching what we are doing but simply *being* fully what we are doing, thinking, and feeling in its smallest, most insignificant detail. It is therefore altogether different from the early 'introspectionist' methods of Wundt and others. One is not looking *for* something, one is not particularly interested in the content of what arises to consciousness as such; one is healing the split between mental contents and knowing those contents rather than deliberately promoting that split as introspection tends to do.

Awareness is acknowledging the quality of sudden openness that comes in when we are fully present. It is a sudden glimpse, a sudden flash of freshness and wider perspective. We cannot discover where it comes from, we cannot hold onto it, and we cannot artificially recreate it. Because it comes from beyond our perceptual process of conceptual projection, this quality of openness brings with it a sense of inquisitiveness, of interest in the environment within which our actions and thoughts take place. From this glimpse, awareness expands to see the associations and causal connections to even the smallest thought or perception, and to unravel and reveal the details and causal processes of thought and perception itself.

This unraveling of the causal process is described as six particular 'discoveries'[3]: first comes discovery of 'meaning,' which means being able to distinguish the meaning of a perception from its name. We become free from the ensnarement of words and language; therefore we are able to have an exact and precise relationship to words, to use them powerfully to cut through mental gossip and ignorance. The second discovery is of 'object.' We begin to see the actual patterning that we are projecting onto our perceptions, and to be able to distinguish a perception that is genuinely in our interaction with the environment from one that is at the level of fantasy or mental creation. The third is the discovery of 'nature,' or 'mark.' We discover how, from the first bare perception, this expands into our projected world, by categorizing and proliferation of concepts.

Fourth is the discovery of 'direction' or 'sides,' which means knowing when proliferations lead toward or away from further awareness. Therefore it means knowing what to do and what not to do from the point of view of awareness. Fifth is the discovery of 'time,' which means realizing how concepts, as memories of the past and anticipations of the future, are entering in to each moment of perception; knowing what you are experiencing now and seeing clearly how past and future are entering into this. Sixth is discovery of 'insight,' which is realizing the deep conceptual frame of reference involved in each moment of perception, which I called 'belief system' in Chapter 1, and therefore not necessarily being trapped in it. You begin to see how each moment of experience is grounded in some relative frame of reference that, until you saw it, you took for granted. You begin to see even beyond the reference of self and other to the entire process of the arising of perception. You see how each moment leads to the next and gives rise, causally, to the next. Therefore it is seeing cause and effect directly, seeing how present action leads to future result. These six discoveries are said to arise after one has become quite proficient at attending to the smallest fluctuations or flickerings of thoughts with their surrounding atmosphere of meanings.

Mindfulness as the identification with thought and perception leads to the direct knowledge of the fundamental peacefulness and wholesomeness underlying all thought, and to the direct knowledge of intuitive insight, vidya. Awareness leads to the understanding of causal relationships and relative reference points and is the development of the sharpness of intellect. Concentration practices similar to mindfulness are common to many contemplative traditions. It was these practices that the Buddha learned in his ascetic years in the forest. It was these practices that were current in the Indian traditions of world denial and the search for a permanent Self that the Buddha was specifically responding to and going beyond. The particular insight of the Buddha was to discover the practice of awareness and, from this, the discoveries of causality and discontinuity. In some early Buddhist schools, the development of mindfulness is carried to its farthest extent before the insight of awareness is cultivated, and joined with mindfulness. In the mahayana schools, the two are cultivated simultaneously from the beginning.

In either case the joining of mindfulness and awareness is regarded as the most important point. It is said that this will bring the discovery of beauty, harmony, and clarity of perceptions that exist beyond ego. This transformation of perception is the view of sacredness in the Buddhist tradition. There is no 'other world' than this one, but this one is said to be immeasurably more vast than our *ideas* of it. It is a transformation that comes from ceasing to ignore what is so close to each one of us that we cannot see it; therefore it is said, "A cow does not taste its own tongue." The discovery of sacredness is not regarded as something to worship, but it is worth celebrating. When perception is less self-centered the world looks at you as much as you look at it.

THE MEDITATIVE AND SCIENTIFIC
METHODS COMPARED

The process of meditation is not the same as the conventional idea of introspection. Meditation differs from introspection in that the meditator is not looking 'inward' at something that is imagined to be 'my mind,' and is not specifically interested in 'consciousness.' One simply allows mind to follow its own course and is directly aware of it as it comes and goes. It is akin to a naturalist looking for hours at a time, for days on end, at groundhogs in a field, popping in and out of their holes, until that naturalist becomes so familiar with their movements that he or she loses any feeling of separateness from them. At this point the naturalist may have direct insight into the behavior of groundhogs. In the case of mindfulness practice, one identifies with the process of one's own mind until one loses the "watcher"; the sense of being separate from one's own mind is lost. At that point the nature of mental process is directly seen.

Mindfulness-awareness meditation is not merely subjective, although it clearly does not make the artificial and ultimately impossible distinction between subject and object that science is conventionally believed to make. It is not 'objective' but it *is* intersubjectively testable. It is a method that has been applied over and over again, with repeatable results. The instruction is analogous to a child learning to read. We usually need merely to introduce a child to letters and sounds and, often with amazingly little instruction that child begins to read. It almost seems miraculous, yet it is quite predictable.

There are of course tremendous variations as to the timing and specific contents of children's progress in learning to read, but the process generally unfolds in a very similar way from child to child. In a similar fashion, with the proper initial directions and guidance, the progress of mindfulness practice unfolds in a quite predictable and repeatable way.

However, because our experimental material is in this case our own minds, and because we may well not like what we find (especially as we come closer and closer to discovering the structure of ego), there is a very strong possibility for self-deception. Therefore mindfulness practice depends on there being a community of practitioners and a guide who has already, at least partially, accomplished the discovery of ego and egolessness. Without such a community and guide, just because of this potentiality for self-deception, mindfulness practice is very much a hit-and-miss affair in which one might very easily get lost.

The intersubjective communal checking by which the practice of mindfulness is kept from becoming mere introspection or dangerous fantasy is almost identical to the way in which the scientific community provides checks for itself. Scientific work is done in a community of practitioners holding a commonly shared and agreed-upon system of beliefs about the nature of phenomena and the way to look. In order to "do science" a young person must be educated for many years—at least seven years beyond the high school level—in order to learn these shared beliefs, to see in the appropriate way, and to learn the language of the community. The validity of that person's work is decided on by the community in the context of the shared belief system. A scientist does not necessarily see directly the object of his inquiry, such as an electron or a gene active in a living cell, nor do his or her colleagues; but the results of this inquiry are always manifested in some way externally. In a similar way, while the community of practitioners and the guide do not directly see a practitioner's mental contents, the development of meditative insight always manifest in physical ways, however subtle and undetectable to nonpractitioners these may be. Thus the community provides a constant support and mirror to the practitioner. From this it follows that the practice of mindfulness can be regarded as a form of scientific method. Thus mindfulness-awareness practice satisfies our criterion of having a method to disclose the operation of mental process as well as to discover the undivided ground of existence and nonexistence.

In discussing the relation between science and religion, Wilber has made the distinction between *method* and *content*. Wilber makes the important point that in comparing science and a religion it is necessary to distinguish these, and, for Wilber, the key point is method. He defines the scientific method as "a method of gaining knowledge whereby *hypotheses are tested* (instrumentally or experimentally) by reference to *experience* ('data') that is potentially *public,* or open to *repetition* (confirmation or refutation) by peers. In bare essentials, it means that the scientific method involves those knowledge-claims open to *experiential* validation or refutation." Wilber points out that this definition of the method does not make reference to the content, that this method can be applied to *any* content that is accessible to it. Therefore, "the only real battle is between genuine science and bogus science, and between genuine religion and bogus religion ('genuine' meaning 'experientially verifiable/refutable'; 'bogus' meaning 'dogmatic, nonexperiential, nonverifiable/refutable'). *There is bogus or pseudo-science just as much as there is bogus or pseudo-religion.*"[4]

STUDIES TO VERIFY THE MEDITATIVE INSIGHTS

Various studies have been done to try to gather some data on the practice of meditation within the context of 'objective' science. Extensive studies have been done on the EEG ("brain-wave") patterns of meditators in comparison with those of nonmeditators. The number and complexity of variables involved in most of these studies, including the type of meditation practiced, the degree of genuine accomplishment of the practitioner, the philosophical viewpoint of the experimenter, and the physiological variables, make it difficult to come to any general conclusions. One thing that is quite clear, however, if one reads the literature with some degree of unbiasedness, is that there is a correlation between physiological state as measured by EEG and the meditative state of the subject. For example, Kasamatsu and Hirai undertook an intensive investigation of forty-eight practitioners of Buddhist meditation from Japanese Zen schools. They found that a short time after beginning the session alpha waves predominated in the EEG records of the practitioners, but not in control subjects who were not meditating; the alpha persisted with the eyes open; there were no EEG similarities between the hypnotic trance state and the meditative state; during and after the session of meditation, the meditators did not exhibit habituation to a click stimulus presented twenty times in succession; and evaluation by the Master of a student's competence in meditation was directly correlated with the amount of alpha present in the EEG record.[5]

Beyond simply showing a correlation between brain activity and meditation, these investigations tend to confirm two of the claims of the meditators. First, alpha activity was not different with eyes open or closed. In fact Buddhist mindfulness-awareness meditation is usually practiced with the eyes open, since the intention is not to enter a trance state in which one is cut off from the world but rather to sharpen and clarify one's senses. This is further corroborated by the lack of habituation to sensory stimuli, in this case a series of clicks. The normal untrained subject does show habituation—if a tap is dripping it disturbs us at first, but then gradually we cease to notice it; city dwellers barely notice the sound of traffic that to a visitor is highly disturbing. The lack of habituation of Zen practitioners during and after a meditation session is a simple confirmation of their claim that their practice makes them more rather than less sensitive to their sensory surroundings.

An extensive and valuable study is that of Daniel Brown, who spent twelve years comparing the meditation practices of three different traditions: the Theravadin Buddhist traditions, the Vajrayana Buddhist tradition of 'Mahamudra,' and the Hindu yoga tradition of Patanjali. The latter is of course purely a 'mindfulness' tradition from the Buddhist point of view, although according to Brown it does have stages roughly corresponding to the Buddhist 'insight' stages. In fact Brown suggests that the path of meditation of each of these traditions can be broken down into eighteen stages, and that there are very significant parallels in the changes of the perceptual process accompanying each stage. He also shows how the very early stages of all three traditions can be interpreted in terms of the stages of perception outlined by cognitive psychology.

Brown points out that although the perceptual change reported at each stage are similar in the three traditions, the way these perceptual changes are experienced depends on the philosophical training provided by the tradition. In particular, each takes a very different approach to the fundamental problem of continuity and discontinuity. All three acknowledge the essential discontinuity of awareness and manifestation. However, the Theravadin tradition sees only discontinuity at the deepest level of the ground of perception, seeing absolutely nothing between moments. The Hindu yoga tradition, because of its eternalistic, dualistic assumptions, sees the discontinuities as fluctuations of a permanent mind-stuff; as Brown says, "For the Hindu, the vicissitudes of mental events are all manifestations of the 'same stuff.' " For the Buddhists, each discretely observable event in the unfolding succession of mental events is "momentary." Whereas both traditions agree that mental events undergo incessant change, the nature of the change can be experienced differently: mental events unfold in a continuous manner for the Hindu yogi and in a discontinuous manner for the early Buddhist meditator. It should, however, be pointed out that Brown is here referring more to the early abhidharmist Buddhist schools. As we will see, the later tantric or Vajrayana schools recognized the continuity of awareness from moment to moment, but did not, like the Hindus, regard it as a separate "stuff." In fact one meaning of 'tantra' is, precisely, 'continuity' or literally 'thread.' This thread of continuity is not other than awareness of discontinuity, it is nonreferential awareness of the entire process *as* process. Another way of saying this is that the gap between experiential moments, the nonduality within which those moments arise and from which they are not separate, is both empty and full. According to these vajrayana-mahayana schools, nonduality is empty of all conceptualization, yet there is primordial intelligence, an aesthetically felt cognitiveness, or 'wisdom-born-within-emptiness.' Thus these later schools declared that they had found a middle way between the eternalism of the Hindus and the nihilism they perceived in the abhidharma schools. We will be examining this claim in detail in subsequent chapters.

The cognitive stages passed through in the formal practice of mindfulness that Brown identifies are: first, discriminatory thinking about the object ceases, the meditation disrupts the categorizing mind and returns to the actual physical features of perceptual objects. For example, a stick is seen as color and form but remains without the attached meaning "stick." The second stage is one in which the object appears to change dramatically in size; there is a destabilizing of the perceptual phenomenon of 'size constancy': for example, normally as you move an outstretched thumb toward you, the thumb appears to move closer without changing in size. This is an important element in the primitive recognition of patterns as definite objects, that at this stage is dropped. Next the meditator observes the reversal of the primary pattern formation. According to cognitive psychologists and on neurological grounds, it appears that, in ordinary perception, a synthesis of the senses occurs first, followed by primary pattern recognition, the first skandha. At this stage of meditation this is reversed so that the primary pattern is lost, followed by the loss of sensory synthesis. At this point the meditator has deconstructed the gross perceptual world altogether. As we have seen, each of these stages has been uncovered by cognitive scientists, providing an excellent 'objective' corroboration of the method of meditation.

The next, more advanced, stages of mindfulness-awareness meditation bring the letting go of subtle thoughts and attachments to the self-construct as well as to the time-space matrix. Awareness rests in brilliance, energy, and clarity, free from concepts of self, of space, or of time. Arising out of this nondual state, the meditator experiences the perceptual world of space, time, and the duality of subject and object returning, and experiences the reconstruction of the gross perception of an 'outside' world with recognizable 'objects.'[6]

Brown's work is merely the barest outline of the wealth of specific details of the process of perception and its unraveling that is to be found in these traditional meditation manuals. Furthermore the fruition type of experience, of resting the mind fully in nonduality, that Brown has described is usually realized only after long preparation, and perhaps completely by only the most capable students. Likewise, only very few scientists really understand Einstein's work, and there are even fewer scientists, if any, of the caliber of Einstein.

Brown, together with Jack Engler, has done some interesting work to try to corroborate some of these descriptions 'objectively.' In one extensive series of tests, meditation subjects at various levels of practice, as designated by meditation masters, were submitted to Rorscharch tests. Brown also traveled to Asia to give similar tests to several meditation masters. The results could quite clearly be correlated with some of the stages Brown has described.

In another series of tests Brown used a tachioscope, a machine that is able to present images to a subject at durations of thousandths of a second, much shorter than a normal subject can detect. These were the type of machine used in many of the experiments on preconscious processing reported in Chapter 12. Brown reports studies of visual sensitivity done on people who had undergone an intensive three-month training in insight meditation. The training seems to have made the meditators more sensitive to perceptual events. For example, in one test a series of lights were flashed for periods lasting just a fraction of a second, some too short to be seen normally. The meditators tested were able to detect much shorter flashes than was possible before they began the training. Their visual detection abilities were also much sharper than were those of people given the same test who had not been in the training course.

In other research, Brown found that some students classified as "adept meditators" were able to describe subtle events in perception that are ordinarily unnoticed. For example, in a test where two lights are flashed in a sequence so quickly that they blend into a single flash on a person's perception, these subjects reported distinctly perceiving as separate moments the beginning of the flash, the flash itself, the ending of the flash and the gap before the next flash, perceptual events that usually go by in a blur.[7]

For someone who would like to verify the reports of practitioners of meditation, this kind of work is really no substitute at all for actually experiencing practice. No amount of looking through a telescope is a substitute for standing on the moon. But at least the telescope convinced skeptics in Galileo's day that the moon was as real as the earth. In like manner we might expect that when cognitive scientists begin to realize the power of the method of mindfulness-awareness to elucidate the processes of perception, this method can become an invaluable tool for the study of the space of the mind.

SEEING THROUGH THE PROLIFERATION OF CONCEPTS

A result of the practice of meditation is the training of attention to be able to note finer and finer time intervals. At a certain point it is possible to note the fading of each perception or thought into nothing, and the arising of each succeeding thought out of nothing. Awareness begins to rest in that gap between perceptions, and the meditator experiences perceptions as they arise, transparent like rainbows in the sky. Perceptions are said to be transparent, because their nature is seen as arising from nothing and returning to nothing. They are experienced as fabrications rather than as manifestations of a solid world because they are seen to be put together out of heaps of dharmas, like a patchwork or a sandcastle.

Nevertheless, because you see a rainbow as merely appearance in the clear blue sky, that does not mean that you no longer see the rainbow. In the same way, because one sees the origin and nature of perceptions, that does not mean that one does not experience one's perceptions. One does not, however, need to grasp onto them as ultimately real. Especially, when the origin of the first split of 'I' and 'other' is seen, one is relieved of the impossible burden of believing in "myself," "my life," "my projects," and in the 'outside world' as a separate reality. Out of this relief a softness, warmth, and friendliness toward oneself and others begins to develop. We can afford, naturally, to be kind because we no longer have to maintain the lie of life as a "harsh struggle for survival," a continual battle of one separate being against another.

Now we might wonder, why is it so difficult to see the nature of our perceptual process and the transparency of the outer and inner worlds? What takes us away from such a simple realization? If we are asking what causes the first split, then the only answer that has been given in the meditative traditions is that we have to find it out for ourselves by the direct experience of meditation practice. If we are asking what keeps us going around in the endless round of consciousness that does not see its origin, one answer that has been given, in the earlier traditions which we are considering now, is that it is the *tendency of consciousness to proliferate concepts.*

All of us have no doubt been in some situation like this: you are sitting in the garden on an early morning in the summer. You have an hour before you have to do something, and you have nothing particular on your mind. For a moment you sit listening to the birds, feeling the soft early sun and the fresh breeze, feeling the vast open sky above and the solid earth underneath, letting thoughts of your family and your profession pass easily through your mind. You experience a moment of a deep sense of well-being. This reminds you of a time two years ago or was it two and a half years ago, when you sat in a similar situation with your secretary, who has now left to have a child; you wonder how her boy is, which leads you to wonder how she will educate him, which makes you think of your own children, who are now in college; thus you think of the difficulties colleges are facing now, difficulties of the "relevance of curricula" and of the cutbacks of government funding, which leads you to think of the present government, other democratic governments around the world, and the world-wide economic and political instability; you think of your own job security, your wish to purchase a new house and the difficulties you have had with the new management at work; this brings your mind again to a question that you have been pondering lately, whether to look for a new job, which in such unstable times at your age would be very risky, but then you are really not completely fulfilled in your present job. . . . You feel an increasing sense of anxiety and restlessness, you look at your watch and realize the hour is passed and it is now time to go to work. Apart from the first moment you were never in that fresh early morning garden at all.

This is a particularly graphic example of the tendency to proliferate concepts. It could have happened in any other situation, while in a meeting, while listening to a lecture, while cutting wood. But according to Buddhist realization it is happening *all the time,* and is the very nature of consciousness in the sense of the fifth skandha. At each moment, some small perception, a moment of direct perception which we are rarely aware of, is suddenly expanded into the proliferation of concepts that is consciousness. This expansion is an energetic one driven by the fundamental affects of ego-centered passion and aggression, the basic energies of feeling.

The whole process of the five skandhas, ending in the tendency to proliferate concepts, is summarized in this delightful and succinct passage from the Theravadin tradition:

> Visual consciousness, brethren, arises because of eye and material shapes; the meeting of the three is sensory impingement; because of sensory impingement arises feeling; what one feels, one perceives; what one perceives, one reasons about; what one reasons about one proliferates conceptually, due to that, concepts characterised by the prolific tendency assail him in regard to material shapes cognisable by the eye, belonging to the past, the future and the present. And, brethren, auditory consciousness arises because of ear and sounds. . . . and so on to mental consciousness arises because of mind and mental objects . . . belonging to the past, the future and the present.[8]

The translator of this passage, Bikkhu Nanananda, points out the interesting change of tense in this passage. At first the tense is impersonal, becoming personal at the skandha of feeling, remaining personal up to the point at which "concepts . . . assail him." Thus the idea of self begins to enter the process at the level of feeling and continues all the way up to consciousness, at which point the self loses control altogether and is "assailed" by the "outside world" in the form of "concepts characterized by the prolific tendency in regard to material shapes," and so on. Feeling assailed, overwhelmed, by an 'outside world' of its own projections, and having to fight that world, is the characteristic anxiety of the self. The self identifies itself with 'consciousness' and becomes lost in 'consciousness,' constantly swept along by the tendency to proliferate. We saw in Chapter 10 that consciousness of 'self' and its 'world' is, according to scientific thinking, located in the proliferating language web. Perhaps, between each experienced moment, itself simply a conglomeration of the skandhas, there is a gap in which the subject-object split dissolves. But this split is only to be recreated a fraction of a second later.

Once again I should emphasize that this analysis need not lead to nihilism. It is not the fact of human awareness, and human aspiration to vastness of awareness, that is being questioned. What is in question is the tendency to limit awareness to an imagined solid, definite, unchanging, aspect of our being, whether it be the conscious 'rational' intellect, the emotional responses of the 'soul,' deeper, more unconscious fixations, or an imagined 'higher Self.' These, if they exist at all, are only minor, superficial parts of the total, primordially intelligent being of mind, heart, and body, which is ever changing and therefore ungraspable by fixed definition. According to the Buddhist analysis and insight, intelligence prior to and beyond dualism already exists at every moment of our experience and pervades that experience. It is directly discoverable at that gap between perceptual moments, when attention is trained to become aware of it. In order to discover it, it is not necessary to struggle in all kinds of solemn and fantastic spiritual pursuits, it is only necessary to turn around on oneself and face the deception of ego. There is a certain irony in this, the self that sets out to accomplish the investigation more than likely wears out somewhere along the way. Perhaps this is why the Buddha is so often portrayed in statues and pictures with a gentle smile, because the best way to see ego is with a sense of humor.

16

Emptiness of Concept

WE MUST NOW FACE a problem that has been simmering in the
background of all our discussion, that no doubt the reader has been
worrying about from time to time. This problem manifests itself in
the Buddhist analysis of the early schools, the dharma analysis, as
well as the various aspects of cognitive science that we have used to
analyze experience. Our analysis has certainly indicated that the self
is nowhere to be found; in other words, there is no reason to believe
that self exists. Likewise our analysis has clearly shown that the
'outside world' as we are conscious of it is a fabrication of the same
process that has fabricated the self. But what then *does* exist? In
Buddhist terms we can ask, to put it bluntly, using our common
sense idea of existence: Is it, or is it not, the case that 'dharmas exist'?
Because, according to this conventional logic, it *must* be true either
that "dharmas exist" or that "dharmas do not exist." Likewise we
could say the same of 'mental representations,' 'literal and final
images,' 'affects,' and 'consciousness,' as well as 'body' and 'mind.'
Are these all real 'things' that actually exist? Or are we somehow
misleading ourselves by the fact that we use nouns to refer to what
may turn out to be nothing other than transient patterns?

We need to take a further, deeper, step. In the scientific tradition
this is the point at which the psychology and the philosophy of mind
must rejoin, as indeed has been happening in the past few decades.
Philosophers have begun to realize that many of the centuries-old
squabbles about 'mind' and 'matter' can be resolved by looking at
what the psychologists and neurophysiologists are discovering about
mental process, and at what physicists are discovering about matter.
Cognitive scientists are beginning to realize that the analyses of the
philosophers are, after all, relevant to the scientific study of mind,
and have been looking back on the work of Plato and Aristotle,
Descartes, Locke, Kant, and others as *psychology* as much as philosophy. In the Buddhist tradition, the deeper step needed led, in the

first century A.D., to a great flowering of new expressions of the teaching known as the Mahayana.

SHUNYATA

A key doctrine that distinguishes the Mahayana from the earlier schools is the direct realization expressed in the Sanskrit term *shunyata*. The word *shunya* has been variously translated as empty, void, nothing, or open. And the suffix *-ta* can be translated as -ness. Therefore the straightforward translation of 'shunyata' would be emptiness, voidness, nothingness, or openness. However, one must as always be very careful when trying to understand a term such as this. The words 'empty,' 'nothing,' and especially 'void' all convey the impression of a blank. 'Empty' and 'void' contrast with 'full'; 'nothing' contrasts with 'something.' Again we are caught in 'thing-thinking.' All these terms convey to us the feeling that there is a blankness where there could have been things, objects, or perceptions. Such a contrast is not the intention of the word 'shunya.' What is meant can be more readily understood if we ask, "empty of what"? The answer is something like "empty of concept, of mental fabrication or projection." Shunyata then means the quality of being empty of mental fabrication. That is, it means *what is*, free from concept.

Now the concept that is the root of all other concepts, the most powerful and central mental imputation we make, is the concept of 'thingness' or 'inherent existence.' Continually we see the world in terms of separate things, each having its own inherent, independent existence. Concepts create distinctions, which are boundaries between one thing and another. They close off one thing from another, because of their tendency to exclude: if a thing is 'A' it cannot also be 'not-A,' according to conventional logic. Therefore things that are 'A' are separated by this concept, 'A', from things that are 'not-A.' If the sky is blue, it cannot also be not blue. If a child is bad, it cannot also be not bad, or good. If a teenager is a punk (bad), she cannot also be a decent citizen (not bad.) If I exist, I cannot also not exist. 'Shunyata' implies that *what is* is not limited by such exclusivity. 'Openness' conveys this better than 'nothingness.' In the world as it is, free from concept, there are not separate things having an existence that comes about by itself not dependent on anything else. There simply is nothing in our entire experience that actually is like this.[1]

As Buddhist scholar Jeffrey Hopkins says in *Meditations on Emptiness*, "Phenomena are empty of a certain mode of being called 'inherent existence,' 'objective existence,' or 'natural existence.' This 'inherent existence' is not a concept superimposed by philosophical systems but refers to our ordinary sense of the way that things exist—as if they concretely exist in and of themselves, covering their parts. Phenomena are the things which are empty of inherent existence, and inherent existence is that of which phenomena are empty."[2] And 'phenomena' here includes dharmas, affects, mental representations, consciousness, minds, and bodies. It also includes you, me, and our friends Peter and Mary or whoever they are. Absence of inherent existence means there is nothing that comes into being by its own power, nothing that has an invariant characteristic and unchanging essence. All of these are the marks of inherent existence that are nowhere to be found.

Emptiness is a very simple truth made complicated by the attempt to elucidate it in words and concepts when it can be pointed to only as direct experience. If a child awakens from a nightmare screaming that there is a monster in her room, we can only point around the room to convince her that there is no monster, we cannot point directly to the nonexistence of the monster. When the child is finally convinced that there really is no monster she smiles and shows great relief. In like manner, we cannot point directly to the nonexistence of inherent existence, simply because there is no inherent existence to point to. We can only search for inherent existence until we are convinced that there is none anywhere to be found.

Emptiness then is not a separate realm or substance or anything existing separately and having its own objective nature. It is a mark or characteristic of every phenomenon, and the ground of all phenomena. Wherever there are phenomena there is emptiness and wherever there is emptiness there are phenomena. Realization of emptiness is precisely also realization of the fallacy of thinking that the things of thought have independent existence. Although it is true that " 'inherent existence' is not a concept imposed by philosophical systems," nevertheless, many philosophical systems do nothing to alleviate this erroneous way of thinking. In fact many of them seem to be designed to shore it up. Classical science certainly seems to do this, many religions do this, and Buddhism itself is by no means immune from this fundamental error.

The principal teacher of shunyata, after the Buddha, was Nagarjuna, who, in the second century A.D., taught the doctrine and practice of shunyata when even the dharmas and their cause-and-effect characteristics were being taken as having self-nature and permanence. Thus Nagarjuna saw that the original teaching of impermanence was being subtly perverted. Dharma analysis had originally been intended to enable the meditator to realize egolessness and the impermanence of all things. But now the dharmas themselves were being taken as real things having inherent existence, and philosophical systems had grown up around them. And in order to ensure that this did not happen in relation to shunyata Nagarjuna proclaimed, "Shunyata has been taught as a remedy for all dogmatic views [i.e., especially belief in inherent existence of anything], but they indeed are incurable who cling to and turn shunyata itself into a view."[3] For shunyata is itself shunya; emptiness too, is empty of inherent self-nature; nothingness is not a thing.

Emptiness can be discovered and experienced when experience is analyzed to try to discover objects having inherent existence. This begins with the recognition that everything one perceives *is* perceived as if it had inherent existence, that is, as if it were a real substantial thing independent of the perceptual process. Having recognized that objects do in fact appear in this way, then, according to Hopkins, "an attempt is made to try to find these objects which so boldly appear to be self-existent; the mind becomes totally absorbed in trying to find an object—among its parts, as the composite of its parts, as something separate from the parts, and so forth. If the search is done with keen interest, the significance of not being able to find the object will be earth-shaking."[4] It is especially earth-shaking if the object one seeks is one's own mind.

In a traditional analysis, a cart is chosen as an example. As Tibetan Buddhist Thrangu Rinpoche says, "We can see that a cart is a very useful thing, a useful worldly object. It has a particular function that everyone can agree on; it is used to carry things from one place to another. But if we examine a cart, we see that this 'cart' is merely a designation that we have placed on something, a convenient mental label. There is no truly existing cart." Thrangu Rinpoche then goes on to analyze the cart from the point of view of a traditional method known as the 'Seven Skills':

1. that there is no essential reality in a thing as a whole, just as there is no reality in a cart as a whole
2. that there is no reality which is distinct from the sum of the parts assembled
3. that there is no real possession of a whole by its parts, or of parts by an imagined whole, just as cartness, which does not truly exist, cannot possess parts or vice versa.
4. that there is no reality on which the parts are dependent

5. that there is no reality dependent on the parts
6. that there is no true self to the mere collection of parts, just as the parts of a cart randomly assembled do not constitute a cart
7. that there is no reality in the shape of an object when the parts are correctly assembled, just as there is no cartness in the shape of the cart, as separate from the parts of the cart which go to make up that shape.[5]

This application of the Seven Skills is a contemplative process, not a philosophical position. The Seven Skills are applied to any cognizable object, including the supposed self and its relationship to the skandhas. One can then go on to examine any event in terms of whether one can find a unique source for that event, whether there is any other event that can truly be designated as the result of it, what is the essential quality of the event and its interdependence on other events. The method in the end points out the logical contradictions and absurdities in any positive beliefs about inherent existence of things, events, their causes, or their results.

IMPUTATION OF INHERENT EXISTENCE

Everything that arises appears to have the characteristic of 'inherent existence' because of imputation, or projection by dualistic self-consciousness. The classical example of this is a necklace of pearls. We may say to our friend, "Oh, what a pretty necklace." But there are actually a number of pearls held together by a string. It is convenient and natural to give this string a name so that we can refer to it, but the necklace does not inherently exist. Its existence is projected onto it by our minds. Similarly, a tree is made up of a large number of cells. Some of these cells form the bark of the tree, some the wood, some the roots, some the leaves. Sometimes a leaf falls off and then a group of cells that we once considered part of the tree we now consider part of a separate leaf falling to the ground. One branch of the tree has partially broken off and some of the leaves on it are dead while others are still living. Some of the leaves that fell off long ago fell to the ground and decomposed and are now providing nourishment for another generation of leaves. If we were to examine the tree at a microscopic level we would find a continual exchange of gases with the atmosphere, of chemicals with the earth, and of other living organisms swarming in it and on it. Yet all this complex concatenation we refer to as "the tree" and we say that the tree certainly exists. Every 'physical object' that we see around us can be analyzed in this way.

'Nonduality,' 'nonseparateness,' or 'emptiness of inherent existence' are equivalent to the interconnectedness of phenomenon in a vast, undivided, causal web. That is to say, every object originates dependent on causes and conditions and its present existence too is dependent. Natural objects such as trees, rocks, and rivers are dependent for their existence on the other objects around them, the geophysical conditions that gave rise to their environment, and the atoms that compose them. A tree is dependent on the earth in which it has roots, on the rain and sunshine that nourish it, on the carbon dioxide in the air, and on the trees around it that protect it. We cannot find an actual electron or a gene that does not depend on the experiment we do to find it, on the theory we have about it, and on the milieu that surrounds it. A relationship such as 'brotherly love,' 'romantic love,' or 'national pride' depends on the people whom it is relating, on the cultural and social conditions that give rise to that particular form of relationship, on the personal conditions that gave rise to that particular expression of the relationship. A state of mind depends on the particular thoughts, feelings, moods, perceptions, and environmental conditions that are contributing to it at that moment. Even our feeling of 'I-ness' at this moment, whether we feel small and insignificant or solid and bloated, depends on our state of mind, our state of emotions, and our bodily sensations, on what has just been said to us and on how we think of responding. When we examine our experience in this way we find that there is nothing whatsoever that arises or exists independently.

Every individual mind can also be analyzed in terms of imputation or projection. A mind is simply a composite stream of thoughts, feelings, perceptions, and sensations, held together by a sense of identity. This composite stream we call a mind or a person and project inherent existence into it. This was pointed out in the sixth century B.C. by the Buddha, in the second century A.D. by Nagarjuna, in the seventeenth century by David Hume, and subsequently in the twentieth century by William James, Bertrand Russell, and Gilbert Ryle and many others. Ryle was particularly focusing on the idea of 'a mind' rather than the idea of personal identity. He called a mind 'the ghost in the machine' and pointed out that the idea of a mind is an error similar to the error made by a visitor to Oxford who, after visiting all the colleges, the administration buildings, the museums, and after being introduced to the professors, asked, "But where is the University?" The University is not a particular building or place or group of people, it is the combination of all these things; yet it has no location or substance. Similarly, according to Ryle, a mind is the combination of all the thoughts, feelings, and perceptions that a person has, while having no inherent nature of its own—'a mind' is not a 'thing.'[6]

Finally, the dharmas also have no inherent existence. *Forms,* the initial sensory input; *feelings,* initial reactivity; *perception,* the first discernment of an 'object' and a self; *formations* of emotional and thought complexes; and *consciousness* with its conceptual proliferations—all co-arise each moment in dependence on interconnected causes and conditions. They are fleeting and insubstantial, and have no inherent existence. In fact, as we have seen in our discussion of the process of perception, concept, or conceptual representation— one thing, a word or other symbol standing for something else—is the determining factor throughout the whole process. Even the view that perception occurs in a series of perceptual 'moments' is conceptual, arising because of the occurrence of memory and anticipation in the present moment.

This analysis is carried out relentlessly until one begins to be convinced intellectually that no inherent existence can be found. And the practice of mindfulness awareness meditation brings this intellectual understanding into the intuitive level of realization. It enters one's perceptual process at the deepest level so that one perceives one's world as projections of emptiness, no longer projecting inherent existence onto it.

The realization of emptiness may be sudden, or it may gradually dawn on one. And before it dawns, such discovery may at first rouse fear and great anger, especially in that mind that finds its identity in the perception and analysis of the world in terms of 'things,' the mind that we take to be a special measure of being human. Beyond fear this realization may bring with it a feeling, or quality, of sadness and loneliness. It is as if you were standing on top of a high ridge, the wind blowing rain in your face, and you hear a dog barking in the valley below. Again it is as if you have just left home knowing you will never return, as you look back your house disappears around the last corner. The 'thing world' that is so familiar to you and that has been your constant companion for so many years is slipping away. And slipping away too is your self-centered concern. Yet, ironically, that very moment of intense sadness is felt as if one were suddenly relieved from an impossible burden. It is said to bring with it great joy, the joy of discovering the truth of nonseparateness, or nonduality.

When we begin to realize the extent to which we are imputing existence into everything at every moment, and the extent to which we think and act in terms of such imputed existences, then we begin to understand emptiness. Emptiness is the unconditioned, undivided, unconceptualized ground of perception and its world-making and its self-making. Emptiness is not simply the fact that we continually make the mistake of seeing inherent existence where there is none. It is also what is seen when we cease to make this mistake. It is 'what is' before the projection of the concept of existence onto 'what is.'

ULTIMATE AND CONVENTIONAL TRUTH

At the same time we should not make the mistake of nihilism, saying that nothing exists at all. It is the *separate existence* of things that is being challenged. Thus the view of emptiness is not at all equivalent to the view that the world is illusion and there is a more real world behind it, nor that there is nothing at all. It is the view of the inherent separate existence of things that we project onto the world that is illusory, and when we see this as illusion, we see the world 'as it is.' To regard the world as illusion would be to project yet another conceptualization onto it and would thereby be compounding the illusion.

The views that the world is illusion and there is something more real behind it, and that the world is illusion and there is nothing real whatever, are regarded from the view of emptiness as the errors of 'eternalism' and 'nihilism,' respectively. Because of its inveterate tendency to thing-think, the thought process tends to swing backward and forward between eternalism and nihilism with many "Yes but's . . .". It is difficult and very unsettling to try not to fixate on either one, like not fixating on either the old woman or the young woman in Figure 12-1. Our minds become uneasy because they want certainty. They want a closed system of belief and cannot accept openness. Even the certainty of nihilism can be preferable to the intellectual uncertainty of openness. In the case of both eternalism and nihilism, one is imputing a something onto the universe: either an eternal something—a God, a One, a Wholeness, the Light, the Universe, and so on; or a Void, a Blankness, Chance, Death. Incidentally, the fact that all of these are nouns is perhaps the most extraordinary example of thing-thinking that we can find. In Victorian English all nouns, including these, were capitalized just to make sure the reader fully understood that all things **EXIST.**

In order to clarify the relation between emptiness and the everyday world, Nagarjuna presented the two truths: ultimate truth and conventional truth. Ultimate truth is shunyata while conventional truth is the ordinary, conventional world in which we live, including the minds that are projecting inherent existence. But ultimate truth is not separate from conventional truth. When perceptions and thoughts, electrons, emotions, and trees manifest out of emptiness, they are not in reality separated from emptiness, their nature continues to be emptiness. They appear to be separate from emptiness because a separate existence is imputed to them by a mind that has forgotten its own projections. To say that phenomena are not in fact separate from emptiness is to say that relative and absolute truth are not separate.

This is brought out in the most well known of all Mahayana Buddhist texts, the Sutra of the Heart of Transcendent Knowledge, in which it is said, "Form is emptiness, emptiness also is form. Form is no other than emptiness, emptiness is no other than form. In the same way feeling, perception, formation and consciousness are emptiness. Thus all dharmas are emptiness."[7] "Form [as well as feeling and so on] is emptiness" refers to the absolute truth, that all dharmas lack inherent existence. "Emptiness also is form" refers to the relative truth, that nevertheless there is form, feeling, and so on. Emptiness is not a denial of the appearance of a phenomenon.

The second sentence says, first, that form is not other than emptiness; that is, there is no higher, more basic, more substantial, or more permanent reality to form, feeling, and so on. Finally, "emptiness is no other than form" means that emptiness, too, is not a philosophical or religious concept that can be projected onto form to make it better, more real, or more true, nor is it some separate realm existing in its own right. As Chögyam Trungpa Rinpoche says, "We see that looking for beauty or philosophical meaning to life is merely a way of justifying ourselves, saying that things are not as bad as we think. Things *are* as bad as we think. Form is form, emptiness is emptiness, things are just what they are and we do not have to try to see them in the light of some sort of profundity. . . . So shunyata in this case is the complete absence of concepts or filters of any kind, the absence even of the 'form is empty' and the 'emptiness is form' conceptualization."[8]

PRAJNA AND COMPASSION

The experience of shunyata cannot be grasped by inferential, analytical knowledge. There is no final literal description of shunyata that can be compared with so-called objective observation to test its truth by 'correspondence.' However, as I pointed out in the previous chapter, through the training of mindfulness and awareness the perceptual process can be deconstructed, or seen through, and thus shunyata can be directly known.

The awareness that knows shunyata is called *prajna*, a Sanskrit word meaning "best knowledge" or "transcendent knowledge." An often used image for prajna is a two-edged sword, one side of which is continually cutting through fixation on concept, the other side of which cuts through itself. Normally we always tend to rest on some concept and come to some conclusion that we have finally "solved" something. This happens at the mundane level of trying to figure out our friends' motivations, or at the scholarly level of academia. At the mundane level we fixate on some aspects of our friends and come to the conclusion that that is how they are, no longer noticing or accepting new sides to them. At the academic level we come to some philosophical, political, or economic conclusion about how the world is and then refuse to analyze any further, and refuse to accept the further analyses of others. Thus our analysis becomes outmoded and we become stuck and opinionated. But prajna has no resting place, no fixed reference points, no conclusions, no conceptualizations. It realizes the relativity of all conceptualizing. This is the highest development of 'intellect' as we discussed it in Chapter 14.

Prajna is not itself a philosophical system or a further concept, but has been defined as "the natural sharpness of awareness that sees, discriminates and also sees through conceptual discrimination." Prajna is sharpened in the training process of analytical study joined with the practice of meditation. At its highest level it is "the awareness that the whole of reality is without origination or basis."[9] It does not dwell on any eternalistic or nihilistic interpretations of reality and transcends even the distinction between dwelling in confusion and liberation into wakefulness.

It is important to understand that the perceptual discovery of shunyata is not some abstract realization. It is a transformation of perception that is said to be like waking up from a dream. Realization of the extraordinary and profound error that one has been making all one's life—the error of imputing existence onto everything—can be, as Jeffrey Hopkins said, "earth-shaking." It is said to be accompanied by great joy and relief as if an unimaginable burden had dropped, and to be the entry into a new way of conducting one's life.

The motivating energy for this new way of life arises naturally from the realization of shunyata as interdependence. Recognizing the truth of dependent coorigination, that no things have separate existence, someone who has realized shunyata also realizes that the anxiety of others is his or her own anxiety. He or she begins to have an empathetic relationship with others who dwell in anxiety and who have not yet discovered the truth of emptiness. The seed of this compassionate attitude, which is said to exist in all biologically sentient beings, is known as *bodhicitta*, or awakened heart. It begins as a heartfelt warmth and feeling of mutual dependency between oneself and one's kin that is epitomized in the love of a mother of any species for her young. And beyond this it can extend toward others. The action of compassion is a natural ethical action that arises from direct knowledge of shunyata. It is not conceptual, philosophical, or religious. It occurs as a result of realizing the mechanism of the imputation of inherent existence onto sentient beings. Because of this, the compassion of helping others goes hand in hand with the prajna of realizing the nonexistence of 'self' and 'other.'

From the point of view of shunyata that I have presented in this chapter we can now go deeper in our analysis of perception. It is clear that the five skandhas as well as the various components into which we analyzed experience from the data of cognitive science do not themselves have inherent existence. They are merely useful conceptual categories that enable us to discriminate the nature of that experience more precisely than we do with our habitual categories of everyday life. And there remain two very fundamental concepts that we have not yet fully dealt with in our analysis, the concepts of 'a mind' and 'a body.' But before we do this it is necessary to turn our language back on itself, to use language to ask, what is the role of language in the covering over and the rediscovery of shunyata?

17

Not Mere Emptiness

FOR SOME MAHAYANA SCHOOLS the teaching of shunyata is the final teaching: samasara and nirvana are not different in that both have the fundamental nature of emptiness, beyond this nothing can or should be said. This is a teaching that points one in the direction of direct intuition of experience, but says nothing of it. These schools had the intention to demonstrate the fundamental incoherence of all speculative philosophy, all philosophical and conceptual systems of every kind, as well as the ordinary concepts and confused beliefs by which we usually live, so that the experience of what is could be realized beyond all this. To speak of what is beyond concept would be bound to wrap the student in yet another layer of self-deception. This is why *belief* in shunyata has been called the 'golden chain,' and, for Nagarjuna, those who *believe* in shunyata are deemed uncurable.

The Prasangika school of Buddhism was particularly adamant about this. According to Khenpo Tsultrim Gyatso, "The Prasangikas argue that to establish emptiness through reasoning is a subtle attempt to grasp the ultimate nature with the conceptual mind. Reason shows the conceptual mind is always in error, it can only ever give a distorted and ultimately self-contradictory version of experience, never the nature of reality itself. Therefore they refuse to use any reasoning to establish the true nature of phenomena. They say that since the ultimate nature is beyond even the most subtle concepts, it is misleading to try to establish or prove this as a description or a concept that expresses the ultimate nature of reality. There is something very profound in this method. It is quite uncompromising in its systematic refutation of all conceptual attempts to grasp the nature of the absolute."[1] The Gelugpa school of Tibetan Buddhism claim to be followers of this approach, although they do after all make statements about the nature of relative reality. The Zen Buddhist school of Japan also takes this approach.

In this sense these philosophers had similar intentions to those modern philosophers classified by Richard Rorty as 'edifying' philosophers in contrast to 'systematic' philosophers. Of these philosophers, Rorty remarks, "Great systematic philosophers are constructive and offer arguments. Great edifying philosophers are reactive and offer satires, parodies, aphorisms. They know their work loses its point when the period they were reacting against is over. . . . Great systematic philosophers, like great scientists, build for eternity. Great edifying philosophers destroy for the sake of their own generation. Systematic philosophers want to put their subject on the secure path of a science. Edifying philosophers want to keep space open for the sense of wonder which poets can sometimes cause—wonder that there is something new under the sun, something which is *not* an accurate representation of what was already there, something which (at least for the moment) cannot be explained and can barely be described."[2]

All these 'edifying' philosophers showed the inherent contradictions in every concept in order to point to what is beyond concept, to cut through the imaginary world of mental projections in order to see beyond them. Nevertheless there are problems even in such an apparently pure approach. Later imitators destroyed that imaginary world and suggested that there is absolutely nothing beyond. This is precisely what happened with the analytic philosophy that followed Wittgenstein, although this was perhaps not Wittgenstein's intention. It is also what happened with some followers of Buddhism. The result is, of course, the extreme of nihilism. And the only way in discourse to avoid this extreme is to try to say *something* about the 'contents' of shunyata.

In order to do this one must state the truth of shunyata and at the same time understand the relative nature of all language. One must understand the difference between using language to *describe*, and using language to *point to*. For 'systematic' philosophers, which includes most philosophers of science at least before the past two decades, its use to describe and to make falsifiable propositions about the world, is language's highest expression. Karl Popper, the grand old man of philosophy of science, who developed the theory of the falsifiability of scientific theories in his ground-breaking work *The Logic of Scientific Discovery*, makes this point over and over again.[3] But for 'edifying' philosophers, poets, and all who recognize a spiritual dimension to people, the use of language to point *beyond* itself is its highest expression. Understanding the relative nature of language and the impossibility of speaking literally of what is beyond concept, we will try to discover in what way it can be said that shunyata is not *mere* emptiness.

THE THREE NATURES

Shunyata is not *mere* nothingness, *mere* non-being. As Masao Abe says, "Emptiness which is completely without form is freed from both being and non-being because 'non-being' is still a form distinguished from 'being'. . . . [The] idea of emptiness is not a mere emptiness as opposed to fullness. Emptiness as shunyata transcends and embraces both emptiness and fullness. It is really formless in the sense that it is liberated from both 'form' and 'formlessness.' Thus in shunyata, Emptiness as it is is Fullness and Fullness as it is is Emptiness; formlessness as it is is form and form as it is is formless. This is why, for Nagarjuna, true Emptiness is wondrous Being."[4]

What is meant by the "fullness' of shunyata? Clearly, in that it is beyond concept, this fullness can only be pointed to, it cannot be literally described. One way in which this "pointing to" has been done, by the fifth-century Buddhist Asanga, was in terms of the 'three natures,'[5] which provide a kind of bridge between the ultimate truth of shunyata and the conventional truth of the mundane world, and separate out the conventional world into two components. There may seem to be an incompleteness to the division between ultimate truth and conventional truth. The designation of all apparent phenomena as 'conventional truth' does not seem to leave room for the distinction between direct perception of 'what is' and the imaginary thing-forms that we impute onto it. This is particularly frustrating for someone interested in scientific inquiry because after our analysis there remains the question, *is* there anything left when thought projections are seen as such and if so how can we talk of it? Nagarjuna did not make this distinction because he wished to point directly to emptiness, in essence saying, "See emptiness. Before you can do this, all is worthless speculation." It is like someone about to take a first parachute jump who tries to find out how an airplane is able to take people up into the air so that people can jump, and why people need parachutes but cannot fly by themselves. The instructor might very well say, "Just jump."

However, after Nagarjuna, the mistake of separateness again reared up. Ultimate became separated from conventional, and more real than conventional. This led inevitably to the wrong views of nihilism or eternalism. It led to nihilism for those who became entangled in the analysis of phenomena as empty. It led to eternalism for those who became immersed in the experience of meditation and began to take emptiness as a 'something.'

So Asanga in the fourth century proposed the 'three natures' as a further understanding of the conventional and the ultimate, and as a further explanation of just what is being denied in the denial of self-nature, or inherent nature. The three natures are (1) false conceptions, (2) dependent truth, and (3) complete perfection. *False conceptions* is just that: false imputation that arises from the tendency to proliferate concepts. *Dependent truth* is 'what is' when the false imputation of inherent existence to things is removed. It is the continuity of awareness of a self and its projected world arising moment by moment and is called dependent truth in reference to the mutual dependence of subject and object. *Complete perfection* is shun-yata, its emptiness and fullness.

A classical analogy for the three natures is the example of walking in the garden one evening and suddenly coming across a snake coiled in the grass in front of you. You leap back in fright, and then gingerly walk forward to see what kind of a snake it is. When you are a few feet away from it you suddenly realize, with a wave of relief and humor, that it is not in fact a snake but a garden hose. The realization that the snake has no inherent existence, but was merely imputed by your imagination, together with your mind suddenly opened on having this realization, is likened to the nature of *complete perfection*. The hose, together with your delight at seeing the hose *as* a hose, is like the *dependent* nature. The snake, which did not exist at all beyond your imagination of it, is like the nature of *false conceptions*.

To give another, similar, example, the wax effigies at Madame Tussaud's Museum in London are so lifelike that it is often very difficult to tell that they are not alive. One day, as a boy, I was visiting the museum and approached a guard standing, in uniform, at the foot of the stairs to ask for directions. As I approached him I began to feel uneasy because he was not smiling at me and looking helpful as I expected, nor was he looking stern and imperious as I felt a guard should. When I was just a few feet from him, I realized that he was wax. I experienced a strong sense of shock and a rather creepy feeling of its *non-person-ness* and that I had not been able to recognize the difference between a live person and this effigy, together with relief that my unease was now understood. In this analogy, the live guard would be the *false conception*, the wax effigy together with my seeing it as wax would be the *dependent nature*, and the absence of a live person the nature of emptiness. This second example is perhaps more close to home because a hint of shunyata may indeed be met with just such a creepy feeling of the *absence* of the familiar world of existing 'things.' But the full experience of shunyata is said to be one of 'great joy' because, at the same time as realizing emptiness of conceptions, there is awareness of complete purity.

The point is that something like this is happening *all the time*. Suppose for example that two people are standing in front of a rose (or, for that matter a pile of fresh horse-manure.) One says to the other, "Look at that rose." The situation itself is a result of a vast web of interconnected causes: the two human organisms arrived in front of the rose as a result of the intercourse of their parents and their whole life history up to that point; their ability to perceive the rose and to recognize and name it is the result of evolution and training; the rose is there as a result of having being planted by a gardener, who took care of it, as a result of the sun shining and the rain falling all those years, and so on. But when one person says to another, "rose," that person is using a symbol that applies not just to that rose, but to all roses, independent of this particular time and place, and he or she is using this symbol to convey a concept to someone else. Then the word "rose" begins to be taken as the thing itself. We begin to regard the actual rose as a separate thing, ignoring its connections to the rose bush, the earth and so on, *and to the perceiver*, just as the word "rose" is separate and distinct from all other words. We begin to associate with the rose all kinds of qualities, of which we may or may not be conscious, coming not from our perception of that actual rose, but from our web of connotations of the word "rose."

It is the conceptualizing, discriminating, imagining function that separates isolated things, then conceives of these things' real independent existences and only afterwards their occasional connections. That is why this aspect of the rose is called its 'false conception.' When we see through this conceptualizing process, when we *see* it as just that—a conceptualizing process—and begin to look directly at this process, looking through it without ignoring it, then we see the interconnectedness of the entire phenomenal world. That is, we see the relative, dependent nature. When we experience this, we cease to believe in the ultimate reality of the object as a real external thing, which is the false conception. We realize instead that the real existence of a subject, myself, and the real existence of an external object, have been projected into what is by our conceptualizing minds. Subject and object in any situation arise in dependence on each other, and this is the relative, dependent nature.

The important point here is that when false conception is removed, by being seen as such, the dependent nature is seen as it is, and this nature is not separate from the ultimate nature, emptiness. The dependent nature is content, fullness, structure of interdependence within emptiness. The interdependent characteristics of phenomena within the dependent nature provide the basis for the process of perceptual discrimination, and for the arbitrary assignment of sounds as names, and therefore the basis for false conception. It is not dependent nature as such that is a problem, or the process of naming, which is simply an aspect of dependent nature. When perceiving dependent nature, one perceives the formation of subject-object split and the projecting process of mind as that split is happening. When perceiving the nature of false conception, one forgets this process and perceives as if things really exist as we think they do, 'out there.'

MISTAKING NAMES FOR REALITY

The problem of believing false conception nature to be all that is lies in the taking of the names as surrogates for a dynamic, interdependent process, like taking snapshots of a turbulent river, and then proceeding to perceive and act as if the characteristics of the names were identical to the characteristics of that process. A person may be a native of the United Soviet Socialist Republics and so we call him a "Russian." We then attribute to that person all the connotations and attributes that we, and our society, have attached to the name "Russian." We may then fear and perhaps hate this person. And we do the same thing with "chairs," "cats," "cups of tea," and our "closest friends" as we do with this unfortunate "Russian."

We react with outrage, hatred, passion, desire, one-up-manship, and so on not to the actual situation as it is, fresh and unknown, at that very moment but to a concept we have of a permanent person with certain characteristics that we know only too well. We act as if there is in everyone a unified agent, "Bertie," "Jeffrey," "Penelope," "Father," or whatever it is we call them, responsible for his or her actions at every moment. Yet there is in reality no such agent at all. Such a belief is false conception existing only in our language-dependent world.

This brings us again to the question of language. According to the study of Diana Paul on language in the Yogacara view, first taught by Asanga and taken to China in the sixth century A.D. by Paramartha, Yogacara Buddhism holds that

> Language fulfills a useful social and communal function,

enabling us to communicate with each other, to have interpersonal relations, and to promote mutual understanding in the societies we live in. Reality, however, must be experienced in a very personal and direct manner, and not through the medium of language. Mental discourse that is influenced by our language is not the personal, direct sort of knowledge the Mahayanists advocate. A prelinguistic [awareness] of reality is free of mental discourse that is based on ideas and formed through false discrimination. Such immediate knowledge enables us to view the world without the distorting medium of language. . . . Yogacarin views on language focus on the communicative function of language, particularly the arbitrary nature of word formation, the intentional nature of reference of language, and the influence of language on our attitudes and behavior.[6]

By the 'intentional' nature of language is meant the fact that words cannot refer to any 'external object' since, as we now know, 'external objects' are created by the perceptual process, and especially the naming process. Words are, rather, constructed by the human mind to express acts of consciousness that 'mean' or are 'about' an object, whether or not that object actually exists. If we say 'I intend to go for a walk,' we mean that we are going to bring 'going for a walk' into our present world. And when we say 'I see a chair,' a very similar process is happening. We mean that our perceptual process has, by naming it at deeply subconscious levels, brought a chair into our present world. This is why Paul refers to the 'intentional reference' of language.

In ordinary everyday discourse when we say, "You are a foreigner, and I dislike you," we forget the role of our own perceptual process in that disliking. We think we mean *that real foreigner* and ignore whether or not he or she 'really' exists. And even when we do understand quite thoroughly that the "foreigner" does not ultimately have inherent existence, we still use words in the conventional way. The same analysis applies not only to rather vague concepts like "foreigner"; it applies equally to supposedly concrete objects, cars, trees, bodies, and so on. "Foreigner," "tree," "car," and "body" then refer to the state of mind that *intends,* or points out, a repetitive perceptual pattern that some group conventionally agrees to call "foreigner," "tree," and so on. This *intending* of things is in fact the essential nature of ordinary language, and the supposed capacity to express the truth about things is not essential to language. However, giving a name to something psychologically predisposes the name-giver to believe in an existing thing corresponding to that name. And so, as Diana Paul says, "The ordinary person is attached to the name and discriminates the nature of the object intended, saying the name is the same as the object intended. This is an incoherent way of thinking."

In these terms the representational nature of language involves us automatically in the view of a world composed of subjects and objects as real entities, because the structure of language itself is this way. We cannot at all derive the nature of the world from the nature of language. However, as Paul says, "If we reflect upon the structure of consciousness, we can become aware of the capacity of consciousness to intend objects over and against subjects. These acts of intending are influenced by the [verbal] distinctions we construct. We can in that way understand how language reinforces a dualistic view of the world, a world of subjects as contrasted with objects."[7] This is the idea of 'false conceptions' and a return of the idea of 'the proliferating tendency of concepts' that we met in our dharma analysis of perception according to the earlier abhidharma schools. This discussion applies not only to the natural verbal languages; it applies also to any symbol system in which a word, image, or sign of any kind is taken to represent, to stand for, and to intend something other than itself. Such representing and intending are the essence of language, verbal or otherwise, and we have seen that it enters the perceptual process at the very first contact between sense organ and sense field, the skandha of *form*.

THE THREE NATURES IN MODERN TERMS

The role of language in creating a nature of false conceptions has clearly been understood by some recent western philosophers, although it must be said that this understanding seems to have remained mostly at the theoretical level. According to Rorty, "On the periphery of the history of modern philosophy, one finds figures who, without forming a 'tradition,' resemble each other in their distrust of the notion that man's essence is to be a knower of essences [inherent existences.] Goethe, Kierkegaard, Santayana, William James, Dewey, the later Wittgenstein, the later Heidegger, are figures of this sort. They are often accused of relativism and cynicism. They are often dubious about progress, and especially about the latest claim that such-and-such a discipline has at last made the nature of human knowledge so clear that reason will now spread throughout the rest of human activity. These writers have kept alive the suggestion that, even when we have justified true belief about everything we want to know, we may have no more than conformity to the norms of the day. They have kept alive the historicist sense that this century's 'superstition' was the last century's triumph of reason, as well as the relativist sense that the latest vocabulary, borrowed from the latest scientific achievement, may not express privileged representation of essences, but be just another of the potential infinity of vocabularies in which the world can be described.

Wittgenstein in his later writing was very much in touch with an understanding of *false conception*, its extent, its power over us, and its creation by language. A great deal of his *Philosophical Investigations* is concerned with the various 'language games' that are played out by individual and society, and the worlds these games create. Yet it would seem that Wittgenstein did not mean this to be a statement of all that there is, but rather it was meant to be a cure for thinking that we can at all *say* all that there is, *precisely*. And it is especially a cure for the problems of philosophy, which are also the problems of 'objective' science, which come from *trying* to say all that there is, or even thinking that one *should* be able to say all that there is in a few limited 'language games.' He says, for example, that "philosophy leaves the world as it is," and "my attitude toward him is an attitude toward a soul. I am not of the *opinion* that he has a soul."[8] The latter statement is a rare kind of statement to find in Wittgenstein, but it indicates that he clearly saw the difference between how we think about someone, our 'opinion,' and how we act toward him as it expresses our 'attitude' to him.

In his younger years Wittgenstein seemed aware of what is beyond language. He ends his first treatise on language and logic saying, "That of which man cannot speak, on that he must be silent."[9] Some of his biographers suggest that in later years he lost this vision in his own obsession with the limits of language. Certainly, those 'linguistic philosophers' who followed him have brought the mainstream of modern philosophy to a state of profound nihilism. But mostly Wittgenstein preferred, like the Prasangika and Zen Buddhists, to say nothing along these lines. After all, to speak of what is outside of or beyond our language games is to use language and therefore, in bringing it into a language game, to lose it.

Harvard philosopher Nelson Goodman has developed the view of the world-making characteristics of words and symbols. He argues that all of the various worlds of scientists, artists, and ordinary men and women are but 'versions' that can be judged 'right' or 'wrong' in terms of various internal characteristics or by comparison of versions with each other. But they cannot be judged 'true' by testing against any foundational 'real' world, because there is no such real world beyond our versions. He summarizes his view thus: "Talk of unstructured content or an unconceptualized given or a substratum without properties is self-defeating; for the talk imposes structure, conceptualizes, ascribes properties."

Goodman continues, "The many stuffs—matter, energy, waves, phenomena—that worlds are made of are made along with the worlds. But made from what? Not from nothing, after all, *but from other worlds*. Worldmaking as we know it always starts from worlds already on hand: the making is a remaking. Anthropology and developmental psychology may study social and individual histories of such world-building, but the search for a universal or necessary beginning is best left to theology. . . . With the false hope of a firm foundation gone, with the world displaced by worlds that are but versions, with substance dissolved into function, and with the given acknowledged as taken, we face the question how worlds are made, tested and known." The Buddhist would agree at every point with this passage, including the implication that the theological search is never-ending, since that search too is simply another 'version' so long as it remains conceptual. The Buddhist simply asserts that when these insights are completely realized personally, by chance or through the practice of meditation, then there is a profound positive change in one's relationship to one's world. But if one merely assents to them intellectually, then nihilism and the egotism that goes along with it may be reinforced rather than diminished.

Goodman's book *Ways of Worldmaking* is dedicated to showing how versions are made with words and other symbols, such as the symbols of art and music. Goodman has described the *false conception nature*, which is what his 'versions' are, but he has here got hold of only one side of shunyata. Like the Prasangikas, he correctly says that talk of unstructured content is self-defeating because such talk imposes conceptual structure. Goodman understands that acknowledging the world-constructing activity of symbol systems could have profound practical consequences for the conduct of the arts, the sciences, and education. In 1967 he founded Project Zero at the Harvard Graduate School of Education, dedicated to arts education.

But, through the practice of mindfulness-awareness, emptiness can be *realized*, not just talked about. Goodman, along with many other modern philosophers who have reached a conceptual grasp of emptiness, does not appear to appreciate this possibility, since he has only theology, itself another version, to offer as a means to go beyond versions. Goodman says, "The overwhelming case against perception without conception, the pure given, absolute immediacy, the innocent eye, substance as substratum, has been so fully and frequently set forth as to need no restatement here. Although conception without perception is merely *empty*, perception without conception is *blind*."[10] Insofar as Goodman is talking here of dualistic perception of an 'outer world' (the pure given) perceived by the mind as a mirror of nature (the 'innocent eye'), this passage is restating the results of our entire analysis of perception. The Buddhists, as well, extensively criticize 'perception without conception' in this sense. But according to the Buddhists, the involvement of conception in perception, and therefore also the ground from which this dualistic perception arises, can be *seen* or *felt* directly. The awareness that sees this process is not blind. This is the ground of *complete perfection*, which they assert is experiential while being beyond concept.

The view of language creations as *false conception* is found, too, in the later Heidegger. He showed that our ideas of *what is* and our ability to describe this idea in language have further and further obscured it. Inauthentic existence is to become caught up in the descriptions, taking them to be *what is*. Over the generations, the intensity of the open mind has been obscured by technical knowledge, by science (in the sense of the standard view), by our gradual revealing, uncovering and explaining *what is*, and finally by our dwelling in our language descriptions.

In its final absorption into science and technology, according to Heidegger, speculative thought as system-building philosophy, has come to an end. People are invited by Heidegger to "have an experience with language,"[11] as he says, rather than merely to dwell in it. By this he seems to mean that we are invited to experience language as it is and to realize the world-making nature of language rather than being lost in it, and thus to work back to the point of view from which *what is* can be glimpsed. This working back brings us to "waiting"—not "waiting for" something, but waiting in openness so that *what is* can come to us unspoken. "Our sole question is, what is it that calls on us to think. How else shall we hear that which calls, which speaks in thinking, and perhaps speaks in such a way that its own deepest core is left unspoken?"

In pointing 'thinking' toward that which is unspoken, Heidegger gradually steers 'thinking' back to the realm of insight. "Thinking is only thinking when it recalls in thought the *eon* [a Greek word meaning what is present, or *what is*], that which this word indicates properly and truly, that is unspoken, tacitly." Unlike Goodman, then, Heidegger acknowledges what is beyond our worlds of descriptions. He expresses this in the following phrase which he translated and interpreted from Parmenides: "Useful the letting-lie-before-us and also the taking-to-heart [of] beings in being." This is a difficult phrase and one which Heidegger takes his entire book to unravel, but nevertheless it conveys something of his realization of the shining ("letting-lie-before-us") out of *dependent nature* ("beings") within *complete perfection* ("being"), as well as its dependence on the perceiver ("taking-to-heart").[12]

SUMMARY

Ignoring the role of language in bringing forth our lived world has serious practical consequences at the level of so-called therapy. Almost all modern therapeutic systems ignore the fundamental role of language in creating the imaginary nature of false conception. Most therapies are in fact means of helping the patient to create a new inner dialogue, and therefore a new imaginary nature, rather than to see through inner dialogue altogether. Thus the imaginary nature, and the ego corresponding to it, is patched up and made to feel more harmonious, but the fundamental problem, the problem of language-based false conception, is not met. Complete healing, or wholesomeness, comes from seeing through false conception to the unbroken ground of complete perfection in which it arises, and this cannot come about in a therapy that is dedicated to smothering the patients' feelings of longing for self-transcendence and trying to make them fully satisfied with mundane existence. A few therapists have acknowledged this—for example Victor Frankl, author of *Man's Search for Meaning*, Jacques Lacan, and R. D. Laing—but it is very rare.

We have seen in this chapter that the fullness of shunyata lies in its potentiality to give rise to all phenomena, unimpededly, as subject and object arise interdependently. We have seen how error arises when the subject-object split is ignored and an "objective" world of things, the world of false conceptions, is projected together with a "subjective" world of "I." And we have seen the role of language and other symbol systems, at a very deep level, in these projections. In the next chapter, we will look further into the tendency of thought to perceive a static world of things, rather than to include itself in a world of constantly changing patterning process.

The basic statement of method in relation to these three natures is that when *false conception* is seen *as such*, then the *dependent truth* is seen within shunyata, *complete perfection*. Shunyata therefore has the potentiality to manifest all appearance. While false conception is altogether without reality, the dependent nature has a relative reality. Forms do appear within shunyata, but as their mutual dependence with the perceiver is felt, they shine with a spacious but self-luminous quality that is at the same time empty of inherent existence. This luminosity that is beyond concept is the fullness of shunyata.

18

No 'Things' of Thought

THE TENDENCY TO REGARD THE WORLD as being made up of separate entities, 'things,' having their own separate existence and identity and only accidentally related to other 'things' is the most deep-rooted characteristic of human thought. We can call it the 'fallacy of separate existence.' This fallacy was termed the "Fallacy of Misplaced Concreteness" by Alfred North Whitehead, the last great system-building philosopher of this century, who anticipated the dawning of a view of the world as process. By the Fallacy of Misplaced Concreteness, Whitehead was referring to the error of mistaking abstract ideas for concrete realities. In particular he was referring to the belief on the part of seventeenth-century scientists up to scientists of the present day that there are, in actuality, lumps of matter with simple location, i.e., at a particular point in space and a particular moment in time. Whitehead says, "This idea is the very foundation of the seventeenth century scheme of nature. Apart from it, the scheme is incapable of expression." And, of course, this belief is now deep rooted in the 'common sense' view of every man and woman in the modern world.

Whitehead then goes on to argue that, ". . . among the primary elements of nature as apprehended in our immediate experience, there is no element whatever which possesses this character of simple location."[1] We do not directly see, hear, smell, taste, or touch small pieces of matter located at specific points in space and time. What we do apprehend in our immediate experience is a complex interweaving of colors, shapes, sounds, smells, and so on that are brought into existence relative to the structure of the human organism and that are organized and correlated into a complete, continually changing moment of experience.

In order to be able to measure this experience and to think about the results of those measurements, Galileo and Newton talked about lumps of matter in space and time. Newton's ideas of space and time:

absolute empty space having no action on its contents, and absolute time flowing independently of all happenings in the universe were abstractions, as we now understand. There is in our actual momentary experience no such space and no such time. Nor, therefore, can there be in our experience lumps of matter moving in this space and time. This does not mean that Newtonian and subsequent mechanical science was altogether wrong—the abstraction certainly bore some relation to experience and was useful. But it is nevertheless an abstraction, not a concrete reality. As Whitehead says, "It does not follow that the science of the seventeenth century was simply wrong. I hold that by a process of constructive abstraction we can arrive at abstractions which are the simply-located bits of material, and at other abstractions which are the minds included in the scientific scheme. Accordingly the real error is an example of what I have termed: The Fallacy of Misplaced Concreteness."

In speaking of the fallacy of separate existence, I have simply extended Whitehead's problem with simple location to the tendency of thought to think in terms of 'things' under almost all circumstances. When fire was first being explained, it was thought of as a thing, phlogiston. When heat was being investigated, caloric was invented. Caloric was supposed to be a fluid substance that entered a piece of matter when that piece was placed in higher temperature. Caloric was supposed to flow from hotter to colder bodies. The caloric theory of heat was a legitimate and widely held theory for a long time, until physicists decided that heat is a form of the motion of the molecules of matter. For the motion of electromagnetic waves, we had the ether, a subtle material that was doing the waving, just as water is the basis for waves on the ocean. Later, again, it was decided that the waves were merely waves of energy, there being no substantial thing underlying them. For life, we had an explanation in terms of a vital force. To explain the forces of nature we had the gods. Nowadays we have elementary particles as the building blocks of matter, we have DNA as the root of life, genes as the unit of inheritance, organisms as the units of living things, species as the units of diversity, computers as individual minds, and the Universe as everything. All these were more or less useful abstractions. The reader might have found himself or herself smiling at the quaint errors of the first half of the list and becoming slightly irritated at the second half. But they are all, equally, examples of 'thing-thinking.' It is necessary for our peace of mind to believe that past generations made the mistakes, not us.

CLOSED SYSTEMS MUST DECAY

The fallacy of separate existence led nineteenth-century scientists to think of the Universe as made up of closed, isolated systems. This led very naturally to the discovery of the idea of 'entropy,' which measures the amount of chaos or disorder in the system. The basic idea of the entropy law is that in a closed-system entropy, the amount of chaos in the system always increases. For example, suppose you have a tray of water and you place drops of blue ink in it, in a circle. In a while the ink circle will have dissipated throughout the water and you will just have a uniformly bluish tray of water. Instead of being arranged in a circle the ink drops are now randomly arranged throughout the water, so there is less order in the uniformly colored water than there was in the original circle. If we had a tray of uniformly dyed water we would not expect to find the dye all gathering together into a circle. In fact if that happened we would think either something 'supernatural' must have occurred, or else the system was not actually closed, that there were some outside forces acting on the water that we were not aware of. Perhaps for example the dye was made of iron particles and there was a circular magnet under the tray that we had not known about. The magnet was outside of the 'closed system' of tray and water but exerting forces on it, therefore the tray-water system was not actually closed.

So the entropy law says that a closed system always changes in the direction of less order. For decades this law was simply applied to all systems we find in nature, and it was said that the order we see around us, the flowers, birds, snow crystals, and cathedrals were all accidents that temporarily managed to defeat the law of entropy but that in the end would succumb to it. And this led naturally to the idea that everything is essentially, inevitably decaying. Everything is moving from states of higher to states of lower order, and eventually everything will completely decay to complete chaos. This is the natural way of nature, and any appearance of order in nature is purely accidental, a temporary blip on the face of chaos.

Little attention was paid to the fact that all the systems we find on earth are open systems, the Earth itself is an open system (receiving constant infusion of energy from the sun and from cosmic radiation), the solar system is an open system, our Galaxy, the Milky Way, is an open system as are all other galaxies and the galactic clusters and superclusters. And to say whether the universe itself is open or closed probably does not mean very much. All the systems we find in nature, plants and animals, trees, flowers, birds, dogs, and humans are all *essentially* open.

The idea of the inevitable decay of everything applies *only* to closed systems. That is, this idea is about systems that are totally isolated from everything else in the universe. *No such system actually exists as part of our universe.* If such a system does exist there is no way we can know about it since any communication between us and it would mean that it was no longer isolated and therefore no longer closed. Nevertheless we can, in abstraction, think about such a thing. There are situations in the world that are almost isolated, and the extent to which they are not isolated can be included in our thinking about them. For example, from the point of view of its mechanical motion around the sun, the Earth is almost isolated; therefore we can calculate in detail its orbit around the sun. And we can also take into account the extent to which the Earth is not isolated because other planets have a small gravitational effect on its motion. A gas in a closed, sealed container is almost isolated from the rest of the world, and the behavior of the gas can be calculated as if that gas were completely isolated.

It should be said that to deal only with closed systems was a perfectly reasonable approach on their part since physicists had no way of knowing how to calculate what would happen in an open system. It was, however, not at all reasonable to extend the work of scientists in this very limited domain to become a Theory of Everything. There is a powerful reason why generally this was done without too much thought: the fallacy of separate existence. If we think in terms of things that are basically separate, that are defined by their own qualities rather than by their interactions with other things, then it is perfectly reasonable to think in terms of closed systems, because this is precisely what a closed system is. A closed system can be defined by its inherent characteristics, its interactions being minor deviations from this. In an open system the interactions between (or within) the system and its environment form a significant part of the definition of that system.

OPEN SYSTEMS CAN EVOLVE

In the past two decades a revolution has been taking place in the understanding of order and chaos in open systems. This revolution has been led by Ilya Prigogine, who received a Nobel Prize for his work in chemistry.[2] This revolution will enable us to unfix our thinking to an extent comparable to the change of thinking brought about by Einstein's revolution. Thanks to Einstein we were able to free ourselves from narrow, fixed ideas about the nature of the space and time we think we live in. Thanks to Prigogine and his colleagues we will have a weapon to begin to free ourselves from the fallacy of separate existence in relation to natural systems. We will be able, if we wish, to begin to free ourselves from the illusion that anything exists in isolation in nature, or that it is even useful to think of 'things' in nature in this way.

Prigogine has shown, essentially, that while closed systems are bound to decay to the state of least order, open systems have an inherent possibility to evolve to states of increasing complexity and order. In other words, we now know that the appearance of order in the natural world is allowed by the laws of nature, and does not require the invocation of any 'supernatural' principle. But this is so only if we think of all the systems exhibiting order as being *essentially* open, *essentially* connected to their environments. Only isolated systems are subject to inevitable decay. A communicating system, a system that exchanges energy or order between itself and other, is not at all subject to decay but may in fact continue to progress to higher and higher levels of complexity, order, and internal energy. Prigogine worked out the detailed thermodynamics of open systems with reference to the analysis of dynamic chemical reactions. However, the analysis was in terms general enough to apply wherever we find order in complex systems: the motion of whirlpools, the cooperative building of hives by termites, the learning and developing intelligence of a child, the organization of a city.

Prigogine showed not only that it is possible, but that it is natural and almost inevitable for open systems to evolve from states of lower to states of higher energetic order. In brief, the way this occurs is like this: Open systems can have high energy states that are stable when there is a small change in the input energy, but unstable under a large change. For example, if you turn the faucet on to the point where the water comes out in a gentle curling pattern, you can alter the setting of the faucet a little either way and the curling pattern will remain. If you open the faucet appreciably, the water pattern will either degenerate to a chaotic splash or change to an altogether different pattern at a higher level of vibration. This is characteristic of all open systems: when these systems are at a stable energy level above the lowest and they receive a large enough change in input, they will either collapse to a much lower level or rise irreversibly to a level of greater order and energy. We see this principle in nature all the time: the way a beehive responds to intrusion, the learning curve of a child, the response of a person or a nation to sudden wealth or economic collapse. All show the tendency, when they are subjected to a sudden energetic shock, to either collapse to a lower, more chaotic, level or to rise to a higher level of order.

All this is much more in accord with the way we intuitively experience our lives than the proclamations of gradual but certain decay. And all of this depends essentially on the idea of open systems, of interconnectedness of systems one with another. We can apply this way of thinking at all magnitudes: elementary particles have all the requirements of open, dynamic systems, as do organisms and the planet Earth, as do galaxies. Prigogine terms these systems 'dissipative structures.' 'Structure' refers to the fact that the systems have internal organization; 'dissipative' refers to their characteristic of *dissipating* entropy (chaos) as their internal structures change in the direction of higher energy and greater self-organization.

Thinking about open systems gives us an entirely different view on how to define life. Rather than being due to the presence of a particular thing—vital spirit or DNA—life could be more appropriately defined in terms of pattern. For example Feinberg and Shapiro in *Life Beyond Earth* suggest, "Life is fundamentally the activity of a biosphere. A biosphere is a highly ordered system of matter and energy characterized by complex cycles that maintain or gradually increase the order of the system through an exchange of energy with its environment."[3] We can see, even in the case of a simple cell, that a definition of life in terms of 'pattern' is clearly more adequate than a 'substance' view. If one takes a single cell and gently breaks the outer membrane that holds it into an organized unit, without destroying any of the other material structures in it, that cell will cease to have the characteristics we normally regard as 'living.' In particular it will not be able to divide and multiply: destroy its pattern of organization and it is no longer living. We saw in Chapter 9 how Maturana and Varela have worked out the details of a view that regards life as self-organization.

According to this view the planet Earth may well be a living system. James Lovelock came to the conclusion that the Earth is a living system through his studies of the composition of gases in the atmosphere, a composition so improbable as to require a global mechanism to maintain it. Lovelock maintains that the entire range of living matter on Earth, from whales to viruses, and from oaks to algae, could be regarded as constituting a single living entity, capable of manipulating the Earth's atmosphere to suit its overall needs and endowed with faculties and powers far beyond those of its constituent parts.[4] The galaxy, too, is a complex system exchanging energy with its environment, and exhibiting order. The scope and time scale of our knowledge is too limited for us to tell by present methods whether the galaxy may be considered a living system. But the present way of thinking says that there is no reason why a galaxy should not be a self-organizing system.

'Bodies' and 'minds,' also, are selected as special patterns in which to discern inherent existence. But, as Owen Flanagan says, ". . . the snag with the traditional formulations of the mind-body problem is the tendency to think that we must frame a solution in which conscious mental life is analyzed as *a thing*, preferably as *The Thing*. It is not at all surprising that this never works. Mental states are functional states and functional properties of the complex commerce we have with the outside world."[5] Unfortunately Flanagan did not have the good sense to place 'outside world' in parentheses; thus he made the mistake corresponding precisely to the mistake he criticizes the traditional view for: the mistake of regarding the 'outside world' as a thing, perhaps even *The Thing*.

A simple illustration of what is meant by a functional state is the state of walking. No matter in how great detail we describe someone's legs: the muscles, bones, blood, nerves, connections to the rest of the body, and so on, we are still not describing "walking." Walking is as 'real' as the legs, but it is not a thing. Similarly, we could describe a clock as that which tells time. There can be a vast array of such instruments: sundials, candles, sand timers, water clocks, pendulum clocks, spring clocks, and quartz clocks. Many of these have no physical resemblance to each other whatsoever, a quartz clock to a candle for example. Yet they all have the function of "telling the time." The relation between the level of patterning we call 'matter' and at least some of what we call mental, particularly thoughts and emotions, can in this view be similar to the relation between legs and walking, or between clocks and the function of telling the time. Both are 'real' but one is an order of patterning different from the other.

Beyond this, we can see that the open-systems way of thinking applies as well to the organization of thought. In the present universe, because we think in terms of static closed systems our way of thinking tends to demand a static, closed, and complete description of our universe. And this indeed has been the goal of science for several generations. With another way of thinking we might realize that our systems of thought too are continually evolving and incomplete and require openness in order to progress to higher order.

UNIVERSE OF PATTERNS

Thinking in terms of open systems along these lines encourages us to think of a universe as interconnected patterns of energy in continual dynamic evolution toward increasing order. Contrast this with the conventional way of thinking of the present universe: built from static lumps of stuff, essentially independent but accidentally taking part in random motion, occasionally bumping into each other, and gradually decaying to utter disorder. Now we know that there is absolutely nothing final or complete about the latter point of view. "Atoms are not things," said quantum physicist Werner Heisenberg.[6] Nor is the universe a thing, nor is anything in between an atom and a universe a thing. Our bodies are not things, and neither are our minds.

Rather than thinking of the natural world as a set of 'things' of various sizes and complexities, it now makes more sense to think of the natural world as interacting domains of open systems, each domain being defined by different principles. There is the domain of the elementary particles of physics; there is the domain of complex molecules, of chemistry; there is the domain of living systems, of biology; there is the domain of intelligent systems, of psychology. This view of reality has also been extended by some writers, particularly Ken Wilber, to include the views of religious and mystical writers. Beyond the realm of mental process, further realms are added that could be called 'soul,' 'spirit,' and 'Spirit,' and that are said to be found in the writings of most religions.[7]

These domains may be ordered into 'hierarchies' according to some principle that we want to emphasize so that each level includes but 'transcends' the previous level in the sense that characteristics observable at the higher levels are not present even in principle at the lower. For example, we may begin by taking atoms as the 'lowest' level. Then molecules are complex combinations of atoms, but molecules are not living, bacteria are living but not feeling, dogs are feeling but not self-conscious, people are self-conscious but generally not saintly. However we might not organize our hierarchy this way at all. We may, as Alfred North Whitehead did, take a moment of experience as the primary level. In this case we have an altogether different hierarchy, a hierarchy of conceptual abstraction in which atoms, far from being elementary, are high-level abstractions. Thus, how such domains are organized into hierarchies depends on the point of view of the organizer.

One way to attempt an explanation of the appearance of these various domains of phenomena, would be to suggest that all these properties are somehow 'contained within' the elementary quarks and leptons as the form of an organism is supposed to be 'contained within' the genetic material. That is to say, it is inherent in the nature of these elementary particles to give rise to the kind of complexity we are talking about, even though the actual forms may manifest themselves by chance. But there is nothing whatsoever in the descriptions of electons, photons, hadrons, or gravitons that implies such hidden complexity. Although it is really the logical consequence of a strict reductionist materialism, it is as 'occult' as any of the writings of the 'mystics' and 'occultists.'

Another alternative is to say that the domains of simple matter, of living organisms, and of mental processes are quite separate realms having separate origins and obeying separate laws. According to this view there is a realm of 'matter' that obeys the laws of physics and chemistry; a realm of 'life' that obeys the laws of biology; a realm of 'mental events' or 'minds' that obeys the laws of psychology, and perhaps 'higher,' 'spiritual' realms obeying the laws of 'God.' These realms are thought to be 'real,' a word having the same root as 'realm.' That is, they are thought to have substantial existence.

In this view the principles of the 'higher' realms are separately created and do not in any sense arise from those of the lower. So, for example, the origin of the organizing principle that gives rise to living organisms is no less or more mysterious than the origin of the organizing principles of matter. Scientists know absolutely nothing about the origin of the *organizing principles* of matter: there is talk of the complete symmetry preceding the Big Bang and the rapid breaking of symmetry that gave rise to the various types of particles after the Big Bang. But all this merely pushes the origin further and further back without at all suggesting how something came from nothing. According to the 'separate realms' point of view it is no less mysterious that we know nothing about the origin of the organizing principles of 'life' or 'mind.' In particular, even where 'life' may be admitted to be a part of the same realm as 'matter,' the mind and the laws governing it are, in this dualistic or multiplistic view, considered to have an altogether separate origin.

However, such a view, of altogether separate realms with separate origins, fragments the universe in a way that is unacceptable to many people. The origin of one universe is mysterious enough. To invent two or more universes, one of matter and one of mind, and then try to find the connecting link between them seems quite unnecessary.

In fact people who hold this view are often so uncomfortable with it that they invent an external God to unify the whole thing.

LEVELS OF OPEN SYSTEMS

Alternatively we may prefer to describe the various domains as open, self-organizing systems. Such a 'systems' view has been elaborated by recent writers, particularly Ervin Laszlo and Erich Jantsch. The idea of a 'general systems theory' was first proposed by Ludwig von Bertalanffy in the 1930s.[8] Over the first few decades of its development, systems theory was not able to do very much more than produce some very general principles that applied to all systems and that were really too general to be of any detailed application. Systems theory was regarded by many scientists as nothing much more than a "hand-waving philosophy." But now, with Prigogine's theory of open systems, the general principles can be supplemented by detailed analysis, which can in turn give rise to verifiable and falsifiable predictions. This approach has been particularly useful and fruitful in elucidating the psychobiology of mind-body interaction and healing in the complex systems of the human body.[9]

One of the key ideas in determining a hierarchy of open systems is that of 'emergence.' This simply means that when we look at systems of increasing complexity and ordering, from molecules to living cells to organisms to brains, we find emerging on each level of complexity properties that are an inherent characteristic of that *complexity*. They therefore do not appear at lower levels and cannot be explained on the basis of the properties of those lower levels.

The higher levels, rather than simply passively arising out of the lower levels, can also act back on those lower levels and causally affect them. In particular the emergent level of mental process can act on and causally affect the lower level of biological organism. This allows also for the possibility of accepting and legitimately investigating psychosomatic illness, which has been for so long excluded from the medical establishment.

The consequence of realizing that the higher levels causally affect the lower is that there is now no more reason to say that the lower level 'causes' the higher or vice versa. And at the same time there is no reason to say that the higher levels are fundamentally separate from the lower. This view has been emphasized, for example, by Roger Sperry, the neuropsychologist who received the Nobel Prize for his work on the different functions of the left and right hemispheres of the brain. Sperry says, "Basic revisions in concepts of causality are involved here; the whole, besides being 'different from and greater than the sum of the parts,' also causally determines the fate of the parts. . . . It follows that physical science no longer perceives the world to be reducible to quantum mechanics or to any other unifying ultra element or field force. The qualitative, holistic properties at all different levels become causally real in their own form and have to be included in the causal account."

In particular in relation to the mental level, Sperry says, "Conscious or mental phenomena are dynamic, emergent, pattern (or configurational) properties of the living brain in action—a point accepted by many, including some of the more tough-minded brain researchers. . . . My argument goes a critical step further, and insists that these emergent pattern properties in the brain have causal control potency—just as they do elsewhere in the universe."[10]

Sperry is saying that the view that causality goes only one way, from the physical level up to the biological and mental levels, is no longer acceptable. The old, reductionist view would say that physical illness can cause depression, but the reverse is impossible. When I have a flu and feel depressed I may be correct in thinking that the flu is causing my depression, but not that my depression is causing the flu. But Sperry's view, representative of the systems way of thinking, says that I could also be correct in my intuitive sense that when I feel depressed I am more likely to catch the flu. My mental process has a causal effect on my body, making my body susceptible to illness.

We are able to think about interactions between the 'mental' and the 'physical' domains because now both mental and physical, rather than being thought of as altogether different kinds of substances, can be thought of as open interacting systems. This view is not, of course, a refutation of materialism. All the various systems and levels of complexity that are being spoken of here *could* still be based on 'matter,' if we knew what that was. Whether all "conscious or mental phenomena are . . . pattern properties of the living brain [i.e., matter]" we will leave at this point as an open question to be taken up again in the next chapter. Suffice it to say at the moment that 'the living brain' is itself a pattern property of the perceptual process, and therefore there is a very clear circularity here: mental characteristics of perception appear to emerge from the properties of the living brain, which is itself an appearance in the perception that we have, in previous chapters, shown to be a dynamic fabricating process.

In this chapter we have examined one way in which scientists are beginning to see through the fallacy of separate existence, or the inveterate tendency on the part of humans to 'thing-think.' We have also seen that thinking in terms of self-organizing open systems rather than static closed systems, or things, enables us to begin to see how the false separation between mental and physical is beginning to break down, insofar as mental and physical can be regarded as patterning. Patterning *in what* remains to be seen.

We must be careful not to begin to think that these kinds of descriptions in terms of hierarchical levels, systems, and 'emergent' properties actually refer to a universe that is more 'real' in an *ultimate* sense than was Newton's mechanical universe of dead particles and little boxlike minds. However, these concepts have certainly provided ways of thinking about phenomena that can include within one conceptual belief system a larger number of experienced phenomena. Now not only the behavior of material atoms but also the behavior of biological organisms and of thoughts and affects can all be encompassed in one conceptual scheme. And its most important aspect is that this scheme provides us with a stepping stone to begin to break down our dependency on 'thing-thinking.' Our world can be thought of as one open, dynamically evolving, self-organizing dissipative structure. And the various open self-organizing systems that we have considered, from atoms to humans, can be thought of as interconnected subsystems of this one world, themselves dynamically evolving. This is, of course, a conceptual framework that itself is not ultimate. However, it is a framework in which dynamic openness and interconnectedness are the dominant principles, in contrast to the static closedness and isolation of the world of 'things.' The reader will no doubt readily see that this is a way of thinking that is more in keeping with the principle of shunyata as we have explored this so far. Furthermore, the Buddhists maintain, the world is actually seen and lived in, not merely thought of, according to these principles when the path of mindfulness-awareness meditation is followed.

The point of this chapter has been not to promote open systems theories as some new conceptualized version of final truth, but rather to show up the fallacy of thinking that, in the words of A. A. Milne, "the world is so full of a number of things," and to point out that there are other ways of conceptualizing experience that do not depend on the projection of inherent existences. In the next chapter we will look at our concepts of body, matter, and the elementary particles which are supposed, in the conceptual framework of 'thing-thinking,' to form the substantial underlying reality. Again we will suggest that 'elementary particle' as well as 'body,' are simply conceptual patternings having no underlying substance, and we will be led to ask: In what, then, do these patternings arise?

19

Joining Mind and Body

IN THE ANALYSIS OF PERCEPTION we saw that the 'outside world' and the 'self' that perceives it are fabrications of a dynamic perceptual process. It was taken for granted during that discussion that this fabrication was taking place in a body and was experienced by a mind. But, of course one of the oldest problems faced by dualistic philosophy is what the connection between body and mind can be. Is one, mind or body, ultimately real, with the other being some kind of derivative of it? From the point of view of shunyata we would now say that both 'mind' and 'body' are concepts to which there is no corresponding inherent existence. But let us examine this mind/body problem on its own grounds. By 'a mind' we mean at this point the conglomerations of representations, images, affects, consciousness, and self-consciousness that we have discussed already. There does not seem to be anything particularly unified or ultimate about any of these. What do we mean by 'a body'? We might think that this is even more obvious than 'a mind.' Yet we find on even a cursory inspection that we mean a number of different things.

First we mean, in relation to our own bodies, our outer perceptions of them: the visual images of our hands moving, of the perimeter of our faces, of our waists and feet, and so on. Second, we mean some inner sensation of warmth and heaviness, tension in the muscles and flow in the breath and blood. These two are the first skandha, form, and the physical side of the second skandha, feeling, in the Buddhist description. Next, we mean our perceptions of other bodies. These perceptions are, of course, subject to all the serious questions we now have, about the relation between perception and a 'world' of which other bodies are a part.

Finally we mean, in relation to both our own and other bodies, an image we have of a whole body, a relatively permanent unity, the biological organism. This is, on the theoretical as well as perceptual level, a concept. In the case of our own bodies, it is this unified image that takes part in conscious events that are remembered. If the reader will, at this moment, reflect on your body as you read this line, you will notice that the first thought is the unified image of your body sitting in a chair. Perhaps secondarily, you noticed the visual image of your hands while reading the book, the tactile image of your backside on the chair, the sound of a dripping tap, etc. And if you try to remember eating breakfast this morning, you remember first the image of your body eating, followed by the memory of the taste of cereal. You might have, in fact, a much harder time recalling the taste than the image of your body as a whole.

What do we mean, then, when we ask, "What is the connection between a mind and a body?" Perhaps, on reflection, we mean all these things, but habitually we usually mean, "What is the connection between the concept of an individual unified mind and the concept of a unified body?" Psychologists and biologists avoid the problem to a certain extent by ignoring this question in relation to their own body/minds and asking it in relation to other, assuming that any answer that applies to other will apply to themselves as well. In doing this they are, of course, reducing the meaning of 'body' from the various intertwined meanings discussed above to just the last, the concept of a whole organism. Nowadays all that is meant by 'a mind' is conceived as being located in the nervous system, especially the brain. So the question becomes "what is the connection between the concepts 'a mind' and 'a brain'?"

The apparent success science has had in explaining physical, chemical, and biological phenomena on the basis of the concept of matter has naturally led to the expectation and hope that mental phenomena will be explainable on the same basis. So most scientists seek to explain mental phenomena without needing to introduce substance that is nonmaterial into that explanation. In a similar fashion, biologists wished to explain life without introducing a substance of fundamentally different type from atomic matter, a substance like the 'vital force.' Up to a point this was successful, but we have seen that a more satisfactory and comprehensive description of life is in terms of dynamic self-organizing pattern rather than in terms of a particular material substance.

On the brain/mind question, the issue has been, Is there one substance or two?[1] If there are two substances, matter-stuff and mind-stuff, do they interact and if they do, how do they do so? If there is only one substance, for scientists it would nowadays generally be 'matter' although for philosophers it could be mind-stuff or something altogether different. If this one substance *is* matter, then how does mind arise from matter? We must of course be careful here to distinguish between the appearance of mental process in others and the first-person experience of our own mental processes. The biggest problem for materialism is how to explain personal experience.

DUALITY THEORIES

In the case of a duality theory one has a very difficult time explaining how mind can influence matter. How does it happen, for example, that when I decide to lift my arm, my arm lifts? Generally two types of ways have been invoked for this interaction. One is to try to locate a place in the body where mind-stuff and body-stuff meet. Descartes suggested the pineal gland, Eccles a region of the cerebral cortex that he calls the *liaison brain*.[2] The other form of solution to the problem of interaction in duality is parallelism. In these theories, mind and matter are said *not* to interact, but to run along in two separate realms in such close parallel that there is an appearance of interaction. That my wish to lift my arm causes my arm to rise is an illusion arising from the fact that the two events happen more or less simultaneously in the two worlds. Such theories seem obviously absurd nowadays, but in a universe in which the heavenly other world was taken for granted it was not so absurd, and a God was there, outside of both, to make sure the two worlds kept in time.

Duality theories are not very popular today among psychologists and philosophers, although some still hold them, notably the Nobel laureate neurophysiologist John Eccles and the philosopher of science Karl Popper.[3] Eccles has, however, tried to introduce some actual interaction between the two realms. Rather than having appearance in the separate realm of mind merely run parallel to material processes, he has proposed that at the link between them, the liaison brain, mental characteristics such as 'will' can actually affect physical processes. And as we saw in Chapter 2, duality theories are quite popular with some physicists. However, even the more sophisticated theories, such as those in which a hierarchy of realms is posited—a realm of 'matter' dealt with by physics, a realm of 'life' studied by biology, a realm of 'mental process' and so on, all such theories have problems similar to the problem of original dualism. That is, first, so long as the realms of mental and material processes are considered to be separate, how can we explain how one realm acts on another, in particular the mental on the physical? Second, we are still left with the problem of what is the nature of the awareness of all these processes.

The most popular view among today's scientists is some version of the view that there is one substance and that that substance is 'matter.' Mind then has to be a derivative of matter. Usually nowadays the question of how does mind arise from matter is regarded as equivalent to asking how does mind arise from the brain. This is not, however, necessary: mind can arise from matter without necessarily being localized in the brain or in the individual body at all. This has to do with the distinction between various meanings of the term 'consciousness' that I introduced in Chapter 10. But before we go further with this, we first have to determine, if we can, what precisely is meant by 'matter.'

MATERIALIST THEORIES

Materialist theories fall again into several kinds: the epiphenomenalist, the behaviorist, and the identity kinds. Epiphenomenalism, popular among nineteenth-century Darwinists, said that mental events are simply useless byproducts of the evolution of matter. Mental events have no evolutionary value and no causal impact on the material world. Behaviorism simply says that mental phenomena do not exist, that descriptions of events using language of mental events are wrong and should be replaced by descriptions using purely physical language. For a behaviorist there is no real difference between sawing a log while lost in a fantasy about you and your favorite film star and sawing a log while being mindful of the movement of the saw and the sensation in your arm. This again highlights the distinction between observable behavior in another to which we attribute mental process, and the personal feeling of mental process. This view dominated Anglo-American psychology and philosophy for several generations, even though, as we have seen, if followed through faithfully it leads to absurdity.

The more recent kind of identity theory says that experience is identical to the activity of neurons or groups of neurons and that one day statements such as "I am hungry" or "Shall I compare thee to a summer's day, thou art more lovely and more temperate" can, if we wish, be replaced by statements about which neurons or groups of neurons are currently firing. These two descriptions are then two descriptions of the same event, just as the description "evening star" and "morning star" are both descriptions of experiencing the planet Venus. Such identity theories suggest that the mental description, "I am hungry," is the direct, inner experience of the 'things-in-them-selves,' i.e., neurons firing. The description in terms of neurons, which we know only theoretically, is description of the same things 'from the outside.' In some ways this is not very different from parallelism or epiphenomenalism in that it gives no hint of what the connecting link could possibly be between the 'inner' and 'outer' views. It just happens to be that way. Again the issue here seems to be that when I say 'I am hungry' I do mean that *I* am hungry, not that some third party is hungry. Therefore to carry out their program the identity theorists must be able to construct measuring instruments that will be able to tell the investigator *himself* which of *his* neurons are firing while he is saying, *and feeling*, 'I am hungry.' And of course these machines must leave the investigator's brain intact. It is more of a promise, an act of faith, than a present actuality: 'some day' descriptions involving terms for mental events will no longer be necessary.

If identity theories are to be genuinely materialist theories of mind, that is, if they are going to say, "the universe, including mental processes, arises from the complex joining together of bits of mind-less stuff," they cannot stop at equating mental processes with the activity of neurons. Such theories have to then go on to say that neurons are complex patternings of organic molecules, organic molecules are complex patternings of atoms, atoms are complex pattern-ings of elementary particles. And what are elementary particles? This is where we begin to lose sight of the pure mindless matter that we were looking for, as we saw in Chapter 2.

Most biologists, neurophysiologists, and psychologists, at least until recently, have been quite ignorant of the problems of quantum reality, and even of the changing nature of elementary particles. For these scientists, materialism probably gets as far as atoms, leaving any level of reality deeper than that to the experts, assuming that the experts will not let them down when it comes to finding the ultimate matter.

WHAT IS MATTER?

Let us nevertheless try to follow the logic of identity theories and try to find the ultimate 'matter.'[4] What, then are the 'atoms' of our observations? Atoms are electrons orbiting nuclei, we say. The nu-cleus is very tiny compared with the size of the atom. If we imagine blowing up the nucleus to the size of a marble, then the atom of which it is the center would be roughly the size of the Houston

Astrodome. Thus it is mostly matterless space, its form being defined by the cloud of electrons. All the phenomena of the physics and chemistry of the ordinary world we see around us, the behavior of solids, liquids, and gases, chemical and biochemical reactions are a result of the forms of the electron clouds around atoms, the forms of surfaces in space.

How thick are these surfaces, that is, how big are electrons? You might be surprised to find out that in order for the equations of the quantum theory of the motion of electrons to work (and they do work very well) physicists have reluctantly had to assume that the size of a bare electron is *zero*. An electron has to be regarded as a dimensionless point. The whole point about matter, so we thought, was that matter occupies a region of space. Not so the electron. The apparent dimensions of the electron come from a cloud of *virtual* particles that is said to surround it, that is a cloud of particles that are continually being created and destroyed out of space. Therefore these surfaces defined by the electron must be said either to have no thickness, or to have a thickness defined by the creative and destructive properties of space.

And what of the nucleus? It used to be thought of as composed of protons and neutrons, which were supposed to be elementary. It is now thought of as composed of at least six different kinds of particles, called 'quarks,' which are thought to be more elementary than protons and neutrons (and all the hundreds of particles similar to protons and neutrons that had physicists very worried until they thought of quarks). There are also at least eight different types of particles, known as 'gluons,' which hold the quarks in the nucleus. One of the most surprising things about quarks is that it is highly probable that quarks are inherently undetectable by any form of direct observation, because they inherently cannot be separated from each other.

Quarks are also very small. If we now think of a quark as the size of a marble, then the nucleus will be somewhere between the size of a barn and the size of the Astrodome. The boundary of the nucleus is defined only by the limits beyond which the quarks cannot be separated. And are the quarks truly elementary? As physicist Heinz Pagels says, "All present evidence supports this view that quarks are a 'rock-bottom' to matter, but no physicist I know would be willing to bet much on that."[5] Some physicists think there are already too many quarks for them to be truly elementary and are already talking about prequarks. In all likelihood such prequarks would also turn out to be so tiny that quarks would again appear to be mostly space.

Logically there is no reason to suppose that there will be any end to this process down to the level at which, according to physicists, space-time itself is discontinuous.

In this presentation I have not used the term 'empty' in reference to space because at this quantum level space, while empty of real elementary particles, is also full. It is filled with particle-antiparticle pairs that normally are 'virtual,' unmanifest or in Bohm's terms implicate, but that occasionally can erupt into the manifest, explicate, world. It is because of a cloud of 'virtual' particles continually surrounding the electron that the electron appears to have size. Because of the wave-particle duality we can equally well describe this 'vacuum state' as being filled with fields, whose wavelike vibrations are the energy of the virtual particle pairs. Whichever way we look at it, it has been calculated that one thimbleful of space contains, in its ocean of virtual particles, as much energy as the energy in all the real mass in the universe.

The overall impression we get from all this is that what we have been calling 'matter' is, at the atomic level, conceptually defined patterns of surfaces within surfaces within surfaces . . . in what we call 'space,' which we must think of as both empty and full. It appears that the definitions of 'matter' and 'space' are mutually dependent. We find, too, a mutual dependency of 'matter' and 'space' in the theory of gravitation of General Relativity, although here the definitions of 'matter' and 'space' are rather different.

These patterns are forming at the quantum level at which all the questions concerning mind and reality that we discussed in Chapter 2 are relevant. We came to the conclusion there that all that we know of the quantum universe arises within the patterns of our human communication. The kinds of patterns produced are dependent on the kinds of questions the observer asks through his or her experimental machines. This then is the 'matter' on which any identity theory of mind rests. Within its own logic, the patterns we call 'matter' are dependent on human observation and communication.

These arguments are not dependent on the particular theories of matter that are current now. The logical inconsistencies that arise in trying to define separate, ultimate inherent existence to 'matter,' 'space,' and 'mind' arise from the fact that such inherent separate existences are, in themselves, logically incoherent. And it also does not do to reply that the inconsistencies arise because we are trying to express in everyday English concepts that are expressible only in high-level mathematical terms. Because at some point, if the mathematics relates at all to the world beyond theory, we are going to want to ask what are the equations *about*? And then we run into just the same logical inconsistencies, and the impossibility of defining anything as truly separately existing.

We might at this point throw in the towel and say, "All this is just unnecessary philosophizing. We *know* what matter is. It is that solid, liquid, or gaseous stuff that the world is made up of. Mind arises in the brain and the brain is made of that soft gray stuff." Then we have to finally acknowledge that "that soft gray stuff" appears within the perceptual process, and there is nothing more real *behind* it at all.

PATTERNS ARE OBSERVER-DEPENDENT

An electron or quark, a molecule, a cell, or a neuron contains a large component that is observer-dependent. The standard view of science is that it is at the level of observation that our patterns can be tested against 'reality.' It is, according to this view, with observation and testing that we come up against the objective, nonmental world. But as we saw in Chapter 3, observations are already inextricably dependent on the theory and the point of view adopted by the observer. What the materialist has to mean by 'matter' is then a conceptual conglomeration of the data taken from photographs obtained on machines built in the human-sized world combined with these conceptual elaborations of the theorists. The surfaces within surfaces are human-dependent, depending on the types of experiments we do and the types of theories we make to do them and interpret them.

As we now try to build the world up from the observer-dependent patterns we call 'matter,' we find another sense in which the patterns we find are observer-dependent at whatever level we are considering. This is a consequence of the understanding of perception that I have developed in the previous chapters.

Observation in the end depends on perception, and this standard view naively assumes that perception is something like a camera, which takes pure pictures of a scene without interpretation or invention. We have already seen that this idea of perception is totally inadequate. And even the more conservative and materialist neurophysiologist will tell us that one thing is certain even from *brain* research, and that is that perception is an abstraction. The typical view of neurophysiology is summed up by Vernon Mountcastle, considered by many the dean of psychobiology: "Each of us lives within the universe—the prison—of his own brain. Projecting from it are millions of fragile sensory nerve fibres in groups uniquely adapted to sample the energetic states of the world about us: heat, light, force and chemical composition. That is all we know of it directly, all else is logical inference. . . . Each of us believes himself to live directly within the world that surrounds him, to sense objects and events precisely, and to live in real current time. I assert that these are perceptual illusions. Sensation is an abstraction not a replication of the real world."[6] By 'the real world' Mountcastle is reverting to a nineteenth-century view of a real world of 'heat, light, force, and chemical composition.' Yet these, too, are conceptual abstractions, items in the physicists' theories.

Our perceptions are patterns that do not in themselves tell what is in the 'real' world behind these patterns. On the level on which patterns create "the world we live in," we saw that 'perception' is just the continual forming of guesses about what is 'out there,' continually pulling out meaningful patterns and finding a fit that will best serve the organism at that moment. Thus the world is perceived in terms of things and meanings, which are the patternings our perceptual process has been able to come up with as adequate guesses. To talk of the 'real,' 'material' world behind these patterns, scientists must make two further conceptual abstractions: abstractions of perceptual inference and abstractions of theoretical inference. There is thus a complete circularity in the idea of a pure mindless matter from which everything is built: the only way we can at all know this matter is by observations, a combination of perception and conception, and perception is a process that itself is largely conception.

The reciprocal self-fabrication of perception is the primary fact, and any philosophy, religion, or science that does not begin here is based on quicksand.

MATTER AND MIND

All this suggests that we could just as easily say that matter, life, and perception are patternings in mental process as that mental process, perception, and life are patternings in matter. And in fact it would seem necessary now to acknowledge that both mental process and matter are conceptual abstractions from immediate experience. Out of the level of patterning of heat, light, force, and chemical composition, which are themselves conceptual abstractions, our perceptual systems form a higher level of patterning that we call "the world we live in." And one of the characteristics of this particular level of patterning is that we think that it is outside of our perceptual systems. Another characteristic of this patterning is that we think it contains 'things.' This is the way we name, and thereby separate out, some special subpatterns of the pattern we call "the world we live in."

We attribute 'thingness' or inherent existence to some patterns rather than to others because of the scale of temporal duration and spatial interval that the untrained human consciousness is capable of attending to. We impute inherent existence into trees and rocks, people and dogs. We impute inherent existence also into rivers and forests, although we more readily admit if questioned that rivers and forests do not 'really' exist as independent entities. A little further removed we project existence into rainbows and clouds, but here we know even as we do this that there really are no rainbows and no clouds. Beyond this we give one spiral of our galaxy a name, the "Milky Way," knowing full well that this cluster is really a group of suns separated by vast distances. And we impute inherent existence into the patterns that we conceive of as 'elementary particles.'

If the time interval in which we are able to detect change were one year rather than one-tenth of a second, we would impute inherent existence into entirely different things. Then a human would be a blip, lasting eight or nine 'seconds' at most, barely noticed. We might see a city, or even an entire society, as one thing slowly changing. We might, from space, detect the changes in the Earth to have patterns that we are quite blind to now, that might lead us to think of the Earth as a unified organism. At even larger time intervals we might see a galaxy as one lump, rythmically changing like a living thing, as galaxies are structurally complex enough to be. We would see inherent existence in entirely different kinds of patterns. Which patterns we now see existence in is dependent on our particular biological, perceptual structure.

Furthermore, when we think in this way, the idea of localizing 'a mind' makes no more sense than the idea of localizing 'walking' or 'the time.' As John Dewey puts it, "Breathing is an affair of the air as truly as of the lungs; digesting an affair of the food as truly as of the tissues of the stomach. Seeing involves light just as certainly as it does the eye and optic nerve. Walking implicates the ground as well as the legs; speech demands physical air and human companionship as well as vocal organs."[7] We might add that being aware of an environment is an affair between environment and organism, as much of the one as of the other. As we saw in Chapter 14, Alfred North Whitehead, Michael Polanyi, and Gregory Bateson, among others, all propose, each in his own way, that we must go beyond such a 'parochialism of the body' if we are to understand how we live in a world of meaning.

The point seems to be that 'mental states' as well as 'bodily states' that are inferred from others, as well as in ourselves when we think of ourselves as an 'other,' are simply different types of patterns with certain characteristics that we call 'mental' or 'bodily.' If we are to ask, What are these patternings *in?*, it is now clear that we cannot imagine that there is some underlying stuff, called 'matter' or 'mind,' which supports the patterns. And in the next chapter I will suggest that the patterns are merely appearances arising within emptiness, that the self that perceives them is simply another co-arising pattern, and that there is nothing supporting them at all. And still we have not yet touched on the issue of immediate experience. If we are forced to go beyond the dualistic view of a pattern we call 'self' perceiving a pattern we call 'the world,' then what is the nature of awareness of the patterning of self and world, at this very moment? In the next chapter we will consider the question of how patternings arise at all, and what might be the nature of awareness in which they appear.

20

Patternings in Emptiness

PATTERNS APPEAR whenever distinctions are made between one side and another. They divide one part of space from another, they distinguish one part of a whole from another. The electron cloud separates one part of space—the 'inside' of the atom—from another, the 'outside.' My skin separates the inside of my body from the outside. My skin is in turn made of cells whose membranes divide space into an inside and an outside. The edge of a cloud distinguishes the blue sky from the gray. The thought of 'liking' and 'not liking' distinguishes my friends from my enemies. George Spencer-Brown has analyzed the making of distinction in *The Laws of Form*, and he succinctly summarizes it thus: "A universe comes into being when a space is severed or taken apart. The skin of a living organism cuts off an outside from an inside. So does the circumference of a circle in a plane. By tracing the way we represent such a severance, we can begin to reconstruct, with an accuracy and coverage that appear almost uncanny, the basic forms underlying linguistic, mathematical, physical and biological science, and can begin to see how the familiar laws of our own experience follow inexorably from the original act of severance. The act is itself remembered, even if unconsciously, as our first attempt to distinguish different things in a world where, in the first place, the boundaries can be drawn anywhere we please. At this stage the universe cannot be distinguished from how we act upon it, and the world may seem like shifting sand beneath our feet."[1]

WHAT IS PATTERNED?

Thinking in terms of patterning we might feel that we now need to ask, But what is this patterning *in*? Generally speaking, attempts in Western speculation to identify mind and matter, without reducing one to the other, have thought in terms of some kind of neutral 'stuff.' This 'stuff,' when viewed from one point of view, seems like

249

'matter' and when viewed from the other point of view seems like 'mind.' And then the question naturally arises, What kind of substance could this 'stuff' possibly be? And there things usually end. All this is just another example of 'thing-thinking.' Trying to find an inherent existence *somewhere* and not now being able to find it in 'matter' or 'mind,' we now push this existence off into the 'neutral stuff.' We then say, "Mind and matter are one," which soon becomes, "Mind and matter are *One*." This 'One' can then be thought of as external to the perceiver, like 'God,' 'Brahman,' 'The Absolute,' and so on.

All this comes from the need to *name*, the need to confine the knowable within the bounds of a complete and consistent language. It is our language system that determines what conceptual distinctions we are able to make. Whenever anything slips through our language system we give that 'thing' a name and thereby try to maintain the completeness of the system. The language system can be a natural language such as English, the language of a particular science, the 'language of thought' of the nervous system, or the language of mathematics, art, or music.

The irony of this is that it has been irrefutably shown that such an endeavor is inherently impossible. This was shown in the 1930s, at about the same time as the work of the quantum physicists was undermining the belief in a 'reality' corresponding to the language of physics. It was shown through a rigorous logical argument, by Godel, that a symbolic system complex enough to include statements that refer to the symbolic system itself cannot be both complete and coherent.[2] Any of the language systems that I have just mentioned are examples of such a complex symbol system. An example of an English sentence referring to the English-language symbol system of which it is a part is, "The English language is not attractive to the ear." It is because in all such complex systems self-referring statements can be found that Godel's theorem applies universally. An example of a self-referring statement in English is, "This sentence will end after the eighth word." The proof of Godel's theorem is too lengthy and tedious to go into here, but the meaning of the result is very clear. It says that any language system has to *either* contain statements that are contradictory, paradoxical, absurd; *or* be incomplete, open-ended, contain statements that are unprovable within that language system. Thus what is outside the entire process of making distinctions within a particular language system cannot itself be determined by making a further distinction in that system. What is beyond language cannot be distinguished by language.

The incessant need to fit everything into our language system, to name whatever arises in awareness, is not only a social issue; it is a constant factor in our personal conscious experience. Whenever we look at a picture, our first thought is "What is it?" or "What is it called?" When we hear an unfamiliar sound, we ask, "What is it?" and feel comfortable only when we have put a familiar name on it. Whenever an emotional energy arises in our being, we try to decide what we are feeling, not simply by feeling it directly, but by naming it. To feel it directly with all its intensity and uncertainty is too threatening—not knowing what to call what we are feeling, we are not even sure of our own identity. So to make that moment safe, we name our feeling.

In Chapter 18 we saw that the patternings of mind, life, and matter are dynamic patternings in contrast to the solid entities formed by thought. At each moment we are immersed in undividedness, which includes our bodies and minds. We process undividedness through multiple levels of perception some of which—perhaps a very large percentage—we are not immediately aware of; and some of which, perhaps also a large percentage, we never ordinarily become aware of.

Some, perhaps a very small percentage, of the results of the processing is experienced as having the components of an observer or experiencer, namely you or me, and what is experienced. Of this portion we say we are 'conscious.' We experience this conscious portion as perceptions or thoughts; and, as we have seen, these are really much the same thing. Thought and perception is the making of distinctions, and thus to a very large extent we *live* in our distinctions, we are *embodied* in them. We feel them as much as think them: our sensory pleasures and pains, our loves and hates, our anxieties and aspirations for self and compassion for others, all are embodiments of perceptual distinctions and, in turn make further distinctions for our actions. We are led again to conclude that *the patternings of appearance, at whatever level they are observed, and the observer to which these patternings appear co-emerge in a mutual fabrication, and there is no more real substance behind these fabrications.*

We are left with the question, How and from where do these discriminations arise at all? Even what we usually call 'present' is based on discriminations arising from the past history of the individual, and, as we have seen in Chapter 12, is actually experienced half a second or so in the past. If, as we found, an individual 'body' and an individual 'mind' are also patternings with nothing more substantial behind those patternings, then the discriminating activity of perception must be more fundamental than 'body' and 'mind.'

Our analysis of perception at first retained the concept of body and mind separate from 'the external world,' but the analysis itself, in the end, undermined this concept completely. We have not so far faced this vicious circle in the logic of perception. Likewise, the dharma analysis of the early Buddhist schools ended at the 'sixth consciousness,' which was the individual mind, coordinating the consciousnesses of the five sense organs. There seems to be a definite need at this point to go beyond the concept of an individual mind as the source of memory and perceptual projection. We are forced by the inevitable course of our logic to go beyond the localization of *all* memory and the origins of *all* mental process in the individual brain, although clearly to *some* extent this localization is justified.

Buddhist insight of the Yogacara school gives some more detail as to how the distinctions of thought and perception arise from a ground that is free from conceptual distinctions. We saw in Chapter 5 that the early schools of Buddhism, the schools of dharma analysis, pointed out six types of consciousness—the five consciousnesses associated with the five usual senses together with the sixth consciousness, which is consciousness of mental contents and which is responsible for coordinating the five sense consciousnesses and grasping them into coherent bundles we call 'things.' The Yogacara schools pointed to two further levels of consciousness, the seventh and the eighth, arising out of a deeper analysis of what is going on in the sixth consciousness of the early schools. In Chapter 5 we saw that there actually are a number of separate concepts compacted into this one.

It might seem rather awkward to be using the term 'consciousness' here to refer to the seventh and eighth levels of patterning. The point seems to be that, although we may not normally be directly aware of such 'levels' or 'consciousnesses,' they are discovered when the first six are abstracted out in analysis, or seen through in meditative experience. They are background levels of patterning process/consciousness that in fact are present, as components of the fifth skandha at every moment. Normally our superficial awareness detects in consciousness only those patterns that draw our attention as highlights—some striking sound, color, shape, smell, emotion or other memory, or some combination of these. Awareness simply does not attend to the ongoing background that is a necessary ground for these highlights. The seventh and eighth levels of patterning process form this necessary ground to consciousness. The work of Bateson, Whitehead, and Polanyi, which I outline in Chapter 14, has begun to provide a possible theoretical basis for this ground of consciousness, normally felt only on the dim periphery of awareness.

BASIC CONSCIOUSNESS

The eighth consciousness (Sanskrit: alaya vijnana), is often known as the 'store consciousness,' but literally translates as 'basis-of-all consciousness.' It is, according to Asanga, a Buddhist scholar and practitioner who lived in the fifth century A.D., the underlying structure in the developing process of consciousness which represents the capacity of consciousness to construct future acts on the basis of past habits and behavior. It is the 'store consciousness' because it stores the impressions or 'seeds' of all past actions as potentialities for the activation of future actions. It is thus also known as the 'retributive consciousness' because from within it all past actions eventually come to fruition in retributive consequences. There is no act or thought that therefore does not produce its corresponding result.[3]

This is the origin of *karma*—that for every action there is a corresponding effect. Karma has ethical consequences in the sense that each action automatically begets its corresponding result and there is no escape from this whatsoever. At the same time it is not 'retributive' in the sense of there being an external being who is watching over us and deciding on appropriate rewards and punishments; in other words, the eighth consciousness should by no means be taken as equivalent to an external deity. It is simply a natural and automatic process.

As the store of all past impressions, this consciousness is like a vast library system, or like the memory storage system of a computer. The eighth consciousness does go beyond individual minds, although there is still a coloration or 'stain' associated with it. This stain is the potentiality for self-consciousness, the action of the seventh consciousness, which we will look at shortly. The eighth consciousness contains stored impressions or memories from the evolutionary history of culture and race as well as species. It is what gives a sense of continuity during dreams and deep sleep. The continuity of the eighth consciousness also goes beyond an individual lifespan, giving rise to the Buddhist version of 'reincarnation.'

To the Buddhist, reincarnation is a very ordinary consequence of the discontinuity of perception and the structure of the five skandhas. The sense of identity, or egohood, is, as we have seen, recreated again and again each moment. It is tied to the sensory or 'physical' body by the first skandha, form, and one side of the second skandha, feeling. Therefore it is neither surprising nor of any special importance that this continuity of the sense of identity continues after the end of a particular physical body and the disintegration of the five skandhas. Since, in the Buddhist view, grasping to the sense of personal identity is the cause of suffering, the Buddhist is not especially excited by the idea of 'reincarnation.' But the eighth consciousness does provide a basis for the sense of continuity—it is in the eighth consciousness that the seed of personal identity resides during the transitions between momentary perceptions, and during the discontinuity of physical death. And the Buddhist tradition does acknowledge some continuity of consciousness for a period of time after physical death.

Particularly in the Tibetan Buddhist tradition the gradual dissolution of the skandha structure after death, and the images that seem to assail consciousness during this period before the lapse into a state akin to deep sleep, has been elaborated in a manual known as the *Bardo Thodol*, or *Instructions on the Intermediary State*.[4] These images, which are of course projections, are said to be at first very peaceful. This may account for the beliefs of some people, who have recovered from short periods of physical death, that they have seen a Deity. Later the images become terrifying, and the *Bardo Thodol*, named in its English translation *The Tibetan Book of the Dead*, provides instruction on how to retain awareness during this intermediary state. Essentially the instruction is the same as the instruction on how to retain mindfulness and awareness in daily life: not to get caught up in believing one's own projections to be real.

Psychologist Carl Jung, appreciating that the store consciousness came from a deeper level than simply individual memory, likened this consciousness to his 'collective unconscious.'[5] This is supposedly a level of consciousness in 'individual minds' that has access, perhaps through genetic inheritance, to racial memory. However, for Jung, this was still a very individual matter, as we can see from Jung's designation of the process of recovering the collective unconscious into personal conscious memory as a process of 'individuation.' But we have already seen that the concepts 'individual body' and 'individual mind' are also patterns in the patterning activity of the undivided ground. Therefore we cannot now go back and say that the store consciousness is merely individual. We have already gone beyond individuality at this point. Jung was perhaps touching on that aspect of the eighth consciousness that is still tainted by the concept of individuality, or separate, inherent existence.

The concept of individuality, the sense of personal identity, arises with the seventh consciousness. The seventh consciousness, known as 'cloudy mind,' 'appropriating consciousness,' or 'the human constant,' is the activity of ego. It is constantly present in all thought and that is why it is known as the 'human constant.' It is known as 'cloudy mind' because its activity is to continually stir up the eighth consciousness and to activate the other six consciousnesses according to patterns arising in the eighth. The 'cloudy mind' derives its feeling of being a self by reflecting back to the eighth consciousness, and the energetic quality of this feeling of self has one of the forms of the three basic emotions of ego: desire or wanting, hatred or rejecting, and bewilderment or confusion. These basic emotions are the fundamental reactions that occur at the earliest level of perception, as we have seen.

'Cloudy mind' is nothing other than this turmoil, and the analogy is often given of wind blowing across a lake stirring up waves—the 'cloudy mind' is the wind as well as the waves it stirs up. It is felt at the periphery of mundane waking consciousness as the edge of paranoia, anxiety, and boredom. Cloudy mind ceases when there are no more seeds in the store consciousness to activate 'karmic' or ego-centered actions.

The seventh consciousness is also known as "appropriating' because, according to Diana Paul, it "is the activity of egotism or of appropriating for 'me.' Through [it] all conceptualizations are intertwined with a false self-identity, and one's existence is then seen in terms of what one acquires or appropriates, whether it be material possessions, other persons, or ideas and values."[6] It is this 'appropriating consciousness' that then feeds back the results of the perceptual processes of the six senses, already contaminated with that 'me-ness,' into the store consciousness, and thus the 'karmic' process continues. Whereas the eighth and each of the first six consciousnesses continue to have an activity in perception even when the 'I' concept is let go, the seventh consciousness does not, because the seventh consciousness *is* the 'I' concept, together with the manipulating self-consciousness associated with it.

The process of normal perception is one of projection that begins with the activation of the energy of a 'seed' in the memory bank of the eighth consciousness. This energy is projected through the seventh consciousness, where it picks up a sense of self colored by one of the three basic emotions. From there it goes out through the five senses, coordinated by the sixth into an impression of an 'outside world of things.' The projecting activity of the eighth and seventh consciousnesses begin at the arising of the first skandha, *Form*, in which all eight consciousnesses are nascent, and proceeds through to the final skandha, *Consciousness*, in which the whole process is recognized as one continuous external world. Even at the deepest level of the eighth consciousness, of memory storage, there is still some primitive concept, some discriminating, symbolizing activity. This whole projective process may well be the nature of the 'hypothesis forming' activity discovered by Gregory and Rock, according to the meditative insight of Buddhism. In terms of the Three Natures (see Chapter 17), the whole process that I have been describing, including the eighth consciousness, is the *dependent nature*.

AWARENESS WITHOUT CENTRAL REFERENCE

The later schools of Mahayana Buddhism speak of the nature of awareness beyond the eighth consciousness and altogether free from ego and individualism. That awareness does not refer back to any central reference point and is therefore called 'nonreferential.' Primordial non-referential awareness is recognized in the Yogacara tradition as *amala-vijnana*, pure consciousness, or 'the fundamentally good structure of mind.'[7] By 'pure' is meant that it is unstained by the conceptual division of subject and object and all the other conceptualizations that arise from this. In the Tibetan vajrayana tradition this awareness is recognized as kunshi-nyangluk-kyi-gewa, which literally means the 'basis of all in the natural state of goodness,' or 'basic goodness.'[8] 'Goodness' does not here refer to moralistic distinctions based on concept. It refers to the quality of openness that accommodates all phenomena without obstruction. It refers also to a quality of primordial intelligence that pervades and penetrates all phenomena. This is the *complete perfection* nature that was introduced in Chapter 16.

The organization of the eight consciousnesses in relation to non-dual awareness, or basic goodness, has been likened to the operation of a film projector, but a 3-dimensional holographic image would be more appropriate.[9] The library of various possible films available to project at any moment, onto a screen (or into space) that is emptiness, is like the eighth consciousness. The movement of the film giving the appearance of continuity is like the seventh consciousness. And the mechanics of the projector is the six sense consciousnesses, with the sound-vision synchronizer being the sixth one. Nonreferential awareness in this analogy is the light shining through the whole thing and not separate from the space. At the same time, the whole set-up of projector and film is itself a projection within that awareness/emptiness. We should understand that the holographic movie is just an analogy. This analogy should not be confused with suggestions, which are in any case not taken very seriously by most brain researchers, that the perceptual mechanisms of the brain are holographic. This is still dealing at the superficial level of the perception of an 'outside' world by the brain. David Bohm's analogy of the ground of wholeness—the implicate order—being like a dynamic 'holomovement' is perhaps closer, but still must be seen *only* as an analogy.[10] There is, in the Buddhist view, nothing that creates the patternings at all, neither a cosmic holograph machine nor anything else. They simply arise within awareness/emptiness. This is, in the Buddhist view, the nonduality of awareness and appearance. Just as clouds seem to form from nothing in the sky, so appearance forms within space, which is nonreferential awareness. This is a step beyond the logic of distinctions that it is difficult for the discriminating intellect to grasp.

That nondual awareness is not separate from appearance and permeates through all eight consciousnesses. It is said to be that awareness that is the basis of intelligence, perception, and cognition. It is what gives to perception the feeling of being 'lighted' rather than 'darkened,' of being directly known rather than inferred, that we usually associate with the idea of consciousness as opposed to unconsciousness. On the ordinary level our conscious perceptions and dreams are immediately known rather than themselves being merely thought about, in an infinite regression; and great meditative practitioners have discovered that this intrinsic nondual perception permeates deep sleep and the state after death and before birth. The seventh consciousness grasps this feeling of knowing to itself and invents the idea of a knowing self. But as we have now amply seen, such a self is merely an idea. Nor should nonreferential awareness be substantialized into anything external like a God or internal like a Self. The capital S makes no difference—Self is still self, and nonreferential awareness transcends any central reference, whatever we call it.

Nonreferential awareness is not separate from appearance, but does not arise *from* a process since it is primordial to and encompasses all processes; it is not produced, manufactured, or created. It does not reside anywhere, in any particular definition, boundary, or distinction; and it cannot be categorized or made into a conceptual reference point. Therefore it is conceptually ungraspable and beyond the range of intellect.

The transcendent aspect of rikpa, intuition, that I introduced in Chapter 14, is the primordial intelligence or energetic knowingness of nonreferential awareness. As Professor Guenther says, "In order to discern the ultimate, man must in some way partake of it." Rikpa is the sense in which man both discerns and partakes of the ultimate which is the nondual and nonconceptual ground of both existence and nonexistence. Guenther says of rikpa:

> Many of us have lost the capacity of understanding that, apart from an intellectual apprehension of the world, there is another one which yields truths just as valuable and valid. This is the aesthetic apprehension or intrinsic perception by the artist, the poet, the seer [and we might add a scientist in his or her creative moments] whose words are a commentary on a vision rather than a futile attempt to establish a system of universal truths over and beyond man's cognitive and sensible capacity, or to reduce the latter to some preconceived scheme demanding the exclusion of everything which the propounder of this scheme is unable to fathom. Aesthetic awareness is certainly subjective in the sense that it must be "felt," experienced by the apprehending subject, but it is not "merely subjective" in the widely held sense of the phrase as being a passing personal whim. Beyond its subjective accessibility as a vividly moving experience the aesthetic fact is the matrix from which all conscious life emerges.

Guenther is using the word 'aesthetic' here not in its rather insipid modern sense of 'artistically pleasurable,' but in its prior meaning of direct sensory awareness, without judgment. Aesthetic awareness is not necessarily pleasurable or painful, but it is totally direct. In this sense there can be aesthetic apprehension of anything including dirty diapers. Guenther indicates that the direct nondual perception of rikpa is the energetic fullness of shunyata: "In the aesthetic experience of rikpa we may say that that of which we are aesthetically aware, before we are aesthetically aware of it is nothing. But this nothing, as the texts again and again assert, is not an absolute nothing which just is not. It is a dynamic nothing which, when we are aesthetically aware of it, has already been given a form and so resides in the vividly present and its meaning."[10]

Finally, rikpa is original knowingness or primordial intelligence (the terms 'original' and 'primordial' are used to indicate that it precedes the subject/object split) in which intellectual knowledge and feeling of quality or value are joined. As Guenther says, rikpa "is a cognition which has the intangible flavor of what we may call 'value,' although this word is likely to create certain misconceptions because under the influence of scientism value is considered to be merely subjective." And again, "The difference between 'ignorance' (ma-rikpa) and 'knowledge proper' (rik-pa) is that in the former case knowledge and emotion have not fused into understanding, because by habit the individual does not let them fuse or is even on guard against their doing so. In the latter case, however, the fusion has come about. Knowledge, in whatever sense we may take it, has a feeling tone."[12] We may recognize here the 'personal knowledge' of Michael Polanyi, discussed in Chapter 13, which transcends subjectivity and objectivity. And, in terms of our discussion in that chapter, this is the level at which 'intuition' and 'intellect' are completely joined.

Language, used literally, is a poor tool for expressing the nature of appearance. When mind rests in nonreferential awareness, poetry far better evokes the flavor of it. This prose poem, by the Buddhist scholar and meditation master Chögyam Trungpa Rinpoche, helps to vividly awaken an impression of perception beyond concept.[13]

THE NAMELESS CHILD

There is a mountain of gold. When the sun's rays strike it, it is irritating to look at. It is surrounded by red, green, yellow, orange, pink, and liver-colored clouds, wafted gently by the wind. Around the mountain fly thousands of copper-winged birds with silver heads and iron beaks. A ruby sun rises in the East and a crystal moon sets in the West. The whole earth is covered with pearl-dust snow. Upon it a luminous child without a name instantaneously comes into being.

The golden mountain is dignified, the sunlight is blazing red.
Dreamlike clouds of many colors float across the sky.
In the place where iron birds croak,
The instantaneously born child can find no name.

Because he has no father, the child has no family line. Because he has no mother, he has never tasted milk. Because he has neither brother nor sister, he has no one to play with. Having no house to live in, he cannot find a crib. Since he has no nanny, he has never cried. There is no civilization, so he cannot find toys. Since there is no point of reference, he doesn't know a self. He has never heard spoken language, so he has never experienced fear.

The child walks in every direction, but does not come across anything. He sits down slowly on the ground. Nothing happens. The colorful world seems sometimes to exist and sometimes not. He picks up a handful of pearl dust and lets it trickle through his fingers. He gathers another handful and slowly takes it into his mouth. Hearing the pearl dust crunch between his teeth, he gazes at the ruby sun setting and the

crystal moon rising. Suddenly, a whole galaxy of stars won-
drously appears and he lies on his back to admire their
patterns. The nameless child falls into a deep sleep, but has
no dreams.

The child's world has no beginning and no end.
To him, colors are neither beautiful nor ugly.
The child's nature has no preconceived notion of birth and
  death.
The golden mountain is solid and unchanging,
The ruby sun is all-pervading,
The crystal moon watches over millions of stars.
The child exists without preconceptions.

In pointing them out it will have become clear to the reader that
these deeper levels of consciousness go beyond what is accessible to
a cognitive science that is concerned dualistically with the mental
processes of others. It is possible that cognitive science may be able
to arrive at similar conclusions by inference, but any method to
become directly acquainted with these processes would seem to
necessitate direct investigation of mind and mental processes on a
first-person basis. It is possible that the methods of analytical psychology may be able to do this when they transcend any idea of
individuality. As we have seen, mindfulness-awareness training is a
way the Buddhists have found to investigate mind and its projections
and to directly realize nonreferential awareness.

21

Awareness Beyond Self-Conscious Minds

NONREFERENTIAL AWARENESS is the quality of awareness in *nowness*, that I introduced in Chapter 13. It is the intelligence or knowingness aspect of the state of being in non-duality that has been referred to as Mind-as-Such, as No-Mind, and as Primordial Mind. These terms together express that it is to be considered neither as an object nor as a subject of experience, since it is prior to both of these. No-Mind cannot be discovered or investigated in a context that presupposes the ultimate duality of subject and object. Thus for the mind of dualism and logic, the response to hearing of Mind-as-Such might well be that it is vacuous, literally empty of all meaning. In fact the mere suggestion of No-Mind, or Mind-as-Such, can cause some irritation if we accept only such methods and only the conceptual knowledge derived from these methods. But when ego-centered consciousness is given up, then, according to Buddhist practitioners, Mind-as-Such is no longer ignored: ignorance (ma-rik-pa) transforms into insight (rik-pa). Although it cannot be comprehended conceptually as an object, it is within the scope of human awareness because it is primordial intelligence, which is all-pervading, like space. The harsh, flat, world of objects and selves appears as a vivid but empty energetic evolving process.

Saraha, the great Indian Vajrayana Buddhist practitioner of the tenth century says on this issue:

> The awareness of the Real [Shunyata], that does not come
> by categorical thinking
> Is free from artifacts and is not stored-up Karma [i.e., it is
> not the eighth consciousness].
> Thus I, Saraha, who know it, declare.
> Yet the heart of the pedants is filled with poison.
> The peace of Mind-as-Such is difficult to understand:
> Untrammeled by limiting concepts, undefiled, the heart
> Can never be investigated concretely in its Being.

If it can, it turns into an irritated poisonous snake.
Things postulated by the intellect are nothing in them-
selves.
Because they are without foundation, they all do not exist.
When one knows the Real free in its reality
Then there is no seeing and hearing, but also not what is
not this.[1]

The reader might wonder why the term 'mind' is used at all after
all we have discussed; and indeed one has to be very careful when
using translated terms not to think too readily that one has immediately understood them. This is especially true in the present case, in
which we are trying to say something about a situation that has
already been said to be beyond concept. As Professor Guenther says
in an article discussing *The Concept of Mind in Buddhist Tantrism*, "The
question, whether the authors of the original texts actually meant the
same as we do by those words about whose meaning we ourselves
are not quite clear, should always be present, not only when translating texts but still more when dealing with a systematic presentation
of Eastern philosophies." If the term 'mind' is used to refer to the
functional stream of perceptual events, the conceptualizations that
we analyzed in our discussion of perception, then 'Mind-as-Such'
perhaps refers to that which, though nothing in itself, takes on
various conditions which appear to divided consciousness as mental
events. As Guenther says, "mind also has the inherent tendency to
assume its 'natural' state when left alone: 'Mind, in the absence of
conditions, is without memory and association and is *shunya*.' This
tendency is compared with what happens when we allow disturbed
water to become calm and transparent again."[2]

Using the terms Mind-as-Such or nonreferential awareness, rather
than simply leaving it as emptiness, does imply that there are characteristics analogous to the 'knowingness' of mind. What, then, are
the characteristics of what is beyond individual projections? The
characteristics of the state of being in nonreferential awareness are
said to be shunyata, bliss, clarity (luminosity), and unimpededness.
Shunyata, as we have seen at length, means that this state is of the
nature of being fully open, without boundary, without conceptual
discrimination, and without perceptual fixation on inherent existence. Thus Saraha says, "Then there is no seeing and hearing, but
also not what is not this." The experiential quality of discovering
such spaciousness has been illustrated by Chögyam Trungpa: "By
relating with the ordinary conditions of your life, you might make a

shocking discovery. While drinking your cup of tea, you might discover that you are drinking tea in a vacuum. In fact, *you* are not even drinking the tea. The hollowness of space is drinking tea. So while doing any little ordinary thing, that reference point might bring an experience of non-reference point. When you put on your pants or your skirt, you might find that you are dressing up space. When you put on your make-up, you might discover that you are putting cosmetics on space. You are beautifying space, pure nothingness."[3]

Bliss means that the energetic aspect of nonreferential awareness has the quality of great joy or bliss. By 'bliss' here is not meant some kind of overindulgent pleasure or 'ecstasy.' It is perhaps akin to the joy of wholehearted loving embrace between man and woman. In this case, however, it is not the union of man and woman that is being spoken of but the union of subject and object, that are the masculine and feminine principles or qualities of awareness. Such bliss is said to be the quality of perception beyond duality, that begins to pervade ordinary appearance as the dualistic mind relaxes. From this point of view, for the Buddhist, the joy that we all seek is found not in some dualistic struggle of one against another, nor in a hedonistic search for excitement, but in realizing the intrinsic nature of perception when the mind opens and relaxes. As we will see in the last chapter, this fundamental reorientation of perception provides the basis for compassionate activity for others. The energetic quality here called 'bliss' is like a fire that burns through conceptual fixation; and through communication of this nonconceptual energy the accomplished practitioner is able to help others to see through their own fixation. The point is, partly, that one need not be afraid that there is 'nothing left' beyond the grasping of ego.

Clarity, or luminosity, means that, in intrinsic perception, appearance shines forth from the openness of shunyata, with inherent brilliance and energy. As Trungpa Rinpoche says, "Such clarity is ostentatious and has immense brilliance. It is very joyful and it has potentialities of everything. It is a real experience. Once we have experienced this brilliance, this far-seeing, ostentatious, colorful, opulent quality of clarity, then there is no problem. It is indestructible. Because of its opulence and its richness, it radiates constantly, and immense unconditional appreciation takes place."[4]

To say that Mind-as-Such, nonreferential awareness, is not separate from the ordinary world of appearance is not, however, the same as saying that mind is *in* nature, which is some kind of pan-psychism. Mind-as-Such, being beyond concept, is beyond 'mind' and 'nature' in the sense of pan-psychism. Trying to join mind with nature, or trying to find mind in nature, is still based on assuming a prior duality of 'mind' and 'nature.' Mind-as-Such is before any such dualistic division ever occurred. This is to say that nondual awareness permeates phenomena and phenomena permeate nondual awareness without obstruction: the phenomenal world and awareness are not-two. So a fourth characteristic of Mind-as-Such is unimpededness, or unobstructedness, which is to say that an endless variety of phenomena arises without obstruction as the 'play' of Mind-as-Such. There is no limitation to the kinds of patternings that can arise, since these patternings are not based on anything.

The nonseparation between Mind-as-Such and phenomenal appearance is expressed in this song of Marpa, the eleventh-century A.D. translator who brought Buddhism from India to Tibet. It summarizes the whole process of unraveling the nature of mind that we have been through:

> Compassion and emptiness are inseparable
> This uninterrupted flowing innate mind
> Is suchness, primordially pure.
> Space is seen in intercourse with space.
> Because the root resides at home [in belief in self]
> Mind consciousness is imprisoned [by thought]
> Meditating on this, subsequent thoughts
> Are not patched together in the mind.
> [the fundamental discontinuity of thought process is
>   realized]
> Knowing the phenomenal world is the nature of mind,
> Meditation requires no further antidote.
> [i.e. no spiritual struggle is necessary]
> The nature of mind cannot be thought.
> Rest in this natural state.[5]

THREE MODES OF EMBODIMENT

From the vantage point of Mind-as-Such, the division of individual existence into mind (the 'inner world' of thought and emotions) and body does not occur. Rather the totality, the inseparability of awareness and energetic process, is experienced as three 'kayas,' or 'modes of embodiment': *dharmakaya, sambhogakaya*, and *nirmanakaya*.[6] In terms of the viewpoint of patterning in emptiness, we can perhaps regard these as three levels of increasing intensity of patterning: from a level of complete openness in which there are no specific patterns, to a level of energetic communication of quality, to a level in which specific conditioned patterns appear as the world of phenomena. But these three levels are not separate from shunyata; they can be regarded as successive perspectives on the nonconceptual fullness of shunyata. The three kayas are related to the four aspects of Mind-as-Such in that dharmakaya is the emptiness aspect, sambhogakaya is the aspect of bliss and luminosity, and nirmanakaya is the aspect of unimpededness.

First is 'dharmakaya,' or 'body of dharma,' which is awareness of shunyata and which corresponds to the level of mind. It is complete openness in which all the dharmas, all the norms and potentialities of manifestation, are not excluded. But these manifestations also cannot be said to exist or to not exist at this level. Mind rests in its natural state and is beyond thought.

However, even though they seem to be "saying the same thing," the popular idea that dharmakaya is somehow the same as the quantum reality, the 'potentia' of Heisenberg or the 'implicate order' of Bohm, is unworkable. These things are known inferentially and can only be known inferentially. By their very definition, there is no possible way that the potentia or implicate order can be directly experienced. Physicists have shown that if the theoretical, inferential logic of physical materialism is pushed far enough a point is reached at which the concept of physical reality becomes paradoxical. This brings us to the point of realizing the problem in trying to conceptualize ultimate reality. But, depending as it does on extremely naive assumptions about perception, 'elementary particle' physics does not touch on the possibility of awareness of what is beyond concept in the world of human experience. And this is what dharmakaya points to. Trying to conceptualize a further level of reality beyond those paradoxes leads the mind into further abstractions, and therefore further away from the direct insight into its own nature that it seeks. These further levels of abstraction are of interest to physicists, but they do not have anything to do with the insight that seeks to overcome the habitual tendency to believe that reality is conceptually graspable.

Niels Bohr's approach probably came the closest, among scientists, to understanding the non-conceptuality of shunyata. As we discussed in Chapter 2, Bohr suggested that at a certain point in trying to conceptually grasp reality, our concepts inevitably highlight aspects that are incompatible. He gave as examples the concepts of wave and particle in quantum mechanics, but he extended this to concepts such as 'thinker' and 'thought' and 'love' and 'justice,' and suggested that this 'principle of complementarity' would turn up throughout human affairs. Bohr's views were regarded as muddle-headed by physicists who still sought a complete and coherent objective world. But Bohr showed a profound understanding of the role of language in world-making as we have discussed it in this book.

The second level of embodiment of Mind-as-Such is 'sambhoga-kaya,' or 'body of complete joy,' corresponding to the level of emotion. This is the level of energy of stimulation of the limitless sense perceptions. It is the level of the awareness of aesthetic qualities and of communication of qualities, of blue*ness*, of red*ness*, of rock*ness*, of water*ness* and so on. Emotions are not experienced as individual expressions, frozen into some conceptualized and personalized anger, or jealousy, or desire. The variety of energies is felt as the qualitative communicativeness of phenomena. And the patterns in which this communicativeness is felt are known as the 'Five Wisdoms.'

When nonduality is realized as the basic ground of perception and the seventh consciousness ceases activity, the energies of the root emotions that activated the seventh consciousness are now transformed into the energies of the 'Five Wisdoms.' Anger is transformed into 'Mirrorlike Wisdom,' which reflects phenomena just as they are, undistorted by 'consciousness'—the need to tie them all together into packages and story-lines about a self and its world. Pride is transformed into the 'Wisdom of Equanimity,' which appreciates the quality and richness of phenomena as they are without the distortion of determining their value relative to a self. Passion is transformed into 'Discriminating Wisdom,' which discriminates the finest details of perception without checking back their relevance to a self. Jealousy is transformed into 'All-Accomplishing Wisdom,' which accomplishes action not dominated by one-upmanship and the fear of failure arising from the self-concepts as philosopher, economist, politician, spiritual person, and so on. And ignorance is transformed into the 'Wisdom of All-Encompassing Space,' which *is* nondual awareness, accommodating all phenomena without exclusion, barrier, or fixation on final inherent existences.

With the sambhogakaya there is an intention toward actual appearance. The third level, corresponding to body, is known as 'nirmana-kaya, or 'body of emanation.' It is the specific appearance at a particular time and place of a particular world. It is the body as lived in, inseparable from the environment of the senses. There is no special emphasis on the individual body as a primary focus. There is no particular emphasis on the individual body because nondual awareness is not localized in space or time, these being the boundary conditions of dualistic consciousness.

Since limitation comes from the conceptualizing, discriminating dualistic view of self, the sense fields are potentially without limit in the space of nondual awareness. As Trungpa Rinpoche says, "You experience a vast realm of perception unfolding. There is unlimited sound, unlimited sight, unlimited taste, unlimited feeling, and so on. The realm of perception is limitless, so limitless that perception itself is primordial, unthinkable, beyond thought. There are so many perceptions they are beyond imagination. There are a vast number of sounds. There are sounds you have never heard. There are sights and colors that you have never seen. There are feelings that you have never experienced before. There are endless fields of perception."[7]

Sense field in Sanskrit is *ayatana*, which means "gate of coming into existence," and in Tibetan *kye-che*, meaning "born and expanding." There is an implication here that the gate opens both ways: that the perceiver comes into existence together with the perceived, and that both are relative. Therefore as the perceiver opens, so do the sense objects; it is a mutual opening, a mutual coming into existence, and a mutual expanding.

When the ayatanas, the doors of perception, begin to clarify, perceptions are felt with the heart as well as cognized by the intellect. Vastness, as well as humor, is felt in the smallest details. The quality of ordinary perceptions might be felt also as joy and sadness mixed, an intense longing pointing beyond them to the unbounded openness of awareness. This is not necessarily a 'higher' state of being or of consciousness at all. It can be quite natural and ordinary. To "rest in this natural state" allows the vastness of perceptions to shine through them and brings direct connection with the power and intrinsic intelligence of the ordinary world. Chögyam Trungpa, Rinpoche, comments thus: "The meditator develops new depths of insight through direct communication with the reality of the phenomenal world. He is able to see not only the absence of complexity, the absence of duality, but the *stoneness* of stone and the *waterness* of water. . . . There is a vast understanding of symbolism and a vast understanding of energy. Whatever the situation, he no longer has to force results. Life flows around him. This is the basic mandala principle."[8]

Since there is no reference point, no center to which such awareness refers back, the notion of mandala principle is invoked here to help understand how perceptions are organized. The Tibetan for mandala is *kuil-khor*, which literally translates as center-fringe. Mandala, or kyil-khor, is often represented as a circle turning around a central dot. This suggests that the mandala is a total, undivided world circulating through awareness, but not directed toward a center or emanating from a center.

Guenther quotes a Tibetan text on mandala (which he translates as "configuration") thus:

> Since the auto-excitatory intelligence [rikpa] has neither a periphery nor a center, it is a point [kyil];
> Since it is this that is experienced, it is the attendant circle [khor];
> Since the auto-excitatory intelligence beautifies itself, it is a kyil-kyor (configuration);
> [Its beauty] does not depend on configurations prepared by colored stone-dust.

Thus phenomenal appearances are experienced as ornaments (the attendant circle) of indivisible nonreferential awareness and space. The reference to colored stone-dust is presumably to the hard, lifeless, artificially colored configurations of the 'object-world.' The following quote, also from a Tibetan text, expresses the manner in which this adornment is displayed:

Energy is the center, the coming-into-presence is the periphery;
Energy and coming-into-presence is complete in (and as) experience.

Invariance is the center, nonartificiality is the periphery;
Invariance and nonartificiality are complete in (and as) experience.

Unorigination is the center, noncessation is the periphery;
The nonduality of unorigination and noncessation is configuration.

Indivisibility is the center, presence-cum-interpretation is the periphery;
Indivisibility and manifoldness is configuration.

Nonduality is the center, nonpremeditation is the periphery;
Nonpremeditation and nonduality is the configuration.

We can paraphrase these two quotes by saying that the unvarying, unoriginated, and indivisible energy of rikpa nondually experiences an adornment of genuine, spontaneous, and unceasing presence. Or, in the words of Trungpa quoted earlier, "You (the hollowness of space [kyil]) are beautifying space [khor], absolute nothingness."

Arising within dharmakaya, which is without center and fringe, total experience can be described as three mandalas: the outer, the inner, and the secret mandalas.[10] The secret mandala is the mandala of the communicative energies, which were felt by ego to be the emotions, but which from awareness of nonduality are transformed into the Five Wisdoms of the sambhogakaya. The inner mandala is the mandala of the body as lived in, its appearance and posture, as well as the breath, blood, and felt, living energy flowing through it. The outer mandala is the totality of the appearance of an outer world, the environment, projected by the perceptual process.

The mandala principle is understanding the vividness and energetic quality of perception beyond concept, that is, beyond a self as center. The symbolic nature of perception is realized. Normally we live in the world of concepts, in which sounds and forms and so on are always symbols for something else. The world we live in is premeditated and not authentic. But in this case, forms, colors, and sounds are symbols, not standing for anything else, but simply symbolizing themselves, the play of energy in space.[11]

THE PRACTICALITY OF THIS VIEW

The mandala principle is another way of talking about dependent nature. And again what is being pointed to is that the realization of nondual awareness as the basis of all does not mean that some fantastic other world appears, nor does it mean that the ordinary world disappears. Rather, when false conception is removed, the ordinary world is transformed by this realization. These topics are not intended as mere philosophy or imaginative poetry; they point to modes of experiencing that are said to be continually present in everyday life, but that are obscured by the reference point of ordinary perceptions. Perception of an ordinary world, transformed in this way, is known as sacredness in the Buddhist tradition. Sacredness, in this view, does not come from another realm, transmitted by authority, nor does it arise only from the blessings of a great teacher. It arises as the result of the disciplined practice of the method of meditation, joined with the intellectual understanding of emptiness.

Sacredness, which opens up from the point of nowness, cannot be examined or described with dualistic methods based on the linear concept of time as past, present, and future. But, especially in the Vajrayana tradition, there are powerful methods available for the transmutation of psychic and spiritual energies leading eventually to the realization of emptiness and the Five Wisdoms. These methods and realizations aid the practitioner to go beyond dualistic thought in actual practice. They go beyond the methods and viewpoint of the sciences so long as these remain based on dualism. They work with the intuitive faculty of mind as well as the intellect. Based on sitting meditation and using visual imagery and the penetrating power of sound, these methods operate directly on the obstructions and impediments to awareness arising from the self-concept at the levels of *form, feeling,* and *perception,* in the terms of skandha analysis. Their power lies in working directly with the energies available when the limitations of ego begin to lift. But whatever special technique is being used to penetrate the deep conceptual obscurations, all have the purpose of bringing awareness to this present moment of nowness. Therefore the simple practice of mindfulness-awareness is the basis of all these techniques.

Many practitioners claim that it is possible, then, by properly guided investigation, to verify and experience for oneself the insights that can only be pointed to but not described. However, because of the need for guidance and because this guidance is of the nature of pointing to rather than describing, this investigation can take place only in the context of a living teaching and teacher. It cannot be learned literally alone, because verbal expression occurs only on the nirmanakaya level. The sambhogakaya and dharmakaya levels of manifestation can be pointed out only in the living moment. Words themselves, as most modern linguists now acknowledge, have a multitude of meanings, or no meaning at all, depending on the context in which they are spoken, and the presence of the speaker. And it is context and presence that enable the discovery of the three kayas to be communicated from one person to another.

The discovery of the various aspects of awareness is not an "all-or-nothing" affair. Each of these aspects is realized in temporary glimpses and hints, however brief they may be, in the continuing path of meditation. As a practitioner opens to such glimpses, his or her perception and the action stemming from this perception, may gradually be transformed. Practice of Buddhist meditation has been likened to someone trying to climb a mountain, the mountain of ego. As the meditator inevitably begins to stumble, the practice and teachings come along and push him so that he or she rolls without struggle down the mountainside, which may be a bottomless pit, continually opening as one relaxes more and more. It is not a state of being to be attained by dualistic struggle, as is the way of both conventional science and conventional religion. According to this teaching, when the struggle to be a something is given up, perceptions can open beyond limitations of the imaginary dualistic world.

The emphasis is on the natural, spontaneous quality of the realization of Mind-as-such.

Devotion of student for teacher and the teachings of egolessness, as well as compassion of teacher for student, is a powerful motivating and energizing factor on the natural path of realization. Of course this is true in any genuine teaching situation. Whether it is parent to child or teacher to student, the realization of the teacher is communicated as much as the verbal information. Especially in the arts, but even in the sciences, apprenticeship is still the only way in which complete understanding can be communicated, so that the student is able to emulate and perhaps go beyond the teacher. In the personal journey of understanding human mind, devotion to an accomplished teacher is even more necessary. This may seem like an external support, until genuine understanding dawns that Mind-as-such is neither one's own nor the teacher's personal possession, but is universal and undivided, so that the teacher is not fundamentally external. If one wished to learn the art of swordsmanship, one would not risk one's life by relying on what one could learn from books or computers. But working toward personal discovery of the nature of mind/body, its perceptual processes, and its powerful energy is far more dangerous as well as potentially fulfilling than swordsmanship. And because sometimes along the way the burden of ego is slightly lifted and correspondingly a hint of the joy of egolessness is felt, devotion for the teacher and compassion for others naturally arise in the process. In the final chapter we will see how devotion and compassion arise inherently within shunyata.

22

Toward a Compassionate Society

WHEN MY DAUGHTER was four years old she attended a preschool based on Buddhist principles. Late that summer, there was a particularly large crop of flies that managed, in spite of the staff's efforts, to get into the school, bother the children, and occasionally settle on the snacks being prepared in the kitchen. After discussion with the Buddhist adviser to the school, the staff decided that it would be better not to hang fly papers, and that they would try to spray only as a last resort. Accordingly they spent one weekend fixing all the holes in the window and door screens and making sure that doors and windows closed tightly. After shooing all the flies out of the building, they scrubbed the whole building extra thoroughly. With some irony they even put down all around it some herbs that someone had heard would ward off flies. In spite of all these efforts, the flies reappeared inside within a few days. They were now in even more abundance so that they became more than a nuisance, they were a definite health hazard. The staff again discussed whether to fumigate the building. They decided this time to go ahead, but to try to be very thorough, especially making sure that all the eggs were destroyed, so that they would not have to do it a second time. A sense of compassion for all sentient beings as well as a practical point of view, that the principle of trying not to kill even flies should not interfere with the basic health considerations of the children, was conveyed to all the children in this and similar little episodes.

Two years later, I was walking with my daughter on the sidewalk of a busy main road. A small cat came up to us, and we bent to stroke it. It walked past us and off the sidewalk, potentially into the traffic. My daughter started to go after it, and I shouted, with some urgency, to her to stop. She said, "But Daddy, we are Buddhists and we always try to save life." I was quite astonished because I had not discussed Buddhism very much with her at all, at least not from the point of view of any particular dogma. Whether she grows up calling herself a Buddhist, or a scientist for that matter, does not seem crucial. But if there is going to be any doctrine that she grows up with, perhaps the best would be that "we always try to save life."

EMPTINESS AND COMPASSION

Along with realization of shunyata, the development of lovingkindness and compassion is the heart of Buddhist meditative practice. Just because it no longer seeks a more real world behind appearance, the viewpoint of shunyata develops great interest in and concern for the world of appearance. It is not blind to the tendency of all sentient beings to become caught in duality and to project inherent existence into themselves and others, thus bringing about profound anxiety. On the contrary, grasping the things of duality and fixating on them, and the resulting anxiety, are seen all the more clearly from the point of view of shunyata. From this clear seeing arises gentleness and friendliness to oneself and to others. In a sense, such fundamental gentleness *is* just the removal of anxiety from concern about one's own existence. And out of friendliness or loving kindness, known as *maitri* in the Buddhist tradition, nonconceptual compassion for others is born.[1] Compassion, born out of awareness of shunyata, is communicative energy that cuts through the barriers of grasping and fixating on duality.

Shunyata is equivalent to dependent co-origination, the fact that all apparently separate things in our perceptual world arise in dependence on each other, have their existence in dependence on each other, and go out of existence in dependence on each other. The 'emptiness' of shunyata is that there is no separate existence; the compassion that is inseparable from shunyata is the appropriate action that makes emptiness and nonseparateness known to others.

EVOLUTION

In order, on the relative level, to appreciate the communicative, cooperative possibility of compassion we might return to science once more. The reader might very well now be saying, "Is there not one thing we know *for sure*, one thing scientists are absolutely certain about: that the natural world is *fundamentally* a world of selfishness, aggression, and a 'struggle for survival'? Therefore is not this idea of compassion simply another religious or moralistic concept smeared on top of a natural world which is, first and foremost, brutish and unkind?" This is indeed the idea that several generations have been taught at their fathers' knees. It is based on a popularized and distorted version of Darwin's theory of evolution and its basic mechanism, natural selection. But is it *true?*

The *theory of evolution* itself has been very successful. It has demonstrated that, by some process, the forms of life that appear on earth now have evolved gradually, or by sudden leaps, from other forms, and that the appearance of a multitude of life forms is understandable without the extra hypothesis of a creator. The theory of evolution has had a varied history since its first proclamation, by Charles Darwin and Russel Wallace, in the mid-nineteenth century.[2] But for the past forty years or so it has become firmly rooted in the popular culture and the lore of mainstream science. The broad principle of evolution can hardly be doubted now. The forms of organic life on earth are continually changing. The vast variety of organic forms we see in the world today has gradually manifested from fewer and less complex forms over the past two or perhaps three billion years. I will not here go into the tremendous wealth of evidence for this: fossil records, experimental breeding, study of hereditary patterns in populations, the elucidation of a chemical basis for heredity. Many details confirm the evolutionary view.

THE DOGMA OF THE 'FITTEST'

Along with the general view of evolution, the dogma began to pervade all of society that competition and struggle for survival was the *one and only* biological basis for the behavior of organisms, including humans, in their natural state. The view of Darwin's staunch and outspoken ally, Thomas Huxley, that "The animal world is on about the same level as a gladiator's show. The strongest, the swiftest and the cunningest live to fight another day . . . no quarter is given" was extended by social philosopher Herbert Spencer to humanity. Spencer, a popular and influential philosopher at the beginning of the century, proclaimed, "The well-being of existing humanity, and the unfolding of it into this ultimate perfection, are both secured by that same beneficent, though severe discipline, to which the animate creation at large is subject. . . . The poverty of the incapable, the distresses that come upon the imprudent, the starvation of the idle, and those shoulderings aside of the weak by the strong, which leave so many 'in shallows and in miseries,' are the decrees of a large and far-seeing benevolence."[3]

This dogma has entered every aspect of our culture starting with the way we bring up our children—teaching them to be aggressive, to 'one-up' others before they 'one-up' you; teaching them that life is the law of the jungle, and the law of the jungle is "red in tooth and claw." It informs our theories of economics and the market place, and our international relations, in which we assume that other nations also obey the law of the jungle and that some of them would wipe us off the face of the earth if they thought they had a chance of survival.

It cannot be emphasized too much how deeply this idea is ingrained into the psyche of modern men, women, and children. We *believe*, deeply believe, that we are aggressive animals. We *believe* that the only way to survive in this world is to *be* aggressive. And this belief has become so deep that we have twisted it around to make it a virtue. The "aggressive" personality has become highly respected and prized. It has been pointed out that even affectionate humor among young Americans is often to put each other down in an aggressive and snide way. This kind of "street humor" is perhaps intended to be a toughening ritual to help them to face the harsh realities of the world of competition and the marketplace.

The misuse of the idea of 'survival of the fittest,' in itself a narrow view of the mechanism of evolution, is leading astray countless millions of "educated" people who learn the scientific certainty of natural selection of the fittest through competition and the basic aggressiveness of nature, not only from their fathers, but in every school class from Grade Four up. The idea of progress through competition and the natural virtue of selfishness has become, of the various motivating ideologies of modern society, the principal one claiming the authority of science. This prejudiced and *anti*-scientific propagation of a half truth has prevented generations of children from appreciating something else that observation of nature teaches: the tremendous harmony, nurturing, and cooperation among all species in their natural habitat.

Selection of the fittest, or the 'struggle for survival' as it is popularly called, is only a very one-sided view of the mechanism by which natural evolution occurs. As I briefly pointed out in Chapter 9, biologists Humberto Maturana and Francisco Varela have shown that, rather than a 'struggle for survival' against the environment resulting in the selection of a 'best fit,' the mechanism could better be regarded as a 'natural drift' in a *coupling* with the environment.[4] In this natural drift, species have many possible paths of internal structural variation open to them that maintain their self-organization. Therefore the idea of 'the fittest,' and the paramount importance of competition, is simply beside the point. Furthermore, in the natural environment it seems almost certain that 'cooperation' within and among species is an equally important factor as 'competition.' And biologists, including Darwin himself, have recognized this since the theory was first proposed.

The idea of competition and struggle for survival arises principally through thinking of organisms as separate things whose main driving motivation is self-preservation and reproduction. But neither individual organisms nor the entire population of a species are really fundamentally separate from each other or from their environment. It is only in the mind of the observer that the essential definition of an organism lies in its separateness. One aspect of all organisms is certainly the tendency to preserve their self-organization and the integrity of their natural boundary, which gives them the appearance of unity and separateness. However, organisms are throughout their lives immersed in an environment and exchanging energy and order with that environment. When it ceases to exchange energy and information, when it becomes that much more separate, an organism is dead.

An organism can be regarded, then, not only as a separate 'thing' always engaged, in isolation, in a struggle for its individual continuation. It can be seen also as an open system, continually exchanging matter, energy, and responses with its environment, embedded in a network of organisms of the same and different species, and within all of this maintaining its self-organization and the self-organization of the various groups of which it is a part.

COOPERATION AMONG SPECIES

Organisms continually interact and communicate with other organisms. Ecologists, who study the interactions among the various species populating an area, as well as ethologists, who study animal behavior, largely assert that by far the most predominant observations they make are of the way in which plants and animals *avoid* competition whenever possible, and tend far more often to support and cooperate with each other. This connectedness of organisms can be very loose relative to the tendency to self-preservation, or it can be so tight that the observer may be uncertain whether he or she is dealing with a single organism or more than one. Such connectedness again means that the unit of self-preservation may not necessarily be the individual organism at all. In fact cooperation balanced with competition seems to be the rule. As Lewis Thomas, biologist and well-known writer, says, ''The urge to form partnerships, to link up in collaborative arrangements, is perhaps the oldest, strongest, and most fundamental force in nature. There are no solitary, free-living creatures, every form of life is dependent on other forms."[5]

Symbiosis is one form of mutual cooperation in which the definition of separate 'things' is dubious. In the case of symbiosis, cooperation occurs between organisms of different species. There are numerous examples of symbiosis in which organisms serve each other by providing a place to stay; helping each other obtain food; providing transport, either of the whole organism or of its seeds; mutual protection; and cleaning.[6] Some crabs live in the rectums of sea urchins, while others are hosts to numerous other smaller species. Some ants grow cultures of fungi for food and others culture aphids. An African bird, the honeyguide, and the ratel, an animal like a badger, cooperate to find and consume beehives. Many species take warning from the alarm cries of other species, while others live in the protective environment of dangerous predators. Cleaning is so abundant, especially in the ocean, that "Littler fish clean bigger fish" could complement the old catch-phrase "bigger fish eat littler fish" that epitomizes the 'struggle for survival' mentality.

And so the list goes on and could be extended almost indefinitely. Wherever there is an ecologic system there are multiple symbiotic interactions and cooperations. In many cases the relationship between the partners has become so intimate that neither one would survive in the same manner without the other. Some symbiotic organisms permit each other to survive in environments far more extreme than each organism alone could survive in, thus opening up entirely new habitats for each other. A well-known example of this is the lichen. Lichens, those tough greenish or bluish patches that colonize rock faces, were for a long time considered single organisms. Then it was found that lichens are in fact a close cooperative arrangement between a type of fungus and a type of algae. The resulting combination has altogether different appearance and behavioral characteristics from the two organisms that compose it. Neither fungus nor algae alone would be able to survive the rugged conditions of a rock face, be able to decompose the rock and take sustenance from the minerals in it. While the fungus and algae have very narrow habitats, lichens are found in deserts and rain forests, all the way from Alaska to the Tropics.

COOPERATION WITHIN SPECIES

Cooperation within species appears to be equally abundant. In fact it appears to be the rule rather than the exception. Simple societies of single organisms interacting cooperatively may behave almost as single organisms, for example the slime mold, a termite colony, or even a migrating flock of birds. And numerous animal species live, hunt, protect each other, and play together in loosely or tightly knit groups. For example, the African elephant, described by John Tyler Bonner, forms groups around a dominant female with her young. The oldest female is dominant, and under attack she will take remarkable risks and often show blind courage. The importance of her role is emphasized by the fact that if she is shot and killed, the group will go into a frenzied disarray for a long period of time. But if another female or a calf is wounded, the whole group, with the old female taking the lead, will try to support and help the injured member away from danger.

Another example, of wolf packs hunting cooperatively, is described by Bonner in this way: "Numerous instances have been described in which the wolves ambush or outflank a large prey animal, such as a caribou or a mountain sheep. They employ clever tactics involving the use of the terrain and the strategic dispersal of individuals to drive the fleeing prey into the clutches of their pack mates. Lest the reader take this merely as an example of "nature red in tooth and claw," it should be added that wolves and other carnivorous predators rarely kill healthy animals in their prime, but almost always the old, sick, or injured. And they rarely kill more than they, or other groups, who in turn depend on their hunting skill, such as vultures, can eat at that time. In fact predator and prey groups can often be seen to coexist in a harmonious and almost symbiotic manner. One example of this is the extraordinary harmony between buffalo and Native Americans, and between Eskimo and caribou, shown in the tremendous caring and appreciation of the humans for their prey. This harmony has now been destroyed by the crass stupidity of the 'progress' mentality.

Finally, there are many examples of cases in which one animal stands guard for the group, or gives a warning cry that draws attention to the danger as well as to itself in a dangerous situation, often at the risk of its own life. For example, according to Bonner, "When a group of red deer flees they form a spindle-shaped pattern with the leader in the front and the second dominant individual in the rear. If they pass into a gulley, the last individual will stop and fix the intruder with her eyes while the group disappears. The moment they emerge into sight again, the leader takes up the sentry duty, and the last individual rushes forward to rejoin the group to reform the spindle."[7]

It seems that the majority of species exhibit some form of cooperative group behavior and communication. Cooperative behavior may have a genetic origin in that it may be advantageous for closely related animals to act in a mutually cooperative way so that their family genes have a higher chance of survival. This genetically based tendency for kin to assist and protect each other means that the unit being preserved is extended beyond the individual to include close family. This is known as 'inclusive fitness' or 'kin selection.' The almost universal caring of one or both parents for their young is the prototype of 'kin selection.'

However, it is not always the case that an animal has an inborn trait enabling it to recognize precisely its close kin. For example, there are several cases of animal species in which a small number of adults join together to care for a group of young, not necessarily their own, almost like a nursery school. In many circumstances animals appear to behave toward each other *as if* they were kin. This is probably the biological basis of animal societies and of "cultural" behavior in animals. Members of the same animal species often have a tendency toward mutual cooperation that may originally have a genetic basis, but that has evolved beyond this into cooperative behavior patterns that are passed from generation to generation by cultural or behavioral, rather than genetic, transmission.

ORGANISMS ARE BOTH OPEN AND CLOSED

The details of evolutionary explanations for any particular case are extraordinarily complex. And any attempt to produce a general evolutionary theory must reflect this complexity. As Pierre Grasse, ex-President of the French Académie des Sciences, says, "By its inextricable complexity, its creations and orientations, its historicity, and, on occasion, its contradictions, evolution is quite unlike the simplified, scaled-down and totally inaccurate picture of it presented by theories. It is so vast as to make one stop and consider that its problems are very far beyond the means of present-day science. Interpretations and explanations advanced by *whomever it may be* can only be partial and tentative."[8]

One might, however, suppose that whatever general evolutionary theory of the biological world appears, it must at least include two basic explanatory principles that are in continuing tension and balance with each other, and a third that harmonizes these two. The first principle is a tendency to self-preservation, to maintain the separate identity of a biological system, to maintain closure. From this point of view individual organisms may couple to form larger units, such as a bee colony or a wolf pack. In this case the coupling is regarded as part of the internal structure of the larger unit that maintains its integrity. The second principle is the tendency to form open systems, and for open systems to evolve to higher and higher levels of complexity through exchange of energy and information with their environment and with each other. This tendency to form evolving open systems, and of open systems to interact responsively with their environment, including each other, is the basis of cooperation. And from this point of view coupling between individual organisms can be regarded as aspects of their openness, or nonseparateness. And the third principle recalls the key point of Niels Bohr, as well as Maturana and Varela, that 'Everything that is said is said by someone.' It is that each of the previous two tendencies depends on the point of view of the observer, and is not in any way an absolute description of what is 'out there.'

In conclusion, far from there being a fundamental obstacle at the biological level to the tendency toward cooperation and openness, there is good biological basis for it, as well as for the tendency toward territoriality, aggression, and closedness. In human awareness, the principle of closedness manifests as the ego-forming tendency and the principle of openness as the tendency to kindness and communication. The third principle, recognizing the role of the describer, is the seed for realization of shunyata.

MAITRI

When the fundamental openness of shunyata is realized, the tendency to cooperative communication is felt as nonconceptual energy of compassion. And before such full realization, on the relative mundane level, the energy of maitri, friendliness or loving-kindness, can itself be an activating principle for transcending ego-oriented perception. On this simple relative level it begins with recognition of the tender caring of parents for their young, extends out to the natural friendship and affection between members of a family, and extends beyond the family to others.

Maitri can be positively and actively cultivated by generally taking the attitude of exchanging oneself for others and specifically by the practice known as sending and taking.[9] This practice consists, basically, in the visualization of taking into oneself the anxiety and suffering of others and radiating out to others a feeling of warmth and friendship. When this is practiced regularly in combination with the practice of mindfulness and awareness meditation, it does actually begin to soften the hard shell of the tendency to closure and to bring about an expansiveness and warmth toward the world. In this way a perception of oneself as fundamentally closed and separate, and of the world as harsh, hostile, and limiting can be gradually transformed. One can begin to feel one's fundamental interconnectedness with others and begin to perceive the world as fundamentally friendly and openended.

At this point we can begin to understand the practical possibility implicit in the detailed analysis of perceptual process and worldmaking that I have presented, which implies the possibility of *actually* transforming the world. The belief context we live by and the world we live in arise in dependence on each other and shift in dependence on each other. If the world is conceived as 'out there' and filled with occupants that are conceived of as separate from each other and engaged in a continual struggle with each other and their environment, then that is how it is. So long as this is the assumed world in which we live, then no amount of political activity, no matter how well intentioned, can fundamentally change anything. But these perceptions arise fundamentally from conception, albeit at a deep cultural and biological level, and therefore they can be transformed. They can be transformed precisely because perception is not a mere reflection of a solid impenetrable world out there with a forever unchanging nature. Perception is discontinuous and creative, with an opportunity at each moment to see our own aggression and allow freshness and gentleness to enter in, or to allow cool space in our passionate grasping.

This transformation cannot, of course, take place merely at the level of trying to change our concepts, our 'paradigms' of the world, although this may be where it has to begin, and conceptual reeducation must certainly be an important part of it. The change can happen only by understanding the three *natures*—false conceptions, interdependence of subject and object, and shunyata—at a level deeper than rational consciousness. This realization is the basis of a natural ethic that goes far beyond the 'struggle for survival' and the type of compromise among self-interests known as the 'social contract.' Such realization is highly energetic and actively directs toward benefiting others, and it does not depend on fame, wealth, or territory. It does depend on the possibility of individual and group practice of mindfulness meditation, and certainly some basic physical and educational needs have to be met before such practice is possible. But it is indicated from all that we have discussed that such a transformation is a real practical possibility at the social, racial, or global level. We

are, in this sense, at a profound turning point in the modern understanding of the nature and potential of humans and of the world we
make.

PRACTICE BEYOND BELIEF

It would be foolhardy to suggest any grand scheme to solve the
world's ills. It must surely be clear by now that conceptual schemes,
however grand, if they are not based on a thorough personal understanding of the world-making nature of perception, can bring only
further divisiveness and separatism. We have come to the end of our
journey that began in the first chapter with the search for a new
'belief context.' And it is perhaps with some irony that we discover
that the 'belief context' proposed by Buddhists turns out to be
freedom, at a profound level, from all reliance on belief, including
belief in shunyata. Let us recall Nagarjuna's warning once more, that
"Those who believe in shunyata are deemed incurable." In this sense
an analogy for the *concept* of shunyata is a ferry that, having got us
across the rough waves of conceptualization to direct experience, is
no longer useful. And so shunyata can hardly be approached without
a sense of irony and humor.

However, it would seem that some form of contemplative or meditative practice that is able to bring awareness of nonduality, and the
inherent compassion that is inseparable from it, would provide the
practical basis for the change of our belief context and of our world
that so many of us urgently seek. It does not really matter whether
the theoretical basis of such practice has its origin in Buddhism,
science, Christianity, or some other doctrine, so long as it recognizes
the nature of dualistic perception, and the possibility of going beyond
this. It is not the theory, but the practice that can bring about a
personal understanding and realization of the nature of perception.
This would seem to be extremely beneficial to our present world.

A society based on such contemplative training and the cooperation
and compassion arising from it is by no means utopian. This is not a
society that is already perfect, in which all its members already
behave like the gods once used to. It is a society that acknowledges
all the facets of being human, the tendencies to being closed as well
as the opening qualities, and the almost unlimited potentialities in
awareness. Most important, it acknowledges the practicality of training to work toward these possibilities.

NOTES

CHAPTER 1

1. James Burke, *The Day the Universe Changed* (Boston: Little, Brown, 1985), p. 337.

2. Thomas Kuhn, *The Structure of Scientific Revolutions* (Chicago: University of Chicago Press, 1962).

3. Jerome S. Bruner, *Beyond the Information Given: Studies in the Psychology of Knowing*, J. Anglin, ed. (New York: W. W. Norton, 1973).

4. Jerome S. Bruner, *Actual Minds, Possible Worlds* (Cambridge, Mass.: Harvard University Press, 1986), p. 46.

5. Douglas Hofstadter, *Metamagical Themas* (New York: Basic Books, 1985), p. 136.

6. Charles Darwin, *The Voyage of the Beagle* (New York: Doubleday, 1962).

7. Michael Polanyi, *Personal Knowledge* (Chicago: University of Chicago Press, 1962), p. 101.

8. Bruner, *Actual Minds, Possible Worlds*, p. 46.

CHAPTER 2

1. Nick Herbert, *Quantum Reality: Beyond the New Physics* (New York: Anchor Press, 1985). For other surveys of the various interpretations of the foundations of quantum theory, see Heinz Pagels, *The Cosmic Code* (New York: Simon and Schuster, 1982), and Bernard d'Espagnat, *The Conceptual Foundations of Quantum Mechanics* (Reading, Mass.: W. A. Benjamin, 1976).

2. Paul Davies, *Other Worlds* (New York: Simon and Schuster, 1980), p. 15.

3. Niels Bohr, *Atomic Physics and Human Knowledge* (New York: Science Editions, 1958); *Essays 1958–1962* (New York: Interscience, 1963).

4. Henry Folse, *The Philosophy of Niels Bohr* (Amsterdam: North Holland, 1985), p. 256.

5. Aage Peterson, "The Philosophy of Niels Bohr," in *Niels Bohr: A Centenary Volume*, A. P. French and J. P. Kennedy, eds. (Cambridge, Mass.: Harvard University Press, 1985), pp. 301, 302.

6. Folse, *The Philosophy of Niels Bohr*, p. 54.

7. Niels Bohr, "Quantum Physics and Philosophy," in *Essays*, p. 7.

8. Niels Bohr, quoted in Gerald Holton, *Thematic Origins of Scientific Thought* (Cambridge: Harvard University Press, 1973), pp. 137, 140.

9. Folse, *The Philosophy of Niels Bohr*, p. 54.

10. Werner Heisenberg, *Physics and Philosophy* (New York: Harper and Row, 1958), p. 186.

11. Nick Herbert, *Quantum Reality*.

12. Eugene P. Wigner, *Symmetries and Reflections* (Cambridge, Mass.: MIT Press, 1970).

13. Bryce deWitt and Neil Graham, *The Many Worlds Interpretation of Quantum Mechanics* (Princeton: Princeton University Press, 1982).

14. David Deutsch, in *The Ghost in the Atom*, ed. P. C. W. Davies and J. R. Brown (Cambridge: Cambridge University Press, 1986), p. 83.

15. David Bohm, *Wholeness and the Implicate Order* (London: Routledge and Kegan Paul, 1980), p. 209.

16. For a discussion of the various responses to Bell's Theorem, see Davies and Brown, eds., *The Ghost in the Atom*.

17. John Wheeler, quoted in ibid., p. 23.

18. Ibid., p. 24.

CHAPTER 3

1. See, for example, Herman Bondi, *Relativity and Common Sense* (New York: Dover, 1980); Nigel Calder, *Einstein's Universe* (New York: Penguin, 1980); Albert Einstein and Leopold Infeld, *The Evolution of Physics* (New York: Simon and Schuster, 1938).

2. See the references for Chapter 2.

3. Karl Popper, *The Logic of Scientific Discovery* (New York: Harper and Row, 1959).

4. Frederick Suppe, *The Structure of Scientific Theories* (Champaign: University of Illinois Press, 1974), p. 4.

5. Richard Morris, *The Nature of Reality* (New York: McGraw-Hill, 1987), p. 4.

6. Bertrand Russell, *Our Knowledge of the External World* (London, 1914), quoted in Richard Gregory, *Mind in Science* (Cambridge: Cambridge University Press, 1981), p. 352.

7. Gregory, *Mind in Science*, p. 352.

8. Paul Churchland, in "Science vs. Reality: A Debate," *Dalhousie Review* 64 (3) (Halifax: Dalhousie University Press, 1984), p. 417.

9. Edward Harrison, *Masks of the Universe* (New York: Macmillan, 1985), p. 1.

10. Ibid., p. 2.

11. Ted Kaptchuk, *The Web That Has No Weaver* (New York: Congdon and Weed, 1983), p. 3.

12. Colin A. Ronan and Joseph Needham, *The Shorter Science and Civilisation in China* (Cambridge: Cambridge University Press, 1978).

13. Morris Berman, *The Reenchantment of the World* (Ithaca: Cornell University Press, 1981), p. 93.

14. Harrison, p. 222.

CHAPTER 4

1. Colin A. Ronan and Joseph Needham, *The Shorter Science and Civilisation in China* (Cambridge: Cambridge University Press, 1978).

2. Herbert Guenther, *Buddhist Philosophy in Theory and Practice* (New York: Penguin, 1972), p. 20.

3. Nolan Pliny Jacobson, *Buddhism and the Contemporary World: Change and Self-Correction* (Carbondale: Southern Illinois University Press, 1983), pp. 137, 121, 122.

4. Walpole Rahula, *What the Buddha Taught* (London: Gordon Frazer, 1978), p. 13.

5. Guy Welbon, *Buddhist Nirvana and Its Western Interpreters* (Chicago: University of Chicago Press, 1968).

6. Rahula, *What the Buddha Taught*; Richard Robinson, *The Buddhist Religion: A Historical Introduction*, 3rd ed. (Belmont, Calif.: Wadsworth, 1982).

CHAPTER 5

1. From the Digha Nikaya in, *The Buddhist Translation*, ed. W. Th. de Bary (New York: Vintage, 1972).

2. A good general introduction to dharma analysis is Edward Conze, *Buddhist Thought in India* (Ann Arbor: University of Michigan Press, 1970). See also Junjiro Takakusu, *The Essentials of Buddhist Philosophy* (Honolulu, 1947); Late Rinbochay and E. Napper, *Mind in Tibetan Buddhism* (Valois, N.Y.: Gabriel, 1980); Geshe Rabten, *The Mind and Its Functions*, trans. Gelong Tubkay (Switzerland: Tharpa Choling, 1978); Herbert Guenther and Leslie Kawamura, *Mind in Buddhist Psychology* (Emeryville, Calif.: Dharma Publishing, 1975).

3. Conze, *Buddhist Thought in India*, p. 97.

4. Jack Kornfield, *Living Buddhist Masters* (Boulder: Prajna Press, 1983).

5. Conze, *Buddhist Thought in India*, p. 107.

6. Herbert Guenther, *Philosophy and Psychology in the Abhidharma* (Berkeley: Shambhala, 1974), p. 180.

7. Steven Goodman, "Situational Patterning," in *Crystal Mirror III* (Berkeley: Dharma Publishing, 1974).

8. Herbert Guenther, *Buddhist Philosophy in Theory and Practice* (New York, Penguin, 1972), p. 75.

9. Quoted in Edward Conze, ed., *Buddhist Texts through the Ages* (New York: Harper Torchbooks, 1964), p. 95.

CHAPTER 6

1. Hermann von Helmholtz, *Popular Scientific Lectures*, ed. Morris Kline (New York: 1962).
2. Helmholtz, quoted in Richard Gregory, *Mind in Science* (Cambridge: Cambridge University Press, 1981), p. 363.
3. H. V. Rappard, *Psychology as Self-Knowledge* (Assen, The Netherlands: Van Gorcum, 1979), p. 84.
4. B. F. Skinner, *Science and Human Behavior* (New York: Macmillan, 1953); *About Behaviorism* (New York: Knopf, 1976).
5. J. M. Wilding, *Perception: From Sense to Object* (London: Hutchinson, 1982).
6. Ibid., pp. 70, 79, 100.

CHAPTER 7

1. Oliver Sachs, *The Man Who Mistook His Wife for a Hat and Other Clinical Tales* (New York: Summit Books, 1985), p. 42.
2. Melvin Konner, *The Tangled Wing* (New York: Holt, Rinehart and Winston, 1982).
3. Robert Plutchik, *Emotion: a Psychoevolutionary Synthesis* (New York: Harper and Row, 1980), p. 144.
4. Paul Maclean, "The Paranoid Streak in Man," in *Beyond Reductionism* (London: Hutchinson, 1969).
5. George Mandler, *Mind and Emotion* (Melbourne, Fla.: Kreiger, 1982).
6. Nyaponika Thera, *Abhidharma Studies* (Kandy, Ceylon: Buddhist Publication Society, 1965).
7. Soshitsu Sen XV, *Tea Life, Tea Mind* (New York: Weatherhill, 1979), p. 72.
8. Donald Hebb, "On the Nature of Fear," quoted in Konner, *The Tangled Wing*, p. 221.
9. Norman Dixon, *Preconscious Processing* (Chichester: John Wiley and Sons, 1981).
10. Ibid., pp. 126, 127.
11. Kahnemann and Tversky, reported in Howard Gardner, *The Mind's New Science* (New York: Basic Books, 1985), p. 371.
12. C. E. Izard, in M. S. Clark and S. T. Fiske, eds., *Affect and Cognition* (Hillsdale, N.J.: Lawrence Erlbaum Associates, 1982).
13. Magda Arnold, *Emotion and Personality* (New York: Columbia University Press, 1960).
14. Magda Arnold, ed., *The Nature of Emotion* (London: Penguin Books, 1968).

CHAPTER 8

1. Jean Piaget, *Six Psychological Studies*, ed. David Elkind (New York: Vintage Books, 1968).
2. Elkind in ibid., p. xii.
3. N. Chomsky, *Language and Responsibility* (New York: Pantheon, 1979).

4. J. Fodor, *The Language of Thought* (Cambridge, Mass.: Harvard University Press, 1975).

5. Howard Gardner, *Frames of Mind* (New York: Basic Books, 1983).

6. John Haugeland, *Artificial Intelligence: The Very Idea* (Cambridge, Mass.: MIT Press, 1985).

7. Ibid., p. 113.

8. Ibid., p. 23.

9. Daniel Dennett in Jonathon Miller, ed., *States of Mind* (New York: Pantheon Books, 1983), p. 79.

10. Margaret Boden, *Minds and Mechanisms* (Ithaca: Cornell University Press, 1977).

11. Hubert Dreyfus, *What Computers Can't Do: The Limits of Artificial Intelligence* (New York: Harper and Row, 1979).

12. Haugeland, *Artificial Intelligence*, p. 222.

13. Howard Gardner, *The Mind's New Science* (New York: Basic Books, 1985), pp. 128, 323.

14. Experiments described in Jean-Pierre Changeux, *Neuronal Man* (New York: Pantheon, 1985), p. 131.

CHAPTER 9

1. Humberto Maturana and Francisco Varela, *The Tree of Knowledge* (Boston: New Science Library, 1987).

2. Francisco Varela, "Living Ways of Sense-Making," in Paisley Livingston, ed., *Disorder and Order* (Stanford: Anma Libri, 1984), p. 213.

3. Humberto Maturana and Francisco Varela, *The Tree of Knowledge: The Biological Roots of Human Understanding* (Boston: New Science Library, 1987).

4. Varela, "Living Ways of Sense-Making," p. 217.

5. Ibid., p. 219.

6. Ibid., p. 221.

CHAPTER 10

1. Donald Griffin, *Animal Thinking* (Cambridge, Mass.: Harvard University Press, 1984), p. 136.

2. John Crook, *The Evolution of Human Consciousness* (Oxford: Clarendon Press, 1983).

3. Nicholas Humphrey, *Consciousness Regained* (Oxford: Oxford University Press, 1983), p. 30.

4. Jack Engler, in *Transformations of Consciousness* (Boston: New Science Library, 1986), p. 21.

5. Thomas McCarthy, quoted in Ken Wilber, "The Spectrum of Development," in *Transformations of Consciousness*, p. 4.

6. Wilber, "The Spectrum of Development," p. 4.

7. John Lyons, *Semantics #1* (Cambridge: Cambridge University Press, 1977), p. 64.

8. George Lakoff and Mark Johnson, *Metaphors We Live By* (Chicago: University of Chicago Press, 1980).

9. E. Rosch and B. B. Lloyd, eds., *Cognition and Categorization* (Hillsdale, N.J.: Lawrence Erlbaum Associates, 1978).

10. Ibid.

11. Crook, *The Evolution of Human Consciousness,* pp. 254, 276.

12. Split-brain research described in John Eccles and Karl Popper, *The Self and Its Brain,* (New York: Springer International, 1981), p. 311.

13. Oliver Sachs, *The Man Who Mistook His Wife for a Hat, and Other Clinical Tales* (New York: Summit Books, 1985), p. 105.

CHAPTER 11

1. F. Heer, *The Medieval World* (New York: New American Library/Mentor, 1964).

2. Guy Welbon, *Buddhist Nirvana and Its Western Interpreters* (Chicago: University of Chicago Press, 1968).

3. F. Heer, *The Medieval World,* p. 64.

4. Ibid., pp. 79, 81.

5. Keith Thomas, *Religion and the Decline of Magic* (London: Penguin, 1971).

6. Carolly Erickson, *The Medieval Vision* (New York: Oxford University Press, 1976), p. 27.

7. Morris Berman, *The Reenchantment of the World* (Ithaca: Cornell University Press, 1981), p. 72.

8. Alfred North Whitehead, *Science and the Modern World* (New York: Free Press, 1967).

9. René Descartes, quoted in Richard Gregory, *Mind in Science* (Cambridge: Cambridge University Press, 1981), p. 465.

10. Descartes, quoted in Howard Gardner, *The Mind's New Science* (New York: Basic Books, 1985), p. 52.

11. John Locke, quoted in Gregory, *Mind in Science,* pp. 339, 489.

12. Quoted in Berman, *The Reenchantment of the World,* p. 121.

13. David Hume, *An Inquiry Concerning Human Understanding* (New York: Liberal Arts Press, 1955 [1748]).

14. Emile Brehier, *The Eighteenth Century* (Chicago: University of Chicago Press, 1967), pp. 199–253.

15. Owen Flanagan, *The Science of the Mind* (Cambridge, Mass.: MIT Press, 1984), p. 181.

CHAPTER 12

1. Edward Conze, *Buddhist Thought in India* (Ann Arbor: University of Michigan Press, 1970), p. 282.

2. G. J. Whitrow, *The Natural Philosophy of Time* (Oxford: Clarendon Press, 1980).

3. Chögyam Trungpa, *Glimpses of Abhidharma* (Boston: Shambhala, 1987), and *Cutting Through Spiritual Materialism* (Boston: Shambhala, 1987); Kalu Rinpoche, *The Dharma*, (Albany, N.Y.: SUNY Press, 1986).

4. David Kalupahana, *Causality: The Central Philosophy of Buddhism* (Honolulu: University Press of Hawaii, 1975), p. 145.

5. Described in John Eccles and Karl Popper, *The Self and Its Brain* (New York: Springer International, 1981), p. 256.

6. Norman Dixon, *Preconscious Processing* (Chichester: John Wiley and Sons, 1981), p. 89.

7. M. R. Harter, quoted in Francisco Varela, Alfredo Toro, E. Roy John, and Eric Schwartz, "Perceptual Framing and Cortical Alpha Rhythm," *Neurophysochologia* 19, (5) (1981).

8. Varela et. al., "Perceptual Framing and Cortical Alpha Rhythm."

9. Weiskrantz, reported in Wilding, *Perception: From Sense to Object* (London: Hutchinson, 1982), p. 160.

10. Wilding, *Perception*, pp. 153, 100.

11. Irving Rock, *The Logic of Perception*, (Cambridge, Mass.: MIT Press, 1983), p. 71.

12. Wilding, *Perception*, p. 79.

13. Rock, *The Logic of Perception*, p. 41.

14. Richard Gregory, in Jonathon Miller, ed., *States of Mind* (New York: Pantheon, 1983), p. 42.

15. Dixon, *Preconscious Processing*, p. 65.

16. Ibid., p. 132.

17. Quoted by George Mandler in H. S. Clark and S. T. Fiske, eds., *Affect and Cognition* (Hillsdale, N.J.: Lawrence Erlbaum Associates, 1982).

18. Wilding, *Perception*, p. 131.

CHAPTER 13

1. Chögyam Trungpa, *Meditation in Action* (Berkeley: Shambhala, 1970), p. 52.

2. Geza Szamosi, *The Twin Dimensions: Inventing Time and Space* (New York: McGraw-Hill, 1987).

3. J. T. Fraser, ed., *The Study of Time* (Heidelberg: Springer-Verlag, 1972, 1975, 1978, 1981).

4. Kenneth Denbigh, *Three Concepts of Time* (Heidelberg: Springer-Verlag, 1981).

5. Ilya Prigogine, *From Being to Becoming: Time and Complexity in the Physical Sciences* (San Francisco: Freeman, 1980).

6. Ilya Prigogine, *The Birth of Time* (Boston: Shambhala, forthcoming).

7. G. J. Whitrow, *The Natural Philosophy of Time* (Oxford: Clarendon Press, 1980), p. 64.

8. William James, *The Principles of Psychology* (New York: Dover, 1950), p. 243.

9. Hans Eysenck and Carl Sargent, *Explaining the Unexplained* (London: Weidenfeld and Nicolson, 1982), p. 183.

10. J. B. Priestley, *Man and Time* (London: Aldus Books, 1964).

11. C. G. Jung, *Synchronicity* (Princeton: Bollingen, 1973); Alex Comfort, *Reality and Empathy* (Albany: SUNY Press, 1984).

12. L. E. Rhine, *ESP in Life and Lab* (New York: Macmillan, 1967).

13. Reported in Eysenck and Sargent, *Explaining the Unexplained*, p. 39.

14. Dame Rebecca West, reported in Michael Shallis, *On Time* (New York: Schocken, 1983), p. 133.

15. Shallis, *On Time*, p. 140.

16. Ibid., p. 198.

17. Chögyam Trungpa, *Shambhala: The Sacred Path of the Warrior* (Boston: Shambhala, 1984), p. 53.

18. J. Krishnamurti, *Krishnamurti's Notebook* (London: Gollancz, 1976).

19. J. Krishnamurti, *Talks and Dialogues* (New York: Avon, 1968), p. 251.

CHAPTER 14

1. Brewster Ghiselin, *The Creative Process* (New York: New American Library, 1937); Arthur I. Miller, *Imagery in Scientific Thought* (Cambridge, Mass.: MIT Press, 1986).

2. Alfred North Whitehead, *Symbolism,* (New York: Putnam, 1955), p. 21.

3. Alfred North Whitehead, *Process and Reality* (New York: Free Press, 1959), pp. 98, 142.

4. Michael Polanyi and Harry Prosch, *Meaning* (Chicago: University of Chicago Press, 1975), p. 38.

5. Michael Polanyi, *Personal Knowledge* (Chicago: University of Chicago Press, 1962), p. 300.

6. Gregory Bateson, *Steps to an Ecology of Mind* (New York: Ballantine, 1975), p. 319.

7. Morris Berman, *The Reenchantment of the World* (Ithaca: Cornell University Press, 1981), p. 132.

8. Chögyam Trungpa, *Seminary Transcripts,* in preparation.

9. Michael Polanyi, *Personal Knowledge*, p. 300.

10. Ken Wilber, *Eye to Eye* (New York: Anchor Books, 1983), p. 202.

CHAPTER 15

1. Herbert Guenther, *Philosophy and Psychology in the Abhidharma* (Berkeley: Shambhala, 1977), p. 95.

2. Jamgon Kongtrul, *The Treasury of Knowledge* (Montignac, France: Dhagpo Kagyu Ling, 1985).

3. Ibid.

4. Ken Wilber, *Quantum Questions* (Boulder: New Science Library, 1984), pp. 13, 21.

5. Kenneth Pelletier, *Toward a Science of Consciousness* (New York: Delta, 1978), p. 154.

6. Daniel Brown, in Wilber, Engler, and Brown, *Transformations of Consciousness* (Boston: New Science Library, 1986), pp. 219–284.

7. Daniel Brown, in *Perceptual and Motor Skills,* October 1984.

8. Nanananda, *Concept and Reality in Early Buddhist Thought* (Kandy: Buddhist Publication Society, 1971), p. 3.

CHAPTER 16

1. Thrangu Rinpoche, *The Open Door to Emptiness* (Manila: Tara Publishing, 1983); Khenpo Tsultrim Gyatso Rinpoche, *Progressive Stages of Meditation on Emptiness* (Oxford: Longchen Foundation, 1986); K. V. Ramanan, *Nagarjuna's Philosophy* (Varanasi: Bharati Vidya Prakashan, 1971); Masao Abe, *Zen and Western Thought* (Honolulu: University of Hawaii Press, 1985).

2. Jeffrey Hopkins, *Meditation on Emptiness* (London: Wisdom Publications, 1983), p. 9.

3. Nagarjuna, *The Mulamadhyanika Karikas,* Kenneth Inada, trans. (Tokyo: Hokuseido Press, 1970), *Karika* 13:8.

4. Hopkins, *Meditation on Emptiness,* p. 10.

5. Thrangu Rinpoche, *The Open Door to Emptiness,* p. 21.

6. Gilbert Ryle, *The Concept of Mind* (London: Hutchinson, 1949).

7. Nālandā Translation Committee, trans., *The Sutra of the Heart of Transcendent Knowledge, Garuda* 3 (Berkeley: Shambhala, 1973), p. 2.

8. Chögyam Trungpa, *Cutting Through Spiritual Materialism* (Boston: Shambhala, 1987), p. 190.

9. Nālandā Translation Committee (trans.), *The Life of Marpa* (Boulder: Prajñā Press, 1982), p. 239.

CHAPTER 17

1. Khenpo Tsultrim Gyatso Rinpoche, *Progressive Stages of Meditation on Emptiness* (Oxford: Longchen Foundation, 1986), p. 65.

2. Richard Rorty, *Philosophy and the Mirror of Nature* (Princeton: Princeton University Press, 1979), p. 369.

3. Karl Popper, *The Logic of Scientific Discovery* (New York: Harper and Row, 1959); *Objective Knowledge* (Oxford: Clarendon Press, 1972), p. 235.

4. Masao Abe, *Zen and Western Thought* (Honolulu: University of Hawaii Press, 1985), p. 126.

5. Janice Willis, *On Knowing Reality* (New York: Columbia University Press, 1979); Herbert Guenther, *Buddhist Philosophy in Theory and Practice* (New York: Penguin, 1972); Gyatso Rinpoche, *Progressive Stages of Meditation on Emptiness*.

6. Diana Paul, *Philosophy of Mind in Sixth Century China* (Stanford: Stanford University Press, 1984), p. 73.

7. Ibid., p. 78.

8. Rorty, *Philosophy and the Mirror of Nature*, p. 367.

9. Wittgenstein, quoted in William Barrett, *The Illusion of Technique* (New York: Anchor, 1978).

10. Ludwig Wittgenstein, *Tractatus Logico-Philosophicus* (London: Routledge and Kegan Paul, 1961).

11. Nelson Goodman, *Ways of Worldmaking* (Indianapolis: Hackett, 1978), p. 6.

12. Martin Heidegger, *On the Way to Language* (New York: Harper and Row, 1982), p. 59.

13. Martin Heidegger, *What Is Called Thinking* (New York: Harper and Row, 1968), pp. 228–244.

CHAPTER 18

1. Alfred North Whitehead, *Science and the Modern World* (New York: Free Press, 1967), p. 58.

2. Ilya Prigogine, *Order Out of Chaos* (Boulder: New Science Library, 1984).

3. Gerald Feinberg and Robert Shapiro, *Life Beyond Earth* (New York: Morrow, 1980), p. 147.

4. James E. Lovelock, *Gaia: A New Look at Life on Earth* (Oxford: Oxford University Press, 1979).

5. Owen Flanagan, *The Science of the Mind* (Cambridge, Mass.: MIT Press, 1984), p. 45.

6. Werner Heisenberg, quoted in Nick Herbert, *Quantum Reality: Beyond the New Physics* (New York: Anchor Books, 1985), p. 22.

7. Ken Wilber, *Eye to Eye* (New York: Anchor Books, 1983).

8. Ervin Laszlo, *Introduction to Systems Philosophy* (New York: Harper Torchbooks, 1972); Erich Jantsch, *The Self-Organizing Universe* (Oxford: Pergamon Press, 1980).

9. Lawrence Foss and Kenneth Rothenberg, *The Second Medical Revolution* (Boston: Shambhala, 1987).

10. Roger Sperry, *Nobel Prize Conversations* (Dallas: Saybrook, 1985), pp. 46, 47.

CHAPTER 19

1. D. M. Armstrong and Norman Malcolm, *Consciousness and Causality* (Oxford: Blackwell, 1984).

2. John Eccles and Karl Popper, *The Self and Its Brain* (New York: Springer International, 1981), p. 355.

3. Ibid., p. 36.

4. Heinz Pagels, *The Cosmic Code* (New York: Simon and Schuster, 1982).

5. Ibid., p. 239.

6. Vernon Mountcastle, quoted in Eccles and Popper, *The Self and Its Brain*, p. 253.

7. John Dewey, quoted in Owen Flanagan, *The Science of Mind* (Cambridge, Mass.: MIT Press, 1984), p. 46.

CHAPTER 20

1. George Spencer-Brown, *Laws of Form* (New York: Bantam, 1973), p. xxix.

2. Douglas Hofstadter, *Gödel, Escher, Bach: An Eternal Golden Braid* (New York: Basic Books, 1979).

3. Diana Paul, *Philosophy of Mind in Sixth Century China* (Stanford: Stanford University Press, 1984), p. 97.

4. Francesca Fremantle and Chögyam Trungpa, *The Tibetan Book of the Dead* (Boston: Shambhala, 1987).

5. Carl Jung, "Psychological Commentary," in W. Y. Evans-Wentz, ed., *The Tibetan Book of the Great Liberation* (Oxford: Oxford University Press, 1954).

6. Paul, *Philosophy of Mind in Sixth Century China*, p. 98.

7. Ibid., p. 99.

8. Chögyam Trungpa, *Seminary Transcripts*, in preparation.

9. Ibid.

10. David Bohm, *Wholeness and the Implicate Order* (London: Routledge and Kegan Paul, 1980), p. 196.

11. Herbert Guenther, *Buddhist Philosophy in Theory and Practice* (New York: Penguin, 1972), p. 96.

12. Herbert Guenther, *Tibetan Buddhism in Western Perspective* (Emeryville, Calif.: Dharma Publishing, 1977), pp. 156, 86.

13. Chögyam Trungpa, *First Thought Best Thought* (Boulder, Shambhala, 1983), p. 33.

CHAPTER 21

1. Saraha, quoted in Herbert Guenther, *The Tantric View of Life* (Berkeley: Shambhala, 1972), p. 86.

2. Herbert Guenther, "The Concept of Mind in Tantric Buddhism," in *Tibetan Buddhism in Western Perspective* (Berkeley: Dharma Publishing, 1977), p. 37.

3. Chögyam Trungpa, *Shambhala: The Sacred Path of the Warrior* (Boston: Shambhala, 1984), p. 155.

4. Chögyam Trungpa, *Journey Without Goal* (Boston: Shambhala, 1985), p. 28.

5. Nālandā Translation Committee, trans., *The Life of Marpa* (Boulder: Prajna Press, 1982), p. 46.

6. Kalu Rinpoche, *The Dharma* (Albany, N.Y.: SUNY Press, 1986).

7. Trungpa, *Shambhala*, p. 101.

8. Chögyam Trungpa, *Cutting Through Spiritual Materialism* (Boston: Shambhala, 1987), p. 223.

9. Herbert Guenther, *Matrix of Mystery* (Boulder: Shambhala, 1984), p. 43.

10. Trungpa, *Journey Without Goal*, p. 31.

11. Chögyam Trungpa, *The Myth of Freedom* (Boulder: Shambhala, 1976), p. 156.

CHAPTER 22

1. Osel Tendzin, *Buddha in the Palm of Your Hand* (Boston: Shambhala, 1987), p. 46.

2. Benjamin Farrington, *What Darwin Really Said* (New York: Schocken Books, 1982).

3. Thomas Huxley, "The Struggle for Existence in Human Society," in *The Nineteenth Century* (February 1888); Herbert Spencer, *Social Statics* (London: Chapman, 1851).

4. Humberto Maturana and Francisco Varela, *The Tree of Knowledge* (Boston: New Science Library, 1987).

5. Lewis Thomas, quoted in Robert Augros and George Stanciu, *The New Biology* (Boston: New Science Library, 1987), p. 117–118.

6. Augros and Stanciu, *The New Biology*.

7. John Tyler Bonner, *The Evolution of Culture in Animals* (Princeton: Princeton University Press, 1980), p. 91.

8. Pierre Grasse, *Evolution of Living Organisms* (New York: Academic Press, 1977), p. 243.

9. Kalu Rinpoche, *The Dharma* (Albany, N.Y.: SUNY Press, 1986), p. 46.

APPENDIX 1

Mental Events *(Cetasika)*, *Sanskaras*, or *Formations**

A. FIVE OMNIPRESENT MENTAL EVENTS, present in every moment of consciousness
   1. Feeling tone (vedanā), feeling (the second skandha)
   2. Conceptualization (samjña), perception (the third skandha), discernment
   3. Directionality of mind (cetanā), motivation, intention
   4. Rapport (sparsa), contact
   5. Ego-centric demanding (manaskāra), attention

B. FIVE OBJECT-DETERMINING MENTAL EVENTS, also present in every moment of consciousness
   1. Interest (chanda), desire, aspiration
   2. Intensified interest (adhimoksa), inclination, appreciation
   3. Inspection (smṛti), mindfulness, recollection
   4. Intense concentration (samādhi), meditation
   5. Appreciative discrimination (prajñā), penetrating insight, intelligence.

C. ELEVEN POSITIVE MENTAL EVENTS (kuśala-mahābhūmika)
   1. Confidence-trust (śraddhā), faith, belief
   2. Self-respect (hrī), shame
   3. Decorum (apatrāpya), bashfulness, consideration for others
   4. Non-attachment (alobha), freedom from greed
   5. Non-hatred (adveśa), freedom from aggression
   6. Non-deludedness (amoha), freedom from bewilderment
   7. Diligence (vīrya), exertion, energy, enthusiasm
   8. Alertness (prasŕabdhi), repose of mind, suppleness

---

*Based on H. V. Guenther and L. S. Kawamura, *Mind in Buddhist Psychology* (Emeryville, Calif.: Dharma Publishing, 1975).

   9. Concern (apramāda), vigilance, conscientiousness
10. Equanimity (apekṣa)
11. Non-violence (ahinṣa)

D. SIX BASIC EMOTIONS (mūla-klésa), or root emotions

   1. Cupidity-attachment (rāga), passion
   2. Anger (pratigha), aggression
   3. Arrogance (māna), pride, self-importance
   4. Lack of intrinsic awareness (avidyā), ignorance
   5. Indecision (vicikitsā), doubt, disturbing indecision
   6. Opinionatedness (dṛṣṭi), fixed or disturbing views

E. TWENTY PROXIMATE FACTORS OF INSTABILITY (upakleśa), or derivative kleśas

   1. Indignation (krodha), anger, wrath
   2. Resentment (upanāha), enmity, vengeance
   3. Slyness-concealment (mrakṣa)
   4. Spite (pradāsa)
   5. Jealousy (irṣya), envy
   6. Avarice (mātsarya), parsimony
   7. Deceit (māya), pretension
   8. Dishonesty (śāṭhya), fraudulence
   9. Mental inflation (mada), pride, self-satisfaction
10. Malice (vihiṃsá), injury, cruelty
11. Shamelessness (ahrí)
12. Lack of sense of propriety (anapatrapya), non-bashfulness, inconsideration for others
13. Gloominess (styāna), low-spiritedness, dullness
14. Ebullience (auddhatya), restlessness, excitement
15. Lack of trust (aśraddhyā), unbelief, faithlessness
16. Laziness (kausīdya), sloth
17. Unconcern (pramāda), negligence, unconscientiousness
18. Forgetfulness (muṣitasmrtitā), absence of mindfulness
19. Inattentiveness (vikṣepa), distraction
20. Desultoriness (asampŕajñā), non-discernment

F. FOUR VARIABLES (aniyata) or indeterminates

   1. Drowsiness (middha), sleep
   2. Worry (kaukṛtya), regret
   3. Selectiveness (vitarka), reflection, general examination
   4. Discursiveness (vicāra), investigation, precise analysis

APPENDIX 2

A Table of Emotion Terms*

tolerant	indecisive	quarrelsome
accepting	rejected	impatient
agreeable	bored	grouchy
serene	disappointed	defiant
cheerful	vacillating	aggressive
receptive	discouraged	sarcastic
calm	puzzled	rebellious
obliging	bewildered	disobedient
patient	uncertain	exasperated
affectionate	confused	demanding
obedient	perplexed	possessive
timid	ambivalent	greedy
scared	surprised	wondering
panicky	astonished	impulsive
afraid	amazed	anticipatory
shy	awed	boastful
submissive	envious	expectant
bashful	disgusted	daring
embarrassed	unsympathetic	curious
terrified	unreceptive	reckless
pensive	indignant	proud
cautious	disagreeable	inquisitive
anxious	resentful	planful
helpless	revolted	adventurous
apprehensive	displeased	ecstatic
ashamed	suspicious	sociable

---

*Based on R. Plutchik.

humiliated	dissatisfied	hopeful
forlorn	contrary	gleeful
nervous	jealous	elated
lonely	intolerant	eager
apathetic	distrustful	enthusiastic
meek	vengeful	interested
guilty	bitter	delighted
sad	unfriendly	amused
sorrowful	stubborn	attentive
remorseful	uncooperative	joyful
hopeless	contemptuous	happy
depressed	loathful	self-controlled
worried	critical	satisfied
disinterested	annoyed	pleased
grief-stricken	irritated	generous
unhappy	angry	ready
gloomy	antagonistic	sympathetic
despairing	hostile	content
hesitant	outraged	cooperative
despairing	scornful	trusting
hesitant	unaffectionate	tolerant

INDEX

ALSO IN NEW SCIENCE LIBRARY:

Awakening the Heart: East/West Approaches to Psychotherapy and the Healing Relationship, edited by John Welwood
Beyond Illness: Discovering the Experience of Health, by Larry Dossey, M.D.
Evolution: The Grand Synthesis, by Ervin Laszlo
Fisherman's Guide: A Systems Approach to Creativity and Organization, by Robert Campbell
The Holographic Paradigm and Other Paradoxes, edited by Ken Wilber
Imagery in Healing: Shamanism and Modern Medicine, by Jeanne Achterberg
The Inward Arc: Healing and Wholeness in Psychotherapy and Spirituality, by Frances Vaughan
The Miracle of Existence, by Henry Margenau
The New Biology: Discovering the Wisdom in Nature, by Robert Augros and George Stanciu
No Boundary: Eastern and Western Approaches to Personal Growth, by Ken Wilber
Order Out of Chaos: Man's New Dialogue with Nature, by Ilya Prigogine and Isabelle Stengers, Foreword by Alvin Toffler
Perceiving Ordinary Magic: Science and Intuitive Wisdom, by Jeremy W. Hayward
Quantum Questions: Mystical Writings of the World's Great Physicists, edited by Ken Wilber
The Second Medical Revolution: From Biomedicine to Infomedicine, by Laurence Foss and Kenneth Rothenberg
A Sociable God: Toward a New Understanding of Religion, by Ken Wilber
Space, Time and Medicine, by Larry Dossey, M.D.
The Sphinx and the Rainbow: Brain, Mind and Future Vision, by David Loye
Staying Alive: The Psychology of Human Survival, by Roger Walsh, M.D.
The Tao of Physics: An Exploration of the Parallels between Modern Physics and Eastern Mysticism, second edition, revised and updated, by Fritjof Capra
Transformations of Consciousness: Conventional and Contemplative Perspectives on Development, by Ken Wilber, Jack Engler, and Daniel P. Brown
The Tree of Knowledge: The Biological Roots of Human Understanding, by Humberto Maturana and Francisco Varela
Up from Eden: A Transpersonal View of Human Evolution, by Ken Wilber
Waking Up: Overcoming the Obstacles to Human Potential, by Charles T. Tart
The Wonder of Being Human: Our Brain and Our Mind, by Sir John Eccles and Daniel N. Robinson